Building the Modern Workplace with SharePoint Online

Solutions with SPFx, JSON Formatting, Power Automate, Power Apps, Teams, and PVA

Second Edition

Hari Narayn

Apress®

Building the Modern Workplace with SharePoint Online: Solutions with SPFx, JSON Formatting, Power Automate, Power Apps, Teams, and PVA

Hari Narayn
Melbourne, VIC, Australia

ISBN-13 (pbk): 978-1-4842-9725-4   ISBN-13 (electronic): 978-1-4842-9726-1
https://doi.org/10.1007/978-1-4842-9726-1

Managing Director, Apress Media LLC: Welmoed Spahr
Acquisitions Editor: Smriti Srivastava
Development Editor: Laura Berendson
Editorial Assistant: Shaul Elson

Cover designed by eStudioCalamar

Cover image by Ash Edmonds on Unsplash (www.unsplash.com)

Distributed to the book trade worldwide by Springer Science+Business Media New York, 1 New York Plaza, Suite 4600, New York, NY 10004-1562, USA. Phone 1-800-SPRINGER, fax (201) 348-4505, e-mail orders-ny@ springer-sbm.com, or visit www.springeronline.com. Apress Media, LLC is a California LLC and the sole member (owner) is Springer Science + Business Media Finance Inc (SSBM Finance Inc). SSBM Finance Inc is a **Delaware** corporation.

For information on translations, please e-mail booktranslations@springernature.com; for reprint, paperback, or audio rights, please e-mail bookpermissions@springernature.com.

Apress titles may be purchased in bulk for academic, corporate, or promotional use. eBook versions and licenses are also available for most titles. For more information, reference our Print and eBook Bulk Sales web page at http://www.apress.com/bulk-sales.

Any source code or other supplementary material referenced by the author in this book is available to readers on GitHub (https://github.com/apress/building-modern-workplace-SharePoint-online-2e). For more detailed information, please visit https://www.apress.com/gp/services/source-code.

Paper in this product is recyclable

This book is dedicated to the loving memory of my dear friend, Jojo Varghese. Your love, your voice, and your laughter will forever be imprinted in our minds.

Table of Contents

About the Author

 **Hari Narayn** is a highly skilled and experienced technology enthusiast with a 13-year track record in developing cutting-edge web and mobile applications. His expertise spans a wide range of technologies, including React, Microsoft 365, SharePoint, Azure, Teams, Power Platform, .NET, Open AI, Angular, and JavaScript. Throughout his career, Hari has successfully delivered numerous web and mobile solutions for clients worldwide, showcasing his exceptional abilities and commitment to excellence.

Hari holds several certifications, including the Certified Power Platform Solution Architect Expert, Microsoft 365 Certified Developer Associate, and Certified Azure Solutions Architect Expert. These certifications demonstrate his in-depth knowledge and mastery of the respective platforms, solidifying his status as a trusted expert in the field. He is also the author of the book *Just React*.

Hailing from Kerala, India, he is currently based in Melbourne, Australia. He is an integral part of the Victorian Public Service, serving as a full-stack engineer. His role entails leveraging his extensive knowledge and experience to spearhead innovative projects and deliver high-quality solutions.

About the Technical Reviewer

 **Vijai Anand Ramalingam** was a Microsoft MVP in Office Apps & Services and Office Development, an experienced modern workplace architect with deep knowledge in SharePoint and Microsoft 365. He is a blogger, author, and speaker and has published 1,300 blogs/articles on C# Corner. Vijai has worked on Microsoft SharePoint on-premises/online, Microsoft 365, and Azure.

Acknowledgments

I am deeply grateful to my incredible wife, Divya, whose unwavering motivation and nurturing support have been invaluable throughout the process of writing this book. I must also express my heartfelt appreciation to our daughter, Ithal, for her adorable interruptions that added joy to the journey. A special thanks goes to my mom for her boundless care and support.

I would like to acknowledge the exceptional support provided by Smriti Srivastava, the acquisitions editor, and Shobana Srinivasan, the project coordinator. Their continuous assistance has been instrumental in bringing this book to fruition. Thanks to Vijai Anand Ramalingam, the technical reviewer, for his invaluable contributions of excellent suggestions and corrections. I extend my heartfelt appreciation to the entire team at Apress for their dedication and efforts in bringing the second edition of this book to life. Their commitment and support have been instrumental in making this edition a reality.

I would like to express my sincere gratitude to the readers of the first edition of this book, whose exceptional feedback and constructive criticism have greatly contributed to its improvement. Their valuable insights and perspectives have played a crucial role in shaping the content and making this edition even more beneficial and insightful. Your continued support and engagement are deeply appreciated.

Lastly, I extend my appreciation to all my wonderful friends and co-workers who have played an integral role in my SharePoint journey. Their support and collaboration have been truly invaluable.

Introduction

Building the Modern Workplace with SharePoint Online is a reader-friendly and comprehensive handbook that is specifically designed to support beginners in their journey with SharePoint Online. It provides clear explanations and step-by-step instructions to ensure that beginners can grasp the concepts and functionalities of SharePoint Online with ease. Additionally, this book serves as an invaluable reference for intermediate and advanced users, offering advanced techniques, best practices, and insights to further enhance their expertise in SharePoint Online. The book takes a design-first approach, emphasizing business analysis and solution planning based on specific workplace requirements.

Starting with an introduction to SharePoint basics, the first chapter familiarizes readers with the platform. The second chapter focuses on conducting a business analysis of a workplace requirement, leading to the design of a tailored solution.

From the third chapter onward, the book delves into the development of individual components that align with the project's requirements. Throughout this process, readers gain a deeper understanding of the underlying concepts, with a focus on incorporating the latest and recommended approaches for each solution. Detailed discussions on JSON formatting, Power Apps, Power Automate, and the SharePoint Framework (SPFx) are provided in the respective chapters.

The penultimate chapter explores modern search, while the book concludes with an examination of Teams and Power Virtual Agents (PVA). By focusing on establishing strong fundamentals, the book equips readers to explore SharePoint Online further. Additionally, the deep-dive approach to requirement analysis, solution design, and development provides valuable insights into successfully implementing modern workplace requirements using SharePoint Online, covering the entire end-to-end process.

CHAPTER 1

Get Online with SharePoint Online

SharePoint Online is a cloud-based service designed primarily for communication and collaboration. It is a superb choice for building a workplace solution because of its endless integration capabilities. Here, you'll learn how SharePoint Online can help you create a modern digital workplace based on your needs.

Throughout this chapter, we will cover the absolute basics of SharePoint Online. We will begin by introducing SharePoint and how it has grown. Our next step is to gain an overview of Microsoft 365, of which SharePoint Online is a part. We'll discuss the platform's licensing plans and the admin center. You will learn how to add users to the Microsoft 365 admin center and create a site. There will also be a discussion of templates, lists, list templates, columns, and content types. Following that, we will look at different developer tools and frameworks.

The next section will focus on permissions and access management. A brief discussion of the Document Library and versioning will follow. During this chapter, we will also talk about web parts and pages and how to add web parts to a page. We will examine a few modern workplace requirements and how SharePoint Online addresses them.

By the end of this chapter, you'll understand the basic concepts of SharePoint Online and the various tools it interacts with. You can skip some sections of this chapter if you are already familiar with the basics of SharePoint Online.

Not Just a "Point" to "Share"

The assumption that SharePoint is just a place to share content, much like Google Drive, has come up in a lot of conversations. That's not true.

© Hari Narayn 2023
H. Narayn, *Building the Modern Workplace with SharePoint Online*,
https://doi.org/10.1007/978-1-4842-9726-1_1

As a communication and collaboration platform, SharePoint allows users to access, author, publish, share, secure, automate, search, collaborate, and do much more on their content. In terms of content presentation and management, SharePoint is an excellent tool. We can configure and customize it to a great extent to meet business needs. In addition, it offers great integration capabilities with Microsoft and non-Microsoft products. It is one of the most effective tools you can use to modernize your workplace.

Offline and Online

The first version of SharePoint was called SharePoint Portal in 2001. In the following years, Microsoft introduced SharePoint Server 2003 and SharePoint 2007. They introduced content management and publishing into SharePoint 2007. With SharePoint 2010, users can take advantage of several new features and a fresh-looking user interface. With SharePoint 2013, SharePoint 2016, and SharePoint 2019, SharePoint continues to grow as an on-premises solution.

Within its 365 suites of products, Microsoft introduced SharePoint as a cloud service in 2014. With SharePoint Online, you can access your content at anytime, anywhere, and you don't need to install anything on a server. This book focuses only on SharePoint Online.

Licensing and Admin Center

Microsoft 365 licenses are required before starting a SharePoint Online project. Licensing plans vary by region. The Microsoft 365 admin center (Figure 1-1) allows you to manage individual licenses.

By joining the Microsoft 365 Developer program, you can get an E5 license for free if you do not already have one. Visit `https://developer.microsoft.com/en-us/microsoft-365/dev-program` to sign up and get online!

After signing up, you can access the Microsoft 365 admin center at `https://admin.microsoft.com`.

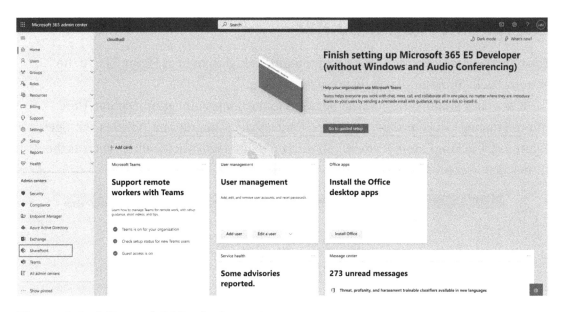

Figure 1-1. *Microsoft 365 admin center*

In the Billing section, you can manage your subscriptions. Groups and individual licenses can be managed from their respective sections.

Users

In the Microsoft 365 admin center, you must create at least one user before you can create your SharePoint site. From this page, you can add a user, remove a user, export users, add multiple users, reset passwords, and set up multifactor authentication. The user licenses and roles can be managed by a specific user from this page (Figure 1-2).

Figure 1-2. *User management*

SharePoint Admin Center

The admin center features a SharePoint option, as highlighted in Figure 1-1. At the bottom, click "Show all" if you do not see anything.

If you click SharePoint, you will be taken to the SharePoint admin center. Here, you can manage all your sites, access, content services, migrations, policies, etc. See Figure 1-3. Clicking "More features" allows you to manage other features such as the Term store, user profiles, search, etc.

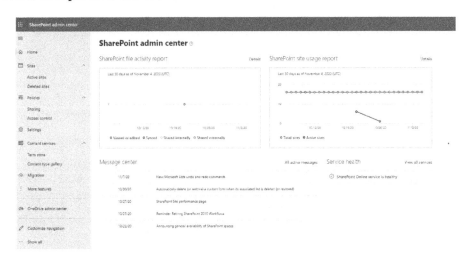

Figure 1-3. *SharePoint admin center*

Site

A *site* is a website that contains different artifacts such as lists, pages, etc. A site will have a home page. Creating a SharePoint site is the first step in starting a SharePoint project. Select "Active sites" and then click Create, as shown in Figure 1-4, to create a site.

Figure 1-4. *Admin interface for sites*

As shown in Figure 1-5, you will be presented with templates to choose from. There are a few options available. Let's start by looking at what a site template is.

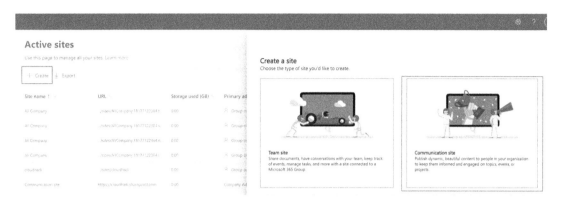

Figure 1-5. *Choosing a site template*

Site Templates

A *site template* in SharePoint is a prebuilt definition of a site. Each of these definitions is tailored to meet a specific business need. On top of these templates, you can build your own customized SharePoint sites.

Teams and communication sites are the two types of templates you will find in SharePoint Online. Team sites connect you and your team to the content, information, and apps you need every day. Team sites are useful for storing files and collaborating on them, as well as storing and managing lists of information. A communication site is a great place to share news, reports, status, and other information visually.

How do you decide between a communication site and a team site? Imagine a research department for COVID-19. Members of the department can collaborate on data and reports via a team site. On the team site, the team can work privately during the data preparation.

A second scenario would be to publish news and other useful information on an intranet for employees. There is no need for employees to understand how the published information is captured; they just need to consume it, provide feedback, etc.

Let's choose the communication site as the site of our example project here, as highlighted in Figure 1-5.

You need to select a design from the left side of the next window. I selected the Blank option. When you select a topic or showcase, SharePoint will add some of the web parts by default. This is a great way to get started with predefined web parts. But for now, let's use the Blank template since we want to focus on the basics.

We can enter the site's name, owner, and language, as shown in Figure 1-6. Advanced settings also provide options for choosing a time zone and adding a description. As soon as you enter the site name, it will be checked to see if it is available.

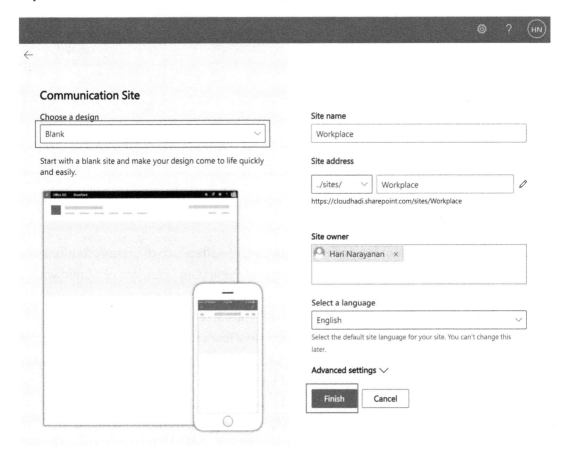

Figure 1-6. *Creating a communication site*

Note   If you click "Advanced settings," you can manage things such as storage quota for a site. Leave it at the default settings in this case.

Click Finish, and SharePoint will create the site. Once the site is created, it will appear under "Active Sites." On the left side, you can select "Active sites" to see the site. Navigate to the site by clicking the URL. Refer to Figure 1-7.

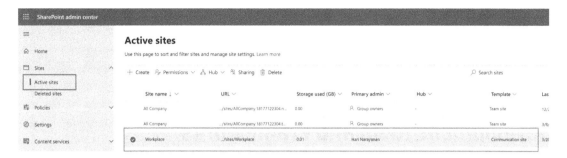

Figure 1-7. *Site displayed in "Active sites" list*

Now you have a communication site. Because you chose the Blank template, it created only the headers and footers, as shown in Figure 1-8.

Figure 1-8. *Home page of the blank communication site*

Configure and Customize

You can customize and configure SharePoint sites in a few different ways depending on the business needs. The following are the few technical areas of the site where you can customize and configure a site:

- Lists
- Libraries
- Columns
- Views
- Pages
- Forms
- Search

- Web parts

- Workflows

- Security

Development Tools and Frameworks

We can customize SharePoint sites using a variety of technologies. The following are some of the most popular and recommended SharePoint customization tools:

- *JSON formatting*: JSON formatting is a powerful tool for customizing SharePoint sites. Using JSON formatting, you can customize columns and views and even have an approval process. By using just JSON code, you can create beautiful user interfaces. In Chapter 3, we will discuss this in more detail.

- *Power Apps*: Power Apps is software that allows you to create a collection of apps, services, and connectors that we can use to build custom apps and forms for SharePoint sites. We can build these apps with a responsive design that run seamlessly on mobile devices and browsers.

- *Power Automate*: With Power Automate, you can automate your workflows. Power Automate can connect to SharePoint Online and integrate it with many other services. Using Power Apps and Power Automate, you can take advantage of artificial intelligence (AI) capabilities and use ChatGPT.

- *SharePoint Framework (SPFx)*: With SPFx, you can create client-side web parts and extensions for SharePoint. The latest updates also allow you to override the form experience in a list or library using SPFx. Among the SPFx developer tools are NPM, TypeScript, Yeoman, Webpack, and Gulp, which are all open source. We can develop a SPFx component using different technologies, such as React, Angular, Knockout, etc.

- *SharePoint REST service*: SharePoint comes with a Representational State Transfer (REST) service that helps you interact remotely with

SharePoint data by using any technology that supports REST web requests. They built Patterns and Practices client-side libraries (PnPjs) and Microsoft Graph on top of this.

- *PnPjs*: PnPjs allows you to consume SharePoint, Graph, and Microsoft 365 REST APIs. Using this open-source initiative, you will consume information from Microsoft 365 and SharePoint alongside the existing software development kits (SDKs) provided by Microsoft. You can use PnPjs within an SPFx component to communicate with SharePoint.

- *Microsoft Graph*: To communicate with SharePoint data, Microsoft Graph offers a single endpoint, `https://graph.microsoft.com`. SharePoint APIs in the Microsoft Graph API support access to SharePoint sites, lists, read-write support for lists, list Items, etc.

- *PowerShell*: An important part of PowerShell is its ability to automate tasks and manage configurations. Numerous SharePoint tasks can be automated using PowerShell. Using PnP modules, REST APIs, or Microsoft Graph, PowerShell can interact with SharePoint.

We will go through all these topics in respective chapters. In addition, we can make use of the Azure software-as-a-service (SaaS) offering, such as Logic Apps and Functions, to customize SharePoint. This is not in the scope of our book. In the "old days," developers used the client-side object model (CSOM), SharePoint designer, JavaScript injection, add-ins, C#, .NET MVC, etc., to customize SharePoint Online. These are not recommended approaches nowadays, so they will not be discussed further in the book.

SharePoint Lists

SharePoint lists are collections of data that can be used to store and manage information such as tasks, contacts, calendar events, and more. Lists are one of the fundamental building blocks of SharePoint, and they provide a flexible way to store and organize data.

Lists are made up of columns that define the type of data that can be stored in each field. For example, a list for tracking tasks might have columns for task name, due date, assigned person, and status. Users can then add their own items to the list, filling in values for each column. Documents are created and stored in SharePoint libraries, which are special types of lists.

SharePoint lists provide a powerful and flexible way to store, manage, and share data within an organization. They can be used to track tasks and projects, manage contacts and customer information, store documents and files, and more.

In the site we created previously, if you click the settings on the right side and then navigate to the site contents, you will see all the lists and libraries created by default. Refer to Figure 1-9. Documents, Style Library, etc., libraries are created by default, and Events is a list created automatically.

Figure 1-9. *Site contents*

Add a Custom List

Custom lists are lists you create, which are internally SharePoint apps. Here you can store and manage content according to your needs. SharePoint sites allow us to create many custom lists, of course, limited to the site storage quota allocated.

Let's inspect the list creation and data entry. The purpose of this is to help you build a good foundation for content management concepts in SharePoint if you are using it for the first time.

Consider a scenario in which you want to store the branch addresses of your company. We can do this by creating a list called Branch Information that contains two columns, Name and Address. You will have 15 rows of information if you want to record information about 15 branches. The rows of the list are called *list items*. Here, you have 15 items on your list.

The first step is to create a list on the site we created earlier. On the top right, click the Chrome button for the settings and select Site Contents. See Figure 1-10.

Figure 1-10. *Settings, Site Contents*

In the site contents, click the New drop-down at the top left and select List. Refer to Figure 1-11.

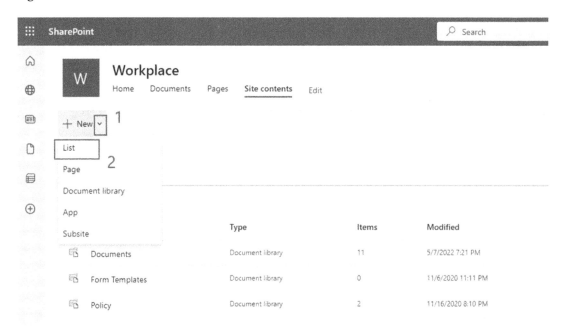

Figure 1-11. *Site contents, new list*

Click the Blank list option from the resulting pop-up. Refer to Figure 1-12.

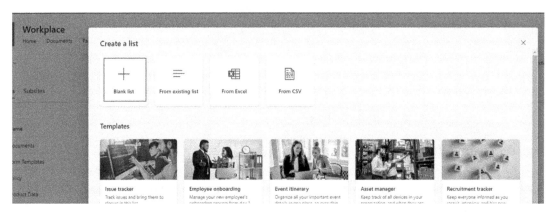

Figure 1-12. *New list, blank list*

Another pop-up appears. As shown in Figure 1-13, provide the name **Branch Information** with an optional description. Click Create to proceed.

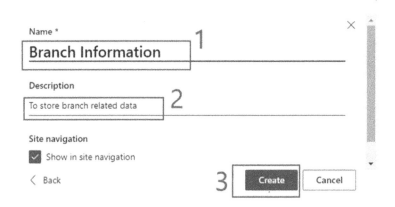

Figure 1-13. *Creating a custom list*

The list will be created, and it will take you to its interface. Also, if you go to the site contents, the list will be displayed there along with the other default content. See Figure 1-14.

Contents   Subsites

	Name	Type	Items	Modified
	Documents	Document library	0	10/24/2020 6:58 AM
	Form Templates	Document library	0	11/6/2020 11:11 PM
	Style Library	Document library	0	10/24/2020 6:58 AM
	Branch Information	List	0	11/7/2020 12:16 AM
	Events	Events list	0	10/24/2020 6:58 AM
	Site Pages	Page library	1	10/24/2020 6:58 AM

Figure 1-14. *List on the site contents*

By clicking Branch Information, it will take you to the list view. See Figure 1-15. In this area, you can add a new list item, edit it, edit the items together in a grid view, export the list items to Excel, etc.

Figure 1-15. *Custom list interface*

Figure 1-15 shows that only the Title column is available on the list. Here, we want to add two more columns, namely, for the name and address. Where are you going to create these columns? We can create them at either the list or site level. It is best to create the columns at the site level if you want to reuse them. To better understand what site columns are, let's create them at the site level.

Add and Manage Site Columns

Site columns are reusable and ensure consistency in metadata across sites and lists. It is possible to add a site column to more than one list.

You can add a site column by selecting "Site settings" from the "Site contents" interface, as shown in Figure 1-16.

Figure 1-16. *Navigate to the site settings from the site contents*

To access the Site Columns interface, click "Site columns" in the site settings, as shown in Figure 1-17.

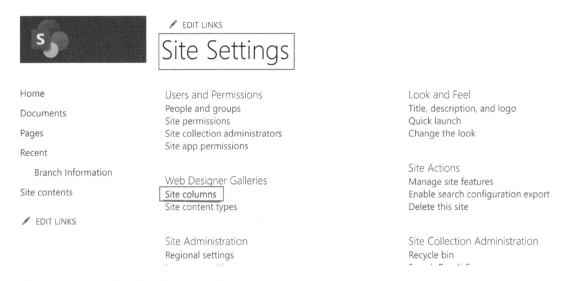

Figure 1-17. *Site Settings interface*

To create a site column, click the Create button at the top on the Site Columns page, as shown in Figure 1-18.

Figure 1-18. *Site Columns interface*

Our example here requires a column called "Branch name" to hold the names of each branch.

As shown in Figure 1-19, fill in the name as **Branch name**, and type **single line of text**. Select the New Group option and name the group **Workplace Columns**.

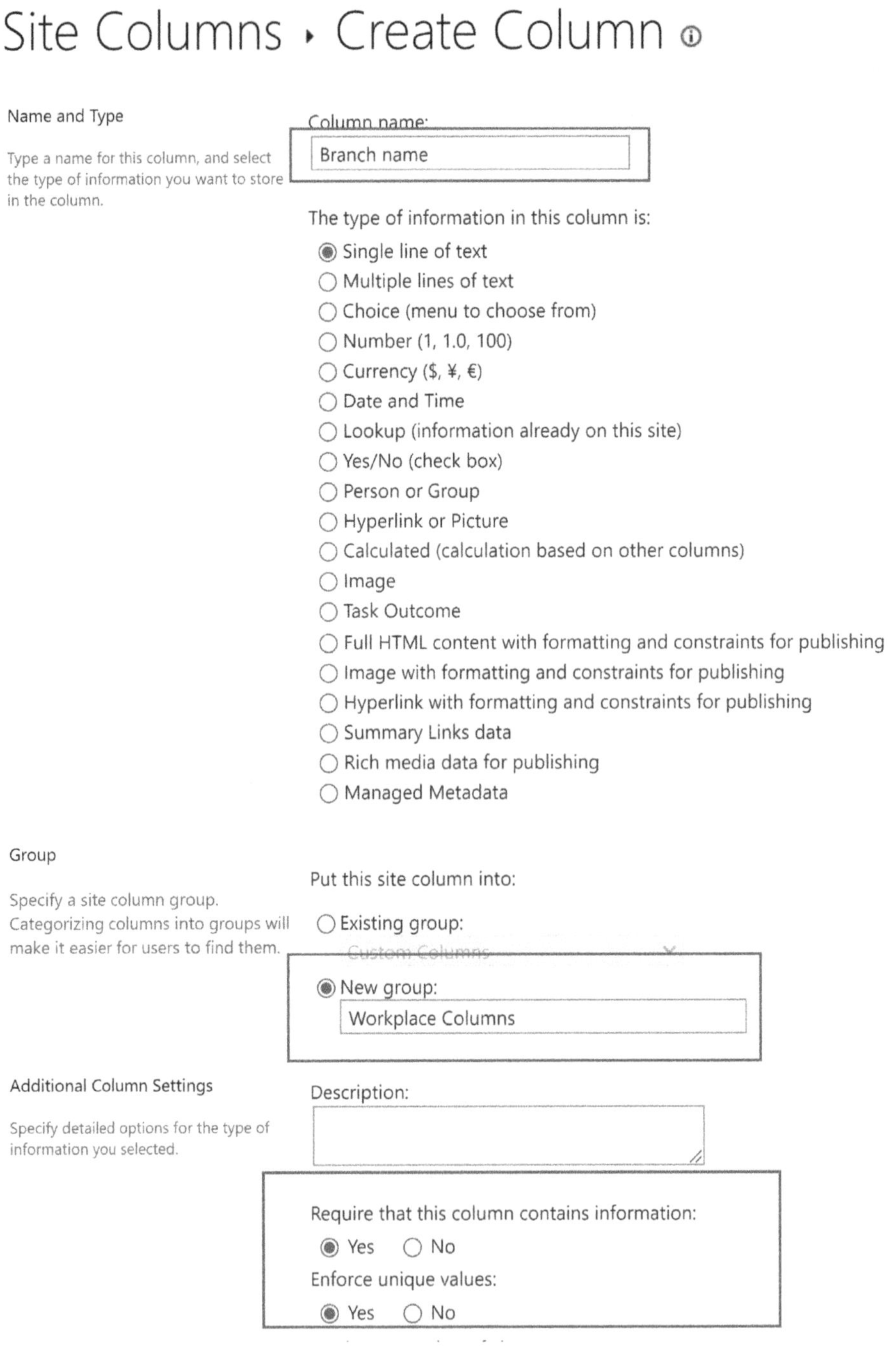

Site Columns ‣ Create Column ⓘ

Name and Type

Type a name for this column, and select the type of information you want to store in the column.

Column name:

Branch name

The type of information in this column is:

- ◉ Single line of text
- ◯ Multiple lines of text
- ◯ Choice (menu to choose from)
- ◯ Number (1, 1.0, 100)
- ◯ Currency ($, ¥, €)
- ◯ Date and Time
- ◯ Lookup (information already on this site)
- ◯ Yes/No (check box)
- ◯ Person or Group
- ◯ Hyperlink or Picture
- ◯ Calculated (calculation based on other columns)
- ◯ Image
- ◯ Task Outcome
- ◯ Full HTML content with formatting and constraints for publishing
- ◯ Image with formatting and constraints for publishing
- ◯ Hyperlink with formatting and constraints for publishing
- ◯ Summary Links data
- ◯ Rich media data for publishing
- ◯ Managed Metadata

Group

Specify a site column group. Categorizing columns into groups will make it easier for users to find them.

Put this site column into:

- ◯ Existing group:
  Custom Columns
- ◉ New group:
  Workplace Columns

Additional Column Settings

Specify detailed options for the type of information you selected.

Description:

Require that this column contains information:

◉ Yes   ◯ No

Enforce unique values:

◉ Yes   ◯ No

Figure 1-19. *Creating a site column*

As you can see, there are many columns in SharePoint, most of which are self-explanatory from its name. When applying the column to a list, the Group property allows you to group a set of site columns for easy reuse. In the Workplace Columns group, let's group all our custom site columns.

A site column has a few other properties. The Required property shows whether a column is mandatory. You cannot have the same branch name for two different branches if you select "Enforce unique values." Let's make the branch name mandatory and unique. Refer to Figure 1-19. Leave the other properties as they are and click OK. You will receive a warning since we selected to enforce unique values as Yes. Ignore this warning and click OK to create the site column. It will now redirect you back to the site columns page. By filtering site columns by group, you can see the new column we created. See Figure 1-20.

Figure 1-20. *Site columns filtered by group*

Like we did earlier, let's create a column for Branch Address. Set Type to "Multiline of text" since we need to input multiple lines of address. Make it a nonrequired column and do not enforce unique values. Select Existing Group and choose Workplace Columns as the group. Specify "Plain text," as illustrated in Figure 1-21. Leave the other properties as they are.

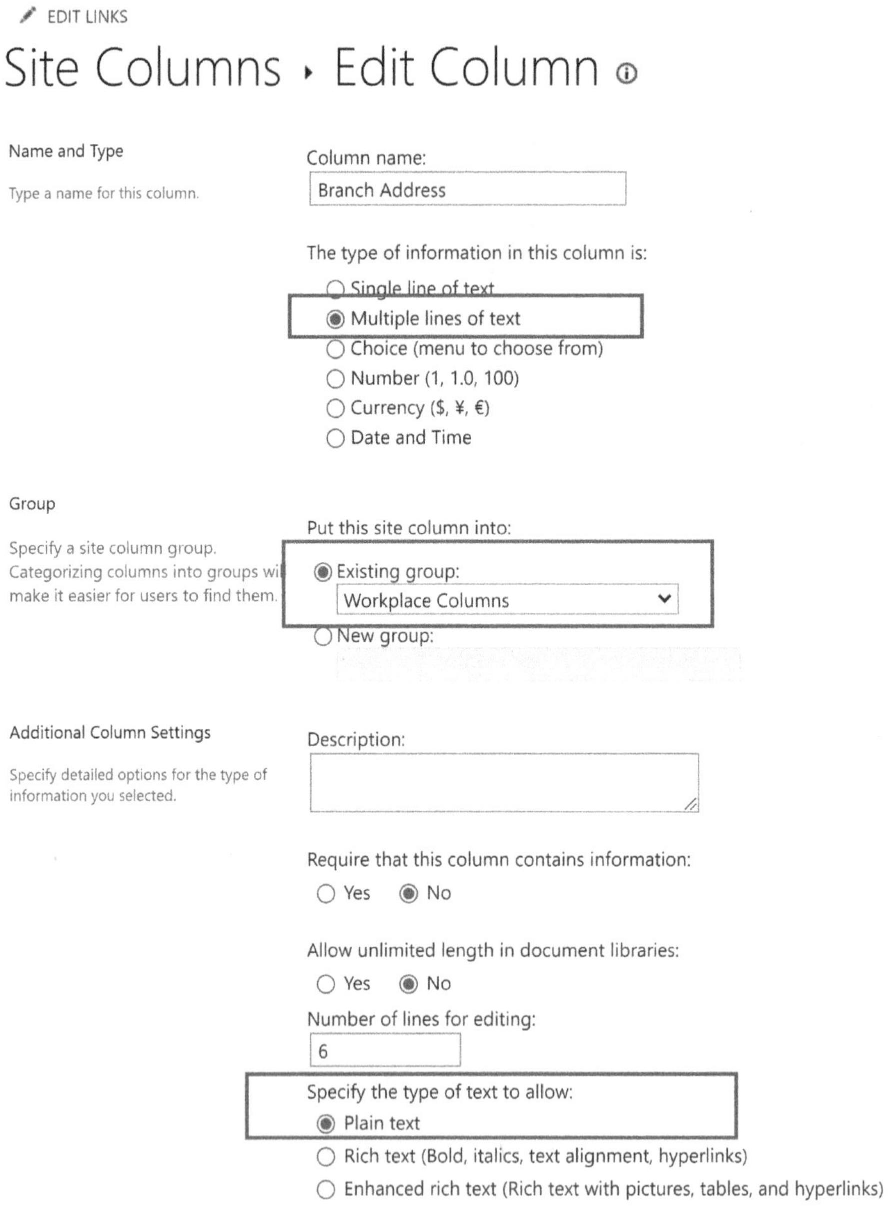

✎ EDIT LINKS

Site Columns › Edit Column ⓘ

Name and Type

Type a name for this column.

Column name:

Branch Address

The type of information in this column is:

○ Single line of text
◉ Multiple lines of text
○ Choice (menu to choose from)
○ Number (1, 1.0, 100)
○ Currency ($, ¥, €)
○ Date and Time

Group

Specify a site column group.
Categorizing columns into groups wil
make it easier for users to find them.

Put this site column into:

◉ Existing group:

Workplace Columns ⌄

○ New group:

Additional Column Settings

Specify detailed options for the type of
information you selected.

Description:

Require that this column contains information:

○ Yes   ◉ No

Allow unlimited length in document libraries:

○ Yes   ◉ No

Number of lines for editing:

6

Specify the type of text to allow:

◉ Plain text

○ Rich text (Bold, italics, text alignment, hyperlinks)
○ Enhanced rich text (Rich text with pictures, tables, and hyperlinks)

Figure 1-21. *Multiple lines of text column*

Once the second column is created, let's add the two columns to the "Branch Information" list. As a result, it will appear in the list for data entry. Go back to the site contents using the left navigation or using the chrome button, as illustrated in Figure 1-22, to add site columns to the list.

Figure 1-22. *Navigate to the site contents from the site columns*

From the site contents, navigate to the Branch Information list. (Refer to Figures 1-14 and 1-15.) As shown in Figure 1-23, select "List settings" from the list interface.

Figure 1-23. *Navigating to the list settings*

On the Settings page, click "Add from existing site columns," as in Figure 1-24.

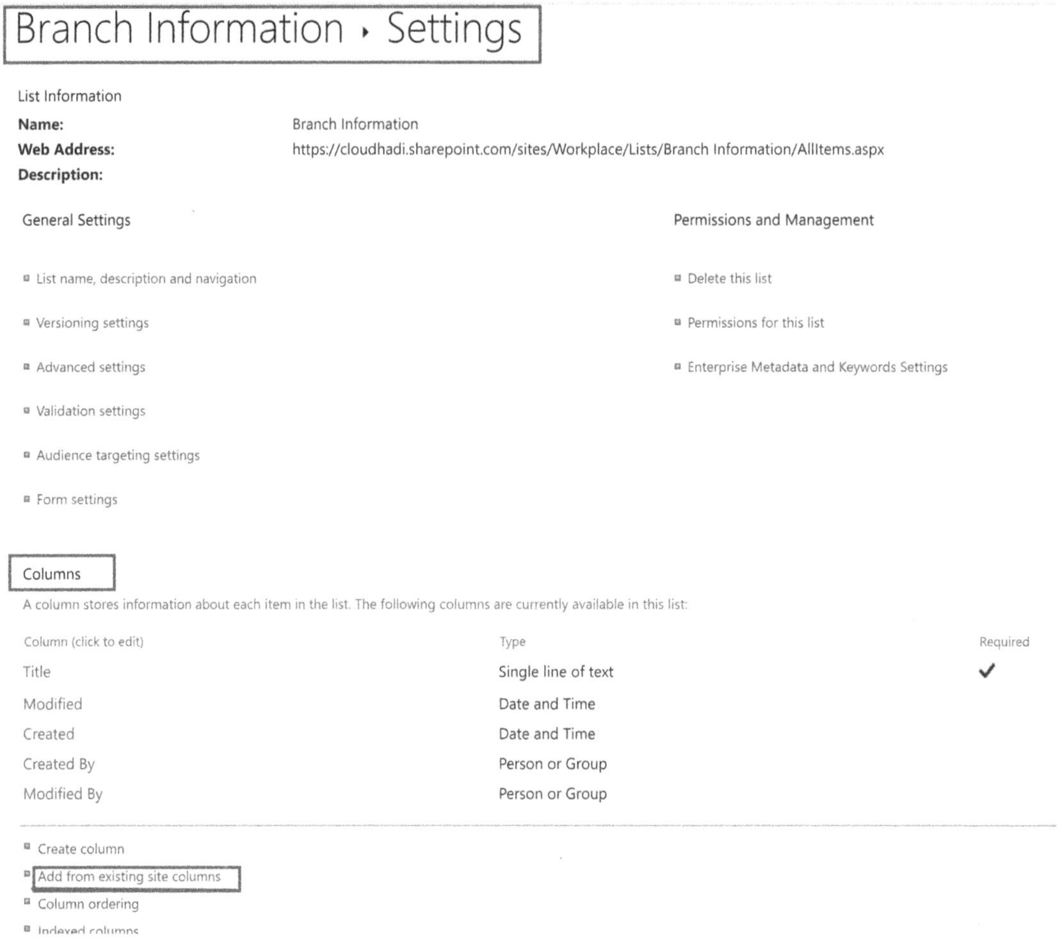

Branch Information ▸ Settings

List Information

Name: Branch Information

Web Address: https://cloudhadi.sharepoint.com/sites/Workplace/Lists/Branch Information/AllItems.aspx

Description:

General Settings   Permissions and Management

▫ List name, description and navigation   ▫ Delete this list

▫ Versioning settings   ▫ Permissions for this list

▫ Advanced settings   ▫ Enterprise Metadata and Keywords Settings

▫ Validation settings

▫ Audience targeting settings

▫ Form settings

Columns

A column stores information about each item in the list. The following columns are currently available in this list:

Column (click to edit)	Type	Required
Title	Single line of text	✔
Modified	Date and Time	
Created	Date and Time	
Created By	Person or Group	
Modified By	Person or Group	

▫ Create column

▫ Add from existing site columns

▫ Column ordering

▫ Indexed columns

Figure 1-24. *List settings*

Choose the Workplace Columns group from the drop-down menu. Select both the "Branch name" and "Branch address" columns and then click Add. You can leave "Add to default view" checked and click OK. Refer to Figure 1-25.

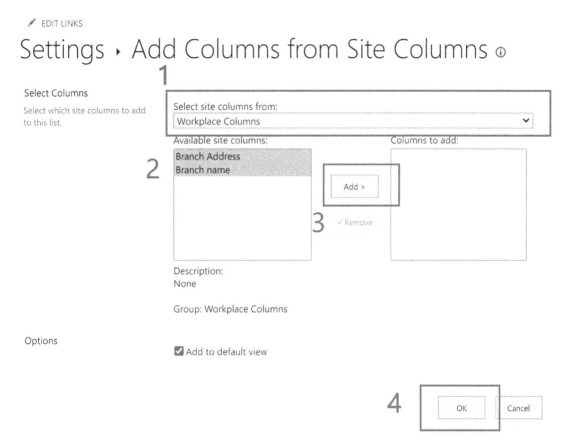

Figure 1-25. *Adding site columns to a list*

Upon being redirected back to the list settings page, you can see both the added site columns under the Columns section.

There will be a Title column on top of the Columns section, which is marked as required by default (refer to Figure 1-24). Since we won't be using that column in our example, let's make it nonmandatory. By clicking Title, change "Require this column contains information" to No and click OK.

Upon being redirected back to the list settings page, scroll down and click "All items" under the section Views. Clicking "All items" will take you to the edit view page. Uncheck the Title box and click OK. Refer to Figure 1-26. A view is a virtual representation of list items, where you can specify which columns to view and in what order. As we will see later, there are also various options for sorting, filtering, and grouping in a view.

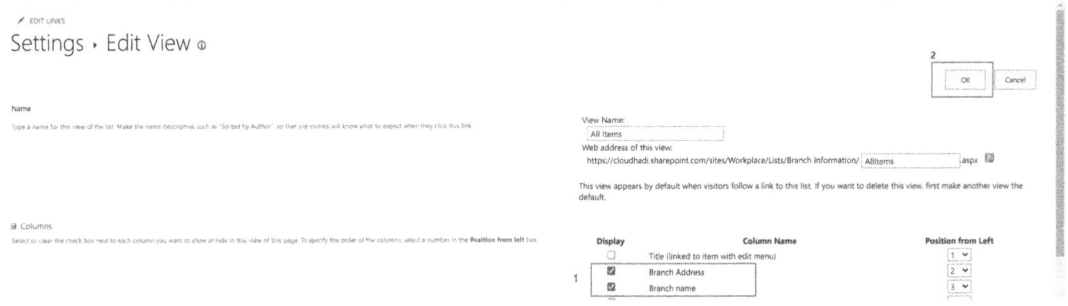

Figure 1-26. *Edit view*

Upon clicking OK, you will be taken back to the list interface, where the two new columns will be visible.

You can always add a column directly from the list settings without adding a site column. In Table 1-1, you'll find out when you can use a site column versus a list column.

Table 1-1. *Choosing Between Site and List Columns*

Scenario	Column	Reason
Column will need to be used only in a single list or library	List column	List column is easy and quick here as it is used only once.
Column needs to be reused across different lists/libraries	Site column	Site column can be reused across list and library boundaries.
Search	Site column	Creating a site column is easier for search as it will create a managed property automatically.

Additionally, site columns facilitate better maintenance.

Instead of adding site columns directly to the list, you can have them added to a content type and later add the content type to the list. The content type is a reusable collection of metadata (columns) for a category of items or documents in a SharePoint list or document library. As an example, you can create a content type called Product and add multiple columns to it. From the list, you can associate the content type Product with it. The list will include all the columns in the content type. By using content types, you can make columns centralized and reusable.

You can create a content type by going to the site settings and then the site content types. Columns can be added to a content type once it has been created. Click "Advanced settings" in the list or library to enable the management of content types. Once enabled, you can add one or more content types. In the upcoming chapters, we will see content types in action.

Having added the columns to our custom list, let's see how we can add a new item.

Data Operations in a Custom List

This section shows you how to add and manage data on a list. You can add a new item to the list by clicking the New button, as highlighted in Figure 1-27. A sliding window appears on the right of the page when you click the New button. This form is called the "new form" of the list.

Let's remove the Title column from the form and move "Branch name" up, on top of Branch Address. You can do this by clicking the Edit form icon (highlighted as step 2 in Figure 1-27). Then, select "Edit columns" (highlighted as step 3).

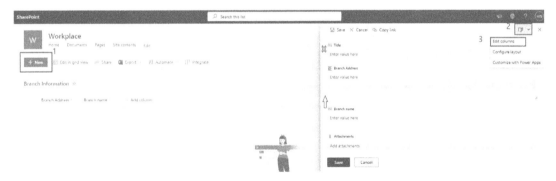

Figure 1-27. *New form of a list*

Once you click "Edit columns," you can uncheck Title. You can move "Branch name" to the top by hovering over it, clicking three dots, and then selecting "Move up." Alternatively, you can drag "Branch name" over Branch Address by clicking it. Finally, click Save to save your changes. Figure 1-28 illustrates this process.

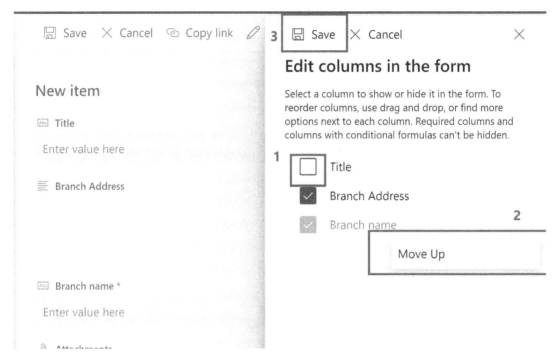

Figure 1-28. *Arranging the columns in the list form*

This will close the "Edit columns" window, allowing you to enter data into the "New item" form. By clicking the Save button at the top or bottom, the item will be saved. See Figure 1-29.

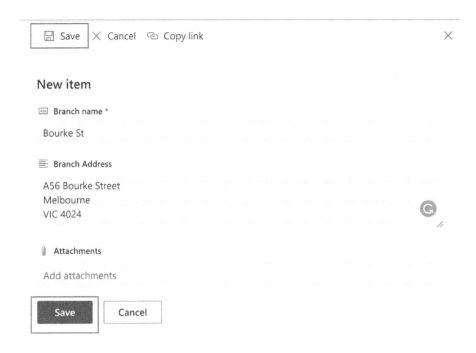

Figure 1-29. *Creating a new item*

The item will be created and will be displayed on the list view, as in Figure 1-30. You can select the item and edit or delete.

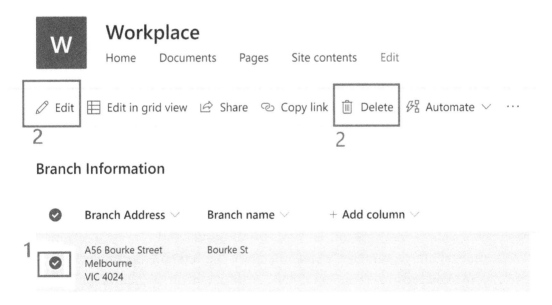

Figure 1-30. *List item operations*

Also, there is an option to edit in grid view next to the Edit option. You can also use the "Edit in grid view" option to create a new item using grid view. The link "Add new item" will appear once you click the "Edit in grid view" option. See Figure 1-31. Once you create/edit an item using grid view, click "Exit grid view" to save the changes.

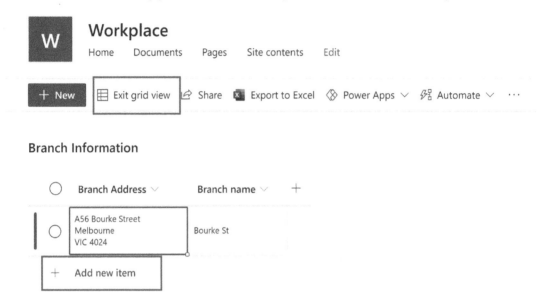

Figure 1-31. *Grid view*

The grid view or the New button can be used to add multiple items to the list.

This gives you a basic understanding of how SharePoint Online's custom lists, site columns, and list forms work. Check out all the options in the list form and list settings to see what you can do.

Document Library

A SharePoint library is a specific type of SharePoint list that is designed to store documents. While both libraries and lists are similar in that they are collections of data, a library is tailored specifically for document management and includes features such as version history, check-in/check-out, and content approval.

A document library is another SharePoint out-of-the-box app. Documents can be stored and managed in a document library. A document library allows you to collaborate and organize documents. It is possible to attach documents to a list item. While discussing the custom list in the previous section, you might have noticed the

Attachment column in the list form. What is the difference between a document in a document library and an attachment to a list item? You cannot search for documents in list attachments, but you can do so using documents in a document library. You can version control a document in a document library, which is not feasible with list item attachments.

There are few out-of-the-box Document libraries available in a communication site by default. Let's create a new one. In "Site contents," click New, just as you did for the list. Choose the option "Document library." Refer to Figure 1-32.

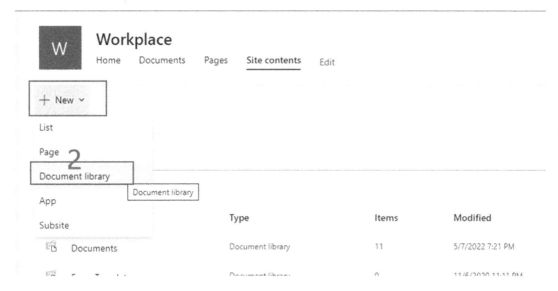

Figure 1-32. *Selecting the "Document library" app*

A slider will appear on the right side. Enter **Policy** as the name and click Create. You will be redirected to the library interface. If you go to "Site contents," you can see the library there also.

Let's add the two site columns we created earlier to this library. In the same way that you navigated to the list settings for Branch Information (see Figure 1-23), go to the library settings here. Add the site columns to the library, exactly as we did for the Branch Information list (see the previous Figures 1-24 and 1-25). The Title field in a library is not a default mandatory field, so you do not need to update it or modify the view. Figure 1-33 shows the library interface after adding the site columns.

Figure 1-33. *Site columns added to library*

From the library interface, you can create a new document or upload an existing document. You can upload using the upload button or drag and drop. Upon uploading a document, you can select it and edit its properties to fill in the metadata, as shown in Figure 1-34. You can also use Edit in grid view, just as we did for the list.

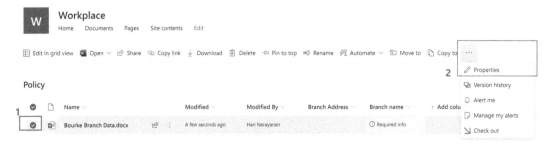

Figure 1-34. *Editing the document properties*

After clicking Properties, the Properties pane opens on the right side. If you would like to arrange the columns or add or remove any column from the properties form, use the "Edit columns" option as explained in the List section (see the previous Figures 1-27 and 1-28). "Branch name" is a mandatory field on the form, so it cannot be removed.

After organizing the columns, click the "Edit all" button and enter the properties data. As you did for the custom list, enter the data. Refer to Figure 1-29 in the previous section.

You can open the document in Microsoft Word by clicking it. The content can be edited in the browser or in a desktop application. Once you have finished editing, save the changes and the document will be updated in the library.

A document library allows you to upload multiple documents. What we did just now is called *content authoring*. The documents have been uploaded, and their metadata has been set. What steps will you take to ensure that the document is visible to end users? How will you ensure that only certain users can read the documents? Is an approval process going to be established before end users can access it? Will you be able to co-author this content with someone else from your organization? As we proceed through this chapter, we'll answer all these questions. Next, let's examine how permissions work in SharePoint.

Permissions in SharePoint

Access to SharePoint content is controlled by permissions. You can specify who can read or update specific information. These permissions can be defined for the entire site, for specific lists or libraries, and even for specific list items or documents.

Permission levels and security groups are two concepts we should understand first.

Permission Levels

A site's default permission levels are as follows:

- *Full Control*: Has full control

- *Design*: Can view, add, update, delete, approve, and customize

- *Edit*: Can add, edit, and delete lists; can view, add, update, and delete list items and documents

- *Contribute*: Can view, add, update, and delete list items and documents

- *Read*: Can view pages and list items and download documents

You can view this full set of permission levels by navigating to Site contents ➤ Site settings ➤ Site permissions ➤ Permission Levels. This is highlighted in the figures in the next section (Figure 1-35 and Figure 1-36).

Security Groups

At a site level, we can classify the user roles into the following three major security groups. The users can be added to the groups. Each group has an assigned permission level. SharePoint permission levels tell the group what users can or cannot do.

- *Site visitors*: Site visitors can only read and download content from your site. The permission level assigned is Read.

- *Site members*: In addition to reading and downloading, site members can add, share, edit, or delete content. Edit is the assigned permission level.

- *Site owners*: Site owners have the Full Control level assigned to them. They can do everything that visitors and members can do. In addition, they can manage settings, security, navigation, etc. They can add users or remove users from the site.

Go to the site settings from "Site contents" interface, and you will see a Site Permissions link in the Site Settings interface (refer to the previous Figure 1-17). Clicking it will take you to the permissions page. You can see the security groups and assigned permissions highlighted. See Figure 1-35.

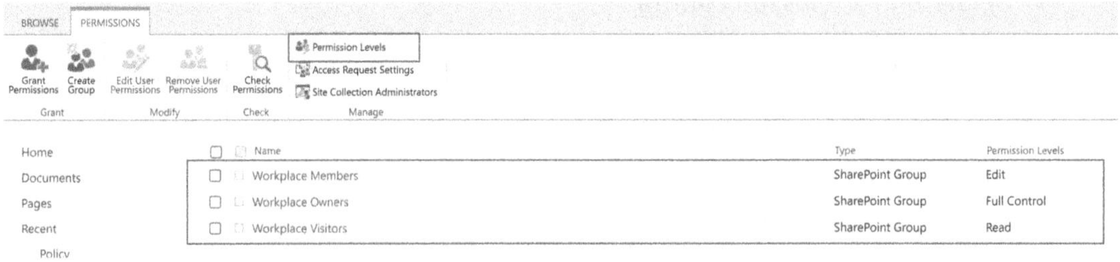

Figure 1-35. *Site permissions*

In addition to these groups, you can create your own group and assign custom-level permissions to it. Like custom groups, you can also create custom permission levels in addition to the default levels we have. But it is recommended to avoid having them unless required.

From the site permission page, if you click the permission levels (refer to the previous Figure 1-35), you will navigate to the permission levels page. You can see the default permission levels and option to add custom-level permissions there. See Figure 1-36.

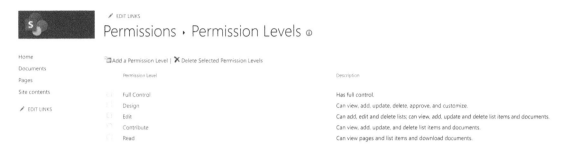

Figure 1-36. *Permission levels*

Unique Permissions

Lists and libraries inherit permissions from the site in which they were created by default. However, a list, a list item, a document library, or a document can form its own permissions if the permissions inheritance is broken.

There are times when we need a list, library, list item, or document to have its own access level. You may want a user to view the workplace site, not branch information, for example. This is where the unique permissions feature comes in handy.

You can define permissions at the list or library level by going to the list or library settings. As an example, let's take "Branch information." Consider that we don't want workplace members to view or edit any of the items in the list. Select "permission for this list" under General Settings under the list settings. Refer to the previous Figure 1-24 to view the list settings page for "Branch Information."

You will be directed to the list permissions page once you click "Permissions for this list." If you click Stop Inheriting Permissions from the top ribbon, it will stop the permissions from inheriting, and you can remove or add security groups. Refer to Figure 1-37.

Figure 1-37. *Permission inheritance*

When a warning pop-up appears, click OK to stop inheritance. You can now remove or add groups or users at the list level. You can, for example, select Workplace Members and use Remove User Permissions to fulfil the requirements discussed earlier. You can also change the permission level of a group using Edit User Permissions. Figure 1-38 illustrates these in rectangles.

The Grant Permissions button can be used to add a user or group only to the list. Click "Delete unique permissions" if you want to inherit the permissions again. As a result, the permissions will revert to inheriting from the site. Figure 1-38 highlights these in ovals.

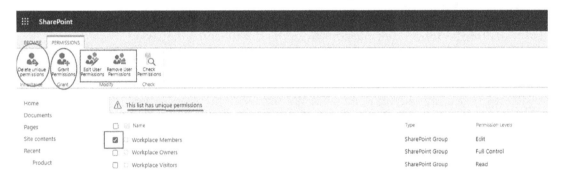

Figure 1-38. *Unique permissions*

Whenever possible and if there is no specific requirement for unique permissions, lists and libraries should inherit most permissions from the site. Permissions can be managed more easily this way. In the upcoming chapters, we will discuss permissions in greater detail.

For the answers to our questions in the previous section, let's return to the document library and discuss versioning.

Version Control

Version control made data tracking and management easier. A version control tool makes it easier to update a document, such as Bourke Branch Data.docx (refer to the previous Figure 1-34), when more than one person wants to update it. As shown in Figure 1-39, you can set versioning in the Library settings by clicking "Versioning settings."

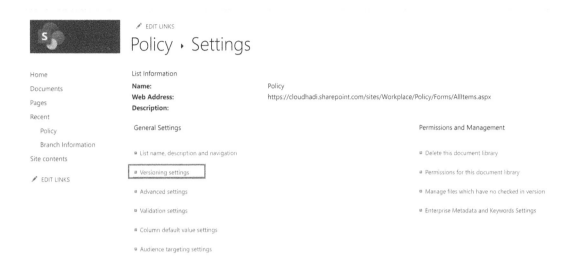

Figure 1-39. *Navigating to the Versioning Settings page*

You will need to set the content approval settings and the requirements for checking out documents to Yes in the versioning settings. The other settings can be left as they are. Click OK. See Figure 1-40.

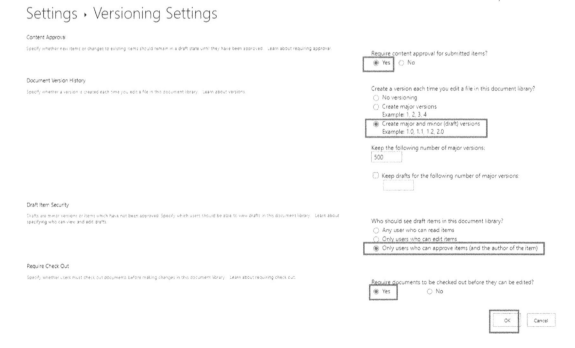

Figure 1-40. *Versioning Settings page*

Now that checkouts have been enabled, the document will be checked out to the user when the user edits it. After making changes to the document, the user can check it in. This will prevent two users from editing the same document at the same time. As shown in Figure 1-40, content approval has been enabled, and the visibility of draft items has been set to only authors and approvers by default. Users with read access will not be able to see the document unless it has been approved. Let's illustrate this with an example.

In the Policy document library, upload a document. By default, the document will be checked out to you. Navigate to the version history by hovering over the document and clicking the three dots, as shown in Figure 1-41.

Figure 1-41. *Navigating to the Version history*

In the version history pop-up, you can see the version is 0.1 and the approval status is draft. Using the top menu, select Properties and then "Edit all," fill in the metadata as you did earlier (refer to the earlier Figure 1-34). As of now, no other user can see the document since it has not been checked in yet. Figure 1-42 shows the steps for checking in a document.

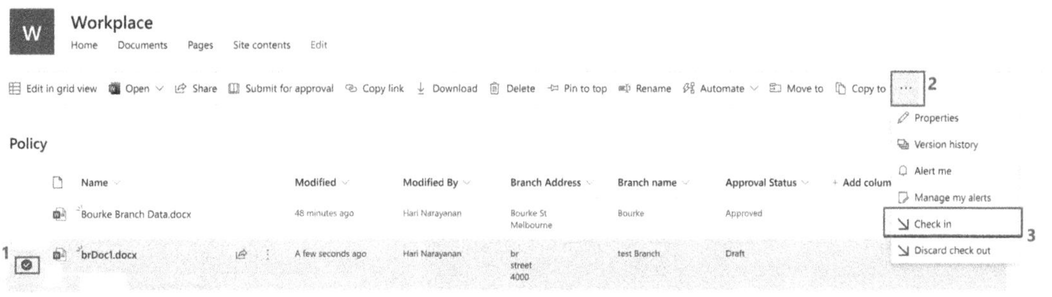

Figure 1-42. *Checking in a document*

When you click "Check in," a pop-up appears. Click "Check in" and select the major version. Optionally, you can provide comments. As soon as the document is checked in, it will be visible to all users who have the Approve permission and you, the author. Refer to the previous Figure 1-40, where it shows the draft visibility by default only to approvers and the item author.

All users added to the "Workplace owners" group have "'Full control" permissions on our site. The Full control permission has been assigned with Approve, permission, so workplace owners can view, edit, or approve this document. Users with Edit or Contribute permission will not even be able to view the document unless it has been approved. As this document has not yet been approved, users belonging to Workplace Members or Workplace Visitors will not be able to view it.

Let's approve the document now. Select the document and click Approve/Reject, as shown in Figure 1-43.

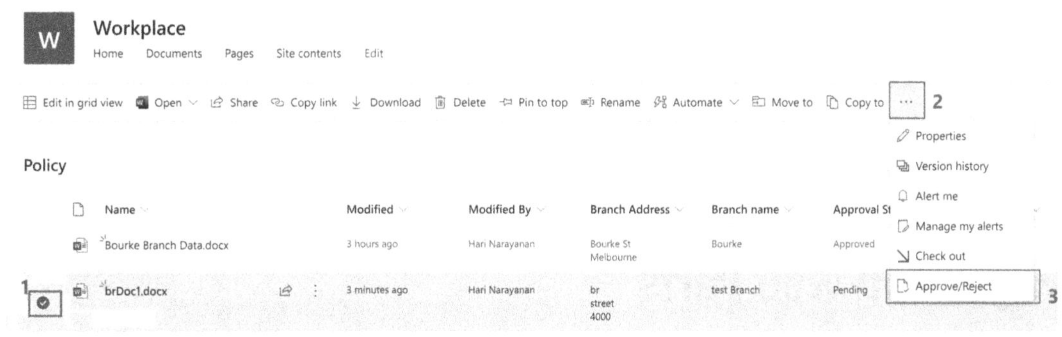

Figure 1-43. *Approving or rejecting a document*

There are three options in the Approve/Reject pop-up, each with its own explanation. As shown in Figure 1-44, click Approved and then click Ok.

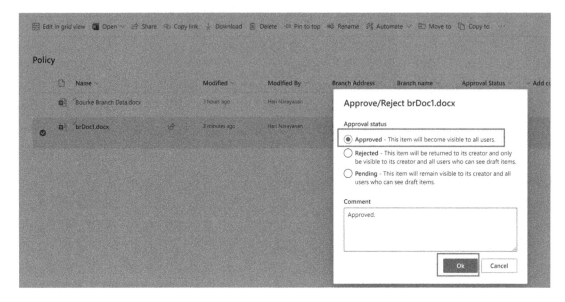

Figure 1-44. *Approving a document*

Now that the document has been approved, all users with read permission can view or download it. The content or the properties of a document can be edited by users with edit/contribute permissions.

Reviewing the version history (refer to Figure 1-41), you can see the current version is published major version 1.0, and the document status is approved.

We just discussed the document management and version control basics. Try to answer the questions on page 30 (Refer to the end of the section 'Document Library') yourself, and you will certainly be able to do so. Now you know about co-authoring, approval, and publishing. In addition, you learned how SharePoint maintains versions of a document and how to define versioning settings. You might want to experiment more with document libraries and version control, such as allowing different users to act on one document, enabling different settings for version control, etc.

Pages and Web Parts

Let's take a quick look at pages and web parts. The purpose of *pages* in SharePoint is to display content. A *web part* lets you display specific content on a page. In other words, an individual web part is a building block for a page. Web parts can be added to a page to display lists, libraries, etc., on a page. Pages are stored by default in a library called Site

Pages, which you can find under "Site content." As we chose the Blank template for the site, our home page was created as a blank page. For a better understanding of pages and web parts, let's create a page and add some web parts to it.

Go to "Site contents," click New, and then click Page, as shown in Figure 1-45.

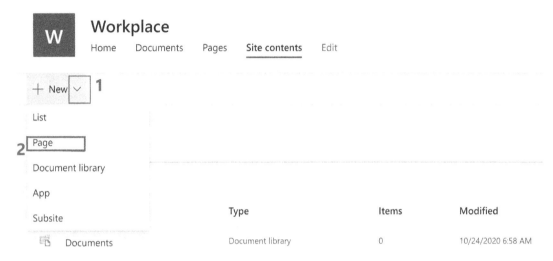

Figure 1-45. *Adding a new page*

A new page will be created, and you can add a title for the page. I titled it "Policy." Figure 1-46 shows how you can change the layout, alignment, etc., by clicking the edit icon on the left. Upon closing the pane, the changes will be automatically saved. If you hover over your name below Title Text, you can remove it with the "x" button if you would like to.

Figure 1-46. *Configuring the title area*

The + button in the middle of the page on the left allows you to add a new section with different layout options, as shown in Figure 1-47.

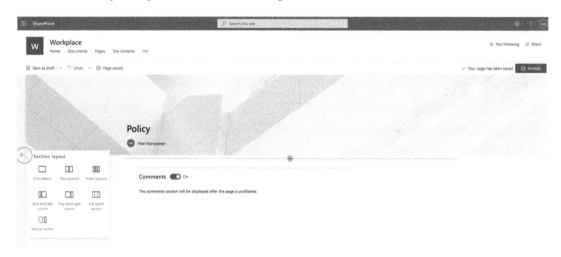

Figure 1-47. *Adding a section layout*

For this example, select the Two columns section. The section will be created and divided into two columns. A pop-up appears when you click the + icon in the first column, displaying the web parts you can add. In our example, let's select the web part Highlighted Content, which displays the most recent documents from the site. Refer to Figure 1-48.

Figure 1-48. *Adding a web part*

As we did for the title area, once the web part is added, you can configure its different properties using the edit icon. Try adding another web part of your choice to column 2. Explore the different web parts available and add multiple sections and web parts to the page. Each web part's properties pane will help you configure it. In the upcoming chapters, we'll go over some of the web parts in more detail.

Click Publish on the top right once you have finished adding the web parts. After the page is published, it will be visible to all users. As shown in Figure 1-49, you can make any further changes to a published page by clicking Edit on the top right.

Figure 1-49. *Edit page*

Once the changes have been made, click Republish. This is illustrated in Figure 1-50.

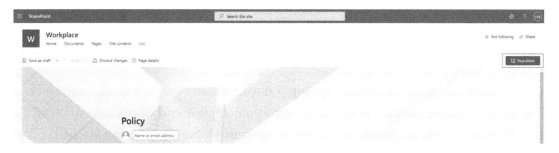

Figure 1-50. *Republishing a page*

We have looked at how to edit a page, add web parts, edit web part properties, and publish. Similarly, you can customize your home page.

Customizing a SharePoint Site

What are the custom requirements for a modern digital workplace, and how can SharePoint Online and various development tools meet them?

You can make a document or page available to site users when you approve it or publish it. What if you want to include a few approvers and a few other conditions before publishing the page? For that, we need customized workflows. *Workflows* are preprogrammed applications used to automate business processes. Power Automate or Azure Logic Apps or third-party solutions can be used to create customized advanced workflows. Chapter 5 will cover Power Automate in detail.

If you want to have a custom user interface or more features on the list or library forms than what the out-of-the-box forms offer, how can you do that? To a significant extent, we can change the look and feel of a form by using JSON formatting. In addition, JSON formatting can be used for a variety of form validation needs. We can use a PowerApps form, SPFx List Form Customizer, or SPFx web parts, based on the specific requirements, if we want to add some complex validation or user interface that JSON formatting cannot provide.

How about creating custom-looking, interactive dashboards for users? That can also be accomplished with JSON view formatting. To accomplish UI and interactive requirements that JSON formatting cannot fulfill, we can combine SPFx web parts and Power Automate.

We also have rich integration capabilities within SharePoint Online with Teams, Power BI, Azure SaaS, and other Microsoft 365 suites.

Summary

In this chapter, we focused on familiarizing you with SharePoint Online in this chapter. This chapter provides a quick overview of SharePoint Online and what you can do out of the box. We began by introducing the admin center. Following that, you learned about site templates and different types of lists in SharePoint. We discussed the different development tools and frameworks that can be used with SharePoint Online. Using a list, we looked at how to add site columns, change a form, and fill out the information. During this chapter, you learned how documents are managed, and we implemented version control in a document library. We discussed SharePoint permissions and security basics. You gained knowledge about different roles and groups and how to set unique permissions. Our next focus was on pages and web parts. At the end of the chapter, we discussed how complex a modern workplace can be and how SharePoint Online can handle it with its rich integration capabilities. Let's look at an application case study in the upcoming chapter and see how all the requirements can be met.

CHAPTER 2

Business Analysis and Solution Design

You learned about the basics of SharePoint Online in the first chapter. SharePoint Online can be integrated with many applications, both inside and outside of Microsoft 365. SharePoint Online offers endless possibilities when it comes to designing an enterprise application. Using the best available and modern technology solutions, let's analyze a business case study.

We will be working together on a project from now on. You will learn most of the modern customization and integration scenarios in SharePoint Online at the end of this project. After we complete the conversion of some requirements to the final solution, we will cover most of the modern customization scenarios and SharePoint Online integration. This includes SharePoint out-of-the-box (OOB) capabilities, SharePoint Framework (SPFx) web parts, PnP provisioning framework, Search, Power Apps, Power Automate, Teams, and Power Virtual Agents. Our objective in this book is not to cover each solution in depth, but to cover the foundation for each so that you can explore it further on your own.

In this chapter, if you cannot understand the high-level solution mentioned for each use case, do not worry, as each solution will be explained in detail in the respective chapters. The use cases are mainly designed to give you an overview of the requirements before we design the solution. As you read through each chapter of the solution, you can always refer to the use case in this chapter.

By the end of this chapter, you will understand how to design a SharePoint Online solution. In this chapter, we will cover the requirements, the design, and the site preparation needed for the upcoming chapters. In the upcoming chapters, we will focus on one technology area while meeting each of the requirements.

© Hari Narayn 2023
H. Narayn, *Building the Modern Workplace with SharePoint Online*,
https://doi.org/10.1007/978-1-4842-9726-1_2

Business Use Cases

A multimanufacturing organization called Cloudhadi produces several products. Their products include food, electronics, and furniture. The company wants to create a portal where employees can collaborate, store, and display product information. The portal must serve as a centralized source of truth for all information, and it must be well presented.

Stakeholders also want a service desk option in the same portal. The home page should also highlight products, achievements, and news.

Let's look at some use cases and how SharePoint Online can meet them. It is possible that some of the requirements can be met with out-of-the-box features. There may be cases where they need customization, and we can use the best option available.

We will list all the use cases and provide a high-level approach for each. Our next step will be to organize the requirements and turn them into a design. The use cases in the following scenarios are denoted by *UC-*, followed by a category and number. In this case, the solution represents the high-level approach to transforming the use case into a business product.

Document Use Cases

In relation to the manufacturing of each product area, many documents need to be stored and published. Here, we have three product areas: food, electronics, and furniture. Document management for these product areas is shown in the following use cases:

UC-D1: As a product executive, I want a place where I can create and upload product-related documents.

Solution: Create a document library called Product Data.

UC-D2: As a product executive, it is important to me that I create, upload, or edit only the documents related to my product area.

Solution: Let's create a folder for each product and set folder-level permissions to a group of users.

UC-D3: As a product executive, I want to read and download documents related to other products.

Solution: Set read access to other product folders by maintaining Contribute access to a person's own folder.

<u>UC-D4:</u> As a product lead, I want to revert to a previous version of a document if there are any errors in the approved current version of the document.

Solution: Enable versioning in the Product Data library settings.

<u>UC-D5:</u> As a product lead, I want to see the history of changes made in a product document.

Solution: Use the version history feature.

<u>UC-D6:</u> As a product executive, I want my documents to be approved by the product lead before they are visible to end users.

Solution: Enable content approval and set the approval permissions to the respective leads at the product folder level.

<u>UC-D7</u>: As a product executive, I want an option to submit a product document for approval.

Solution: Use JSON formatting to create a button to submit for approval.

<u>UC-D8:</u> As a product executive, I want an option to choose a product lead from a set of product leads from the respective product area.

Solution: Create SharePoint groups for product leads for each product area and create a person field to choose from the respective group.

<u>UC-D9:</u> As a product lead, I want to be notified if any user submits a document for approval.

Solution: Use a Power Automate automatic flow to trigger a notification to the respective product lead when the product executive clicks the button from the SharePoint interface.

<u>UC-D10:</u> As a product executive, I want an option to choose an inspection lead from any of the product leads in case the document needs their approval.

Solution: Create a person field like UC-D8, again restricted to the specific product lead groups.

<u>UC-D11:</u> As a product executive, I want the inspection lead to be visible only if inspection is required.

Solution: Create a conditional formula and apply it to the Inspection Lead field based on "Do inspection required."

<u>UC-D12:</u> As an inspection lead, I want to be notified if any user submits a document for approval.

Solution: Use a Power Automate automatic flow to trigger a notification to the selected inspection lead when the product lead approves the document.

UC-D13: As a product executive, I want to enter information about the document that I am uploading and want to do basic validations for the metadata.

Solution: Use a SharePoint OOB form with JSON formatting.

UC-D14: As a product executive, in my documents view, I want to view product names in different colors according to the product type selected.

Solution: Use JSON column formatting to set the colors according to the product type.

UC-D15: As a product lead, I want to have a dashboard where I can see the document information of my pending documents and approve or reject them.

Solution: Use JSON view formatting to create a dashboard view and approvals.

Product List Use Cases

The stakeholders want to store product information, such as information about all the products that have been manufactured, those whose manufacturing is in progress, and those whose manufacturing is pending. To store this data, we can use a SharePoint list.

UC-PL1: As a product lead, I want to enter project-related information into a product list and update the status. I want to have checks such as displaying data in a column based on another.

Solution: Use a SharePoint OOB form with JSON formatting. With its advanced validation and layout capabilities, JSON formatting is an ideal solution for this. We don't ideally require bringing in a Power Apps form or SPFx.

UC-PL2: As a product lead, I want to manage products from the home page. I need an interface where I can view, create, edit, and delete products from the home page.

Solution : Develop a Power Apps canvas app.

Page Use Cases

Stakeholders want to set up pages like the home page, About Us, etc. Let's look at these use cases.

UC-P1: As a business user, I want to view the recent company updates in a visually appealing way on the home page.

Solution: Use an out-of-the-box Hero web part.

UC-P2: As a business user, I want to view the most recently manufactured products and details on the home page.

Solution: Use a highlighted content web part with product information.

UC-P3: As a business user, I want to see the recent news and events on the home page.

Solution: Use out-of-the-box news and event web parts.

UC-P4: As a site administrator, I want to configure news and recent company updates on the home page.

Solution: Create a SharePoint group with the Full Control permission to configure the information.

UC-P5: As a site administrator, I want to configure the About Us and Employee Offers pages in the site.

Solution: Create pages and provide a SharePoint group with the Full Control permission to configure the information.

Service Portal Use Cases

Within the same site, stakeholders would like to set up a service portal where employees can request services such as machines, licenses, etc. Afterward, the service desk team can handle the service requests.

UC-SD1: As a business user, I want an interface where I can submit a request and view the status of my existing requests.

Solution: Add an SPFx web part to a page. Store the requests in a SharePoint list. Because of the need to create a form with multiple tabs and handle complex validations, OOB JSON formats are not suitable for this web part. Power Apps is also an option. Creating and retrieving service requests will be faster with SPFx. On the other hand, Power Apps makes it easier to develop and provide easy integration with many data sources, which is not a specific requirement in our case. We can implement the web part using SPFx since it fits our scenario better.

UC-SD2: As a business user, I want to have a live chat option where I can ask questions and create service requests through Teams.

Solution: Create a chatbot using Power Virtual agents and deploy it to Teams.

UC-SD3: As a business user, I want to be notified via email when I raise a request and when my request is actioned.

Solution: Create a Power Automate flow to notify the user.

UC-SD4: As a service desk executive, I want an interface where I can view all pending requests and take action on them.

Solution: Implement this feature in the SPFx web part.

UC-SD4: As a business user, I want an interface in Teams where I can create requests and view all my requests.

Solution: Sync the SPFx web part to Teams.

Navigation Use Cases

It is important to have good navigation on the site. Users should be able to navigate to the desired location, and access should be restricted according to their roles.

UC-N1: As a business user, on my home page, I want to have a link to view all the products and a link to the service portal.

Solution: Use the out-of-the-box top navigation.

UC-N2: As a product executive, only I should be able to upload documents related to my product area.

Solution: Use the SPFx Application Customizer to create a navigation link based on the current user. This requires an SPFx extension since we need to add a link to the navigation and customize it based on the logged-in user.

UC-N3: As a site administrator, I want to add links to About Us and other information about the company at the bottom of the site.

Solution: Use the out-of-the-box footer settings.

_UC-N4:_ As a business user, I want to move to the About Us and Employee Offers pages from my home page.

Solution: Use the out-of-the-box footer links.

UC-N5: As a business user, from the home page, I should be able to notify the service executive team immediately if any urgent issue arises, before raising a service request.

Solution: Use the SPFx Application Customizer to create a footer link that posts urgent issue messages to the Teams channel for service executives. This requires communication with Teams, so we'll use the SPFx extension.

Search Use Cases

As part of the requirements, search plays an important role. A user should be able to search for documents or products and refine their search results.

UC-S1: As a business user, I want to search for all documents related to all products from the home page.

Solution: Use the out-of-the-box SharePoint Online Search box and configure the search results page.

UC-S2: As a product executive, I want to search for documents related to my product only.

Solution: Build a custom search results page with a custom result source configured to filter for each product.

UC-S3: As a product executive, I want to see specific information related to my product documents while searching for them.

Solution: Use the PnP Modern Search solution and update the display templates to display the required information.

UC-S4: As a product executive, I want to filter documents based on a specific property.

Solution: Use the PnP Modern Search filters.

High-Level Design

We identified use cases and a high-level approach for building Cloudhadi's new modern digital workplace. Let's now put these requirements into a high-level design in the following sections.

We will be using a communication site for Cloudhadi in this project, as the site will be used for sharing information with broader organization users.

Identifying the Roles

Through all the use cases, you can identify that there are few roles, and each role requires its own access level. Let's look at the roles.

- _Business User_: All Cloudhadi employees fall into this category. All information on the site can be viewed by these users, except the location information. Additionally, they should have "Add item" access to the service portal list for raising service requests. However, these users should not be able to edit service requests. Business User is the most basic level of access required in the site. Other roles require permissions in addition to Business User permissions.

- *Product Executive*: All employees working for a particular product, including its product lead, are considered product executives. A Product Executive must have Business User access. Furthermore, this role will need access to create and upload documents.

- *Product Lead*: The Product Lead is responsible for approving the documents. The Product Lead needs Product Executive access. Inspection Leads also fall into this category. For a specific document, some Product Leads will have the Inspection Lead role. However, access to the site and library remains the same. In addition, Product Leads have Edit access to the product list where they can add or edit items.

- *Service Executive*: The Service Executive needs Business User access. In addition, to handle service requests, they must have Edit access to the service portal list.

- *Sales Manager*: Sales Managers can read, add, and update location-based sales information, in addition to the Business User access they have.

- *Site Administrator*: Site Administrators are the power users and need to have Full Control access to the site, to configure pages, to grant access, etc. They can add, edit, or view any information/settings on the site.

Security Design

Let's determine the SharePoint groups and permission levels. Here are the steps we plan to follow to design the site security. In the following settings, permissions are set according to the principle of least privilege (PoLP). As a result, a user will have access only to the bare minimum of privileges they need to perform their intended task.

- *Stage 1*: Create the following SharePoint groups at the site level with the access. (They are listed here in Group Name – Access format.)

  - Cloudhadi Users – Read

  - Food Executives – Read

- Electronics Executives – Read

- Furniture Executives – Read

- Food Leads – Read

- Electronics Leads – Read

- Furniture Leads – Read

- Service Executives – Read

- Sales Managers – Read

- Site Administrators – Full Control

- *Stage 2*: Set unique permissions for the Sales list, and remove access from all users. Give Edit access to Sales Managers.

- *Stage 3*: Set unique permissions for the Products list. Maintain Read access for Cloudhadi Users and remove all other access. Set Read access for Cloudhadi Users and set Edit access to Food Leads, Electronics Leads, and Furniture Leads.

- *Stage 4*: Set unique permissions for the Service Portal list, and give Edit access to Service Executives. Provide "Add item" access to Cloudhadi Users so they cannot edit any other items. We will see how we can set this in detail.

- *Stage 5*: Create three folders in the library Product Data, one each for one product type. Set unique permissions for each folder; provide Edit permission only to the respective executive group, and provide approve permission only to the respective lead group. For example, provide Edit access to Food Executives and Approved access to the Food Leads for the Food product folder. Maintain Read access for Cloudhadi Users.

We have a total of 10 groups. Except for the Site Administrators group, all other groups will have only Read permission at the site level. This is our base design for the security level. If required, we can make any adjustments during our project development and update the design accordingly.

Identify and Design Artifacts

In this stage, we need to identify all the artifacts that need to be created.

Lists and Libraries

Table 2-1 shows the lists and libraries for the solution.

Table 2-1. *Lists and Libraries*

List/Library Name	Content Type	Purpose
Products	Clouhadi product	List to capture the product information
Product Data	Cloudhadi document	Document library for document upload, approval, and publishing
Service Portal	Cloudhadi service	List to capture service request information
Sales	No content type	List to capture location-based sales information

Content Types

A content type is a reusable collection of site columns. Content types can be inherited by a list or library. Here we need to create three content types: a Cloudhadi product for the Product list, a Cloudhadi document for documents in the Product Data document library, and a Cloudhadi service for the service portal. For the Location list, let's create columns at the list level so that we can illustrate that as well.

Table 2-2 shows the content types required for the solution.

Table 2-2. *Content Types*

Content Type	Category	Parent Content Type	Site Columns
Cloudhadi product	Cloudhadi content types	Item (list content types)	Refer to Table 2-1.

(*continued*)

Table 2-2. (*continued*)

Content Type	Category	Parent Content Type	Site Columns
Clouhadi document	Cloudhadi content types	Document (document content types)	Refer to Table 2-1.
Cloudhadi service	Cloudhadi content types	Item (list content types)	Refer to Table 2-1.

Site Columns

Table 2-3 shows all the site columns we need to create for the portal. During development, we may need to alter some columns or add some columns. Accordingly, we will update the design. Let's begin by using the information we already have from designing the solution.

In Table 2-3, the first column displays the column name, the second column displays the type of column, the third column displays any special requirements for the column, and the last column displays the type of content the column should belong to.

Note   You might be confused with some of the terms here if you are a new user to SharePoint. As we proceed through the development, you will gain more clarity. It is always possible to refer to the design during that time.

Table 2-3. *Site Columns*

Site Column	Type	Special Conditions	Content Types
Product Name	Single line of text	Mandatory	Cloudhadi product, Cloudhadi document
Product Type	Choice	MandatoryPossible values: Food, Electronics, Furniture No default value	Cloudhadi product, Cloudhadi document, Cloudhadi service

(*continued*)

Table 2-3. (*continued*)

Site Column	Type	Special Conditions	Content Types
Product Lead	Person or group	Single person, restrict to product lead group, mandatory	Cloudhadi document, Cloudhadi product
Materials Used	Multiple lines of text		Cloudhadi product
Inspection Completed Date	Date	Mandatory	Cloudhadi product
Manufactured Date	Date	Mandatory	Cloudhadi product
Expiry Date	Date		Cloudhadi product
Product Features	Multiple lines of text		Cloudhadi product
Product Status	Choice	Mandatory Possible values: New, In production, Completed; the default is New	Cloudhadi product
Review Date	Date	Mandatory	Cloudhadi document
Do inspection required	Boolean	Yes or No toggle	Cloudhadi document
Inspection Lead	Person or group	Single person, restrict to product lead group	Cloudhadi document
Document Type	Choice	Mandatory Possible values: Product Information, Product Inspection details, Product Tooling Data, Product Materials Information, Other	Cloudhadi document

(*continued*)

Table 2-3. (*continued*)

Site Column	Type	Special Conditions	Content Types
Request Title	Single line of text	Mandatory	Cloudhadi service
Request Description	Multiple lines of text	Mandatory	Cloudhadi service
Related to	Choice	Possible values: Access, Materials, Equipment, General	Cloudhadi service
Request Status	Choice	Mandatory Possible values: New, In progress, Resolved, Completed, Rejected, Reopened;the default is New	Cloudhadi service
Request Assigned To	Person or group	Person only, restricted to service executive groups	Cloudhadi service

List Columns

Table 2-4 shows the list columns. In our project, we have decided to use list columns for the list Sales.

Table 2-4. *List Columns*

Column Name	Type and Conditions	List
Product Type	Choice; mandatory	Sales
Location	Choice; mandatory, populates based on selected product type	Sales
Quantity	Number; mandatory	Sales
Date	DateTime; mandatory	Sales

Site Pages

Table 2-5 shows the possible pages we need to create for the solution.

Table 2-5. *Site Pages*

Page Title	Web Parts	Purpose
Home	Hero, News, Events, Highlighted Content, SPFx Application Customizer	Home page of the site
About Us	Text	About Us page
Employee Offer	Text	Employee offers page
Service Portal	SPFx custom web part	To display the service requests by pulling data from the service list
Search Product	PnP Modern Search box, search filter, and search results web parts	Custom search results page for products

Custom Web Parts and Extensions

As per the use cases, a few custom web parts and extensions need to be developed. Let's identify them. See Table 2-6.

Table 2-6. *SPFx Components*

Web Part/Extension	Purpose	Use Case
Quick Updater	An extension for a quick update of metadata of documents from the library interface	UC-D14
Navigator	Application customizer extension for creating navigation links based on current user	UC-N2
Notify App Customizer	Application customizer extension for notifying service executive team on urgent issue	UC-N5
Location List Form Customizer	List form customizer for location list	UC-LL1
Service Portal	SPFx web part for service portal page to display the service request	UC-SD1

Custom App (Power Apps)

Table 2-7 identifies some of the list/library forms that can be developed using Power Apps.

Table 2-7. *Power Apps Forms*

Form	Purpose	Use Case
Manage Products	Solution for managing products from home page	UC-PL2

Workflows (Power Automate)

Table 2-8 describes some scenarios where we need to develop Power Automate flows.

Table 2-8. *Power Automate Flows*

Flow	Purpose	Trigger
Product document publishing	This flow is for the document approval process, which includes inspection and product leads approval and notifications.	Product Data – On item modified with approval field modification
Product document reset	Reset document status on editing the document.	On file modified
Service request	To notify the service desk via Teams and email on raising a service request.	Service Portal list – item created
Service action	To notify the requester once a service request is actioned.	Service Portal list – item modified

Teams and Power Virtual Agents

Regarding the service chatbots, we do have some requirements for integrating Teams and Power Virtual Agents. Refer to Table 2-9.

Table 2-9. *Teams and PVAs*

Action	Purpose
Chatbot	Create a chatbot using Power Virtual agents and deploy to Teams
Integration	Sync the service portal web part in Teams

A Quick Recap

To summarize what we have done so far, we have planned how to build the solution. We discussed security, artifact creation, and customization scenarios. If necessary, we can make minor changes to this design during development.

This business analysis and design exercise is meant to familiarize you with the process of designing a SharePoint Online solution. As part of this requirement, I also included the technical areas I intend to cover in the book. Throughout the following chapters, we will discuss each section's technical solution and its actual implementation. For each of the technical areas, such as Power Apps, Power Automate, SPFx, Teams, etc., we will implement at least one use case.

Preparing the Site

Let's prepare the site by creating all the artifacts from the SharePoint interface.

Site Columns

To start, refer to Table 2-1 and create all the site columns. We saw how to create a site column in Chapter 1. Create all columns under the group Cloudhadi Columns. Once all site columns are created, you can add all the site columns under Site Contents ➤ Site Settings ➤ Site Columns and filter by the group Cloudhadi Columns, as you can see in Figure 2-1.

Figure 2-1. *Site columns*

Content Types

To create content types, refer to Table 2-2 and create all the content types. For each content type, add site columns to it by referring to Table 2-1. Let's look how to create a content type and add site columns to it, as we didn't discuss this in Chapter 1. We will use the example of Cloudhadi service.

Go to Site Contents ➤ Site Settings ➤ Site Content Types. Click "Create a content type." Refer to Figure 2-2.

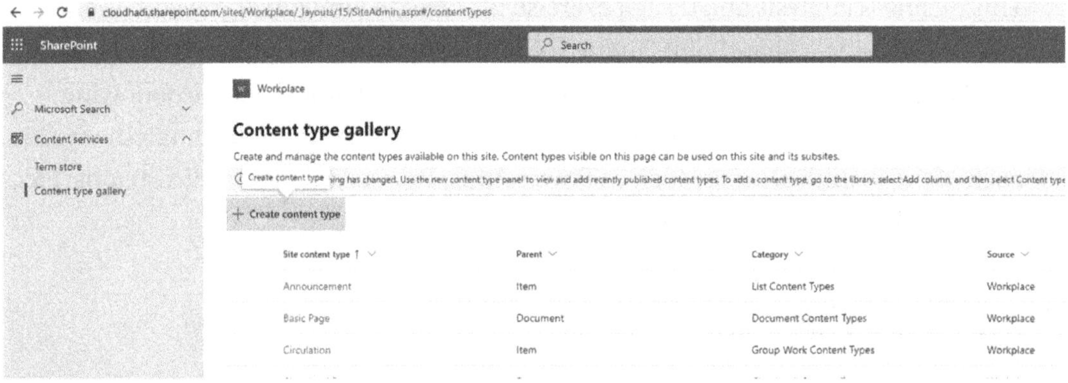

Figure 2-2. *Content type gallery*

A sliding pane will open. Enter the name **Cloudhadi Service**. For Category, select "Create a new category" and provide **Cloudhadi Content Types** as the name. Refer again to Table 2-2 and Figure 2-3 for other details.

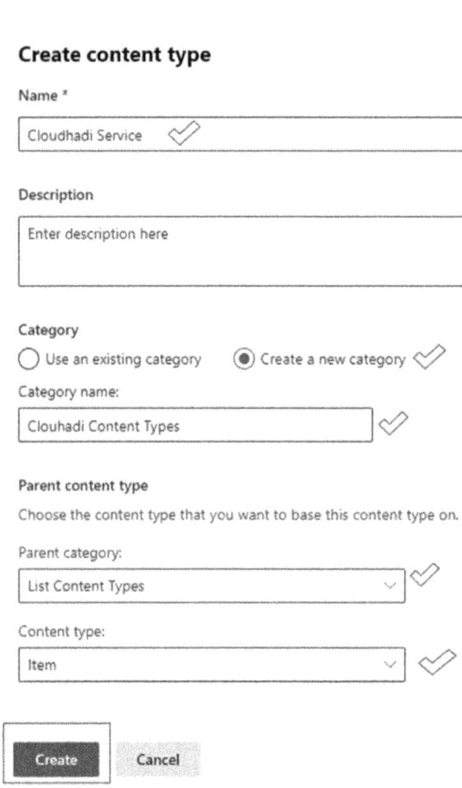

Figure 2-3. *Creating a content type*

Click Create. The content type Cloudhadi Service will be created, and you will be taken to an interface where you can add site columns. To add site columns, click Add site column ➤ Add from existing site columns. Refer to Figure 2-4.

Content type gallery > **Cloudhadi Service**

✎ Edit   ⚙ Advanced settings   🗑 Delete content type

Cloudhadi Service
Category
Cloudhadi Content Types

Parent
Item ⓘ

Content Type ID
0x010036DF314B855F73428645944444E85A5C

Site columns
Add and manage the site columns that are a part of this content type.

＋ Add site column ⌄

Create new site column

Add from existing site columns	Type	Required	Source
Title	Single line of text	Yes	Item

Figure 2-4. *Adding a site column*

From the resulting pane, for "Select site columns category from existing category," select Cloudhadi Columns, and add all the site columns for this content type (refer to Table 2-1). Then add the required site columns for the Cloudhadi Service content type, one by one to the right column. Once all site columns are added, click Save. Refer to Figure 2-5.

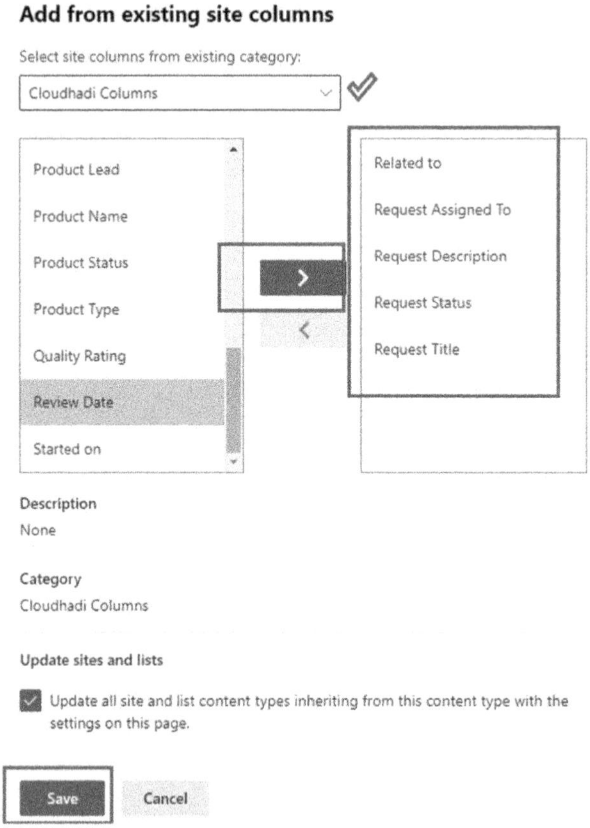

Add from existing site columns

Select site columns from existing category:

Cloudhadi Columns

Product Lead		Related to
Product Name		Request Assigned To
Product Status	**>**	Request Description
Product Type		Request Status
Quality Rating	**<**	Request Title
Review Date		
Started on		

Description
None

Category
Cloudhadi Columns

Update sites and lists

☑ Update all site and list content types inheriting from this content type with the settings on this page.

Save   Cancel

Figure 2-5. *Adding existing site columns*

The Cloudhadi Service content type will be updated with all the columns now. Select the default Title column and uncheck "Show this column in lists." Save. We don't use this default column. Refer to Figure 2-6.

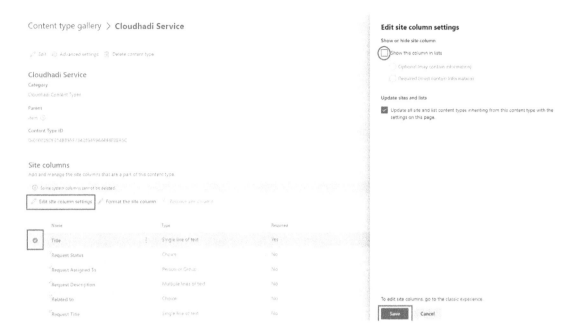

Figure 2-6. *Changing the site column settings*

Now repeat the steps for other content types listed in Table 2-2. You can refer to Table 2-1, Table 2-2, and the earlier figures for help.

Lists, Libraries, and List Columns

We went through how to create a list and a library in Chapter 1. Follow those steps to create all the lists and libraries listed in Table 2-3. You can see all the lists and libraries under the site contents once they're created.

To create list columns for the list Sales, follow these steps:

1. Go to the "Site contents" tab, and click the Sales list to go to its interface. Click "Add column," select Choice, and click Next. Refer to Figure 2-7.

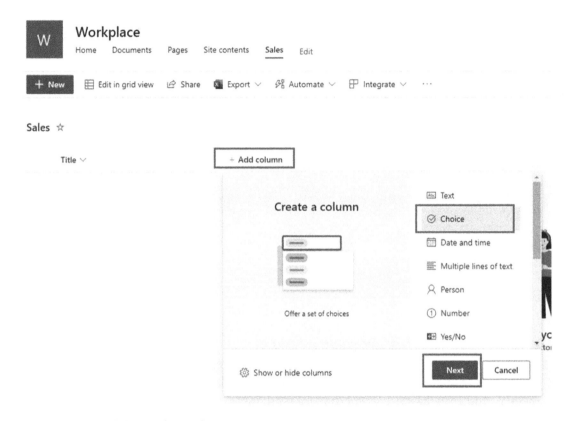

Figure 2-7. *Adding a list column, step 1*

2. Fill in the name and values as in Figure 2-8 and click Save.

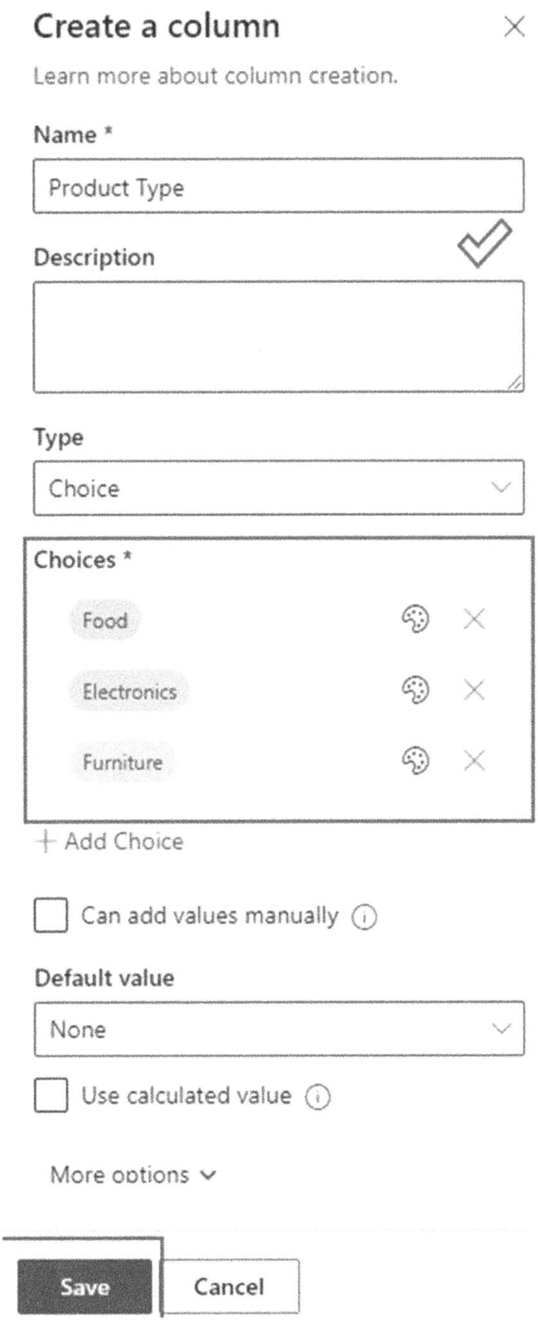

Figure 2-8. *Adding a list column, step 2*

This creates a list column called Product Type. Repeat this for all the columns listed in Table 2-4. Choose the type as per the table. Leave the default Title column as it is.

Add a Content Type to a List

For the Products and Service Portal lists and the Product Data library, we need to add the respective content type. Let me show you how to add a content type to a list by adding the Cloudhadi Service content type to the Service Portal list.

1. Go to the "Site contents" tab, click Service Portal, click the three dots, and select Settings. Refer to Figure 2-9.

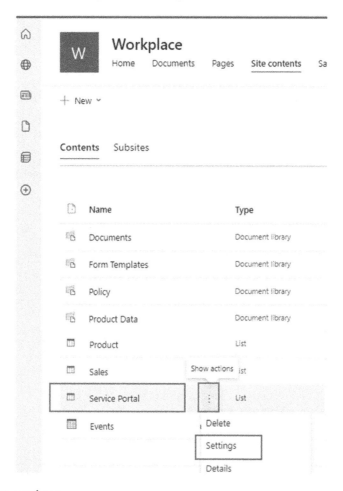

Figure 2-9. *List settings*

2. From the Settings page, click "Add from existing site content types" under Content Types. From the resulting page, select the content type group to filter, choose the Cloudhadi service, and click Add. Then click OK. Refer to Figure 2-10.

Figure 2-10. *Adding a content type to a list*

Now, the content type is added to the list. Follow similar steps for adding the respective content type to the Products list and the Product Data library. Refer to Table 2-3 for which content type to add to which list.

Site Pages

Create all the site pages listed in Table 2-5. Refer to Chapter 1 for the steps to create a page.

Security

Let's now create all the groups, assign the respective permission levels, and set the unique permissions. Before creating the groups, ensure that you have created a few users (at least five) in the Microsoft 365 admin center in the Active Users section (refer to Chapter 1's "Users" section and specifically Figure 1-3).

Execute the stages described in the section "Security Design." For stage 1, I will show how to create the Cloudhadi Users group as an example.

1. To create a group, go to the "Site contents" tab, click Site Settings, and click Site Permissions ➤ Create Group. Refer to Figure 2-11.

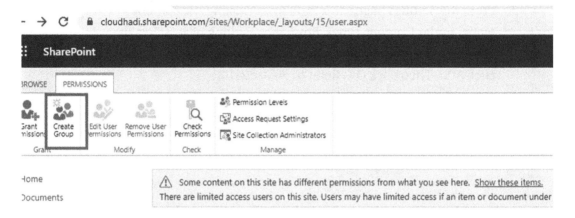

Figure 2-11. *Creating a group, step 1*

> 2. Add the group name, fill in the group owner, choose the
>   permission level, and leave the other settings as they are. Refer to
>   Figure 2-12.

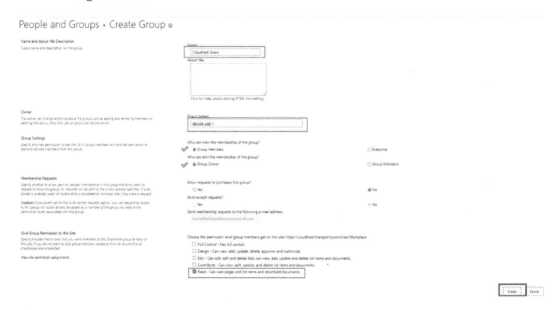

Figure 2-12. *Creating a group, step 3*

Create the remaining nine groups in the same way. Provide the group name and
permission level as mentioned in "Security Design" for stage 1.

Let's move on to stage 2. Go to the Sales list, go to the list settings, and then go to the permissions settings. Set the unique permissions for the list as described in the "Security Design" section. (Refer to Chapter 1's "Unique Permissions" section for the steps.)

Repeat the previous steps for stages 3 and 4 for the Products and Service Portals lists, as described in the "Security Design" section.

For stage 5, create three folders in the library Product Data. Go to the "Site contents" tab and then Product Data. Click New. Select Folder from the drop-down menu and name it **Food**. Repeat and create two more folders, named Electronics and Furniture. See Figure 2-13.

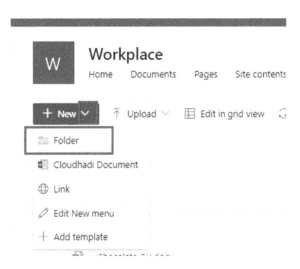

Figure 2-13. *Creating a new folder*

Click the three dots next to the Food folder and click "Manage access." Refer to Figure 2-14.

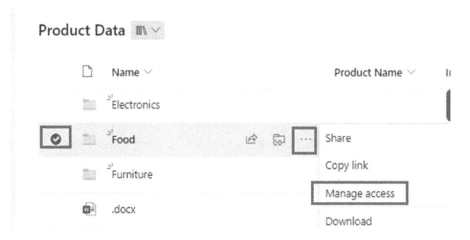

Figure 2-14. *Managing folder access*

In the pop-up, scroll to the bottom and click Advanced. This will take you to the permissions page where you can set unique permissions on the folder like you did for the lists and library before.

This completes the requirement analysis, solution design, and site preparation for our project.

Note   If you have any queries on this solution design or any queries on site setup, reach out to me by creating an issue in the Github repository of the Product: `https://github.com/apress/building-modern-workplace-SharePoint-online-2e`. I will respond to you as soon as I can.

Deployment Overview

You learned in Chapter 1 how to create site columns, lists, etc. We will have three or four environments in a real project. Artifacts can be created and deployed in multiple ways.

In the development site, we could create all artifacts from the SharePoint interface and then run a PnP PowerShell command to extract them. To accomplish this, we can use `Get-PnPSiteTemplate`. To deploy all the artifacts to the test and production environments, run another PowerShell command: `Invoke-PnPSiteTemplate`. Alternatively, you can use a third-party tool like ShareGate for the deployment.

PnP PowerShell and XML Provisioning Schema

As mentioned, using PnP commands, you can extract artifacts of a SharePoint site into a template XML file and use this to deploy all the artifacts to another environment. PnP XML Provisioning Schema is an open-source solution. The SharePoint PnP Community is an open-source initiative coordinated by SharePoint engineering. The PnP Provisioning schema is available at `https://github.com/pnp/PnP-Provisioning-Schema`.

The latest schema available while writing this book is the October 2022 version. You can refer to it here: `https://github.com/pnp/PnP-Provisioning-Schema/blob/master/PnP.ProvisioningSchema/ProvisioningSchema-2022-09.xsd`.

PowerShell PnP PowerShell allows you to connect to SharePoint and extract and deploy SharePoint artifacts. PnP PowerShell requires PowerShell 7.2 or later. To install PnP PowerShell module, use the following command at your command prompt:

```
Install-Module PnP.PowerShell.
```

Summary

The purpose of this chapter was to thoroughly examine the project requirements, strategize the solution design, and identify the necessary development components. Throughout this chapter, we explored various capabilities of SharePoint Online, both out-of-the-box and custom features, and discussed how they align with the specific business requirements of the project. As a result, we now have a clear understanding of the project scope and the planned design.

In addition to understanding the project, we also created the foundational artifacts such as site security, site columns, content types, lists, and libraries. With these essential elements in place, we are now ready to dive into the next chapter, where we will focus on developing out-of-the-box forms using JSON formatting techniques. Furthermore, we will delve into the exciting realm of JSON-based column and view formatting. These topics will empower us to enhance the user experience and customize the display of data within SharePoint.

Let's move forward to the next chapter as we start on the journey of creating dynamic and visually appealing forms using JSON formatting in SharePoint Online.

CHAPTER 3

JSON Formatting

The JSON formatting feature in SharePoint Online allows you to customize forms, columns, and views. The previous chapter discussed a few form requirements, so let's look at how JSON formatting can be used to meet those requirements. Most requirements for a SharePoint Online site can be met with out-of-the-box features and JSON formatting. That's the power of JSON formatting in SharePoint development.

SharePoint serves as both the front end and back end of our application. Various types of information are stored in lists and libraries, which serve as a back end. Forms and pages are the front ends where you enter data, validate data, etc. In SharePoint Online, there are many ways to customize forms. The JSON formatting technique is the fastest and easiest way to customize a form. JSON formatting also supports advanced formatting techniques for columns and views. In this chapter, we will also discuss these topics.

Many functionalities are available with SharePoint Online's out-of-the-box forms. They look good, but there are some limitations when it comes to custom requirements. You can customize forms using Power Apps, SPFx List Customizer, SPFx web parts, and third-party forms like Nintex forms. However, JSON formatting allows you to customize forms to a significant extent without complex development or third-party tools. The loading time of JSON-formatted forms is quite fast. The JSON format also offers the benefit of maintaining the same theme for the form as the underlying SharePoint site theme, without having to do any styling separately.

Using JSON, you can format columns in SharePoint lists and libraries. You can also update field values. Creating a button with the text *Approve*, for example, can change another column's value, e.g., a status from Pending to Approved when a user clicks it. In this chapter, you'll see how this works.

You can create beautiful views with JSON by using view formatting. Creating dashboards where users can view and act on data is possible. We'll also demonstrate this with an example.

© Hari Narayn 2023
H. Narayn, *Building the Modern Workplace with SharePoint Online*,
https://doi.org/10.1007/978-1-4842-9726-1_3

This chapter discusses forms, columns, and views and how to format them using JSON. By the end of this chapter, you will be able to customize SharePoint Online forms, columns, and views using JSON. You will also learn about setting up validations and performing updates using simple JSON formatting.

Forms

Our requirements for the Cloudhadi modern workplace consist of four forms: document properties, product list form, sales list form, and service portal list form. For the service portal and sales, we will be using a custom SPFx solution. Before looking at the JSON formatting of a form, let's configure an out-of-the-box form for product data and document properties. After that, let's discuss column and view formatting before we explore some formatting techniques to customize the product list form.

Document Properties Form

The Product Data library is where the user uploads documents. The documents will be uploaded into three different folders. Let's start with uploading a document to the library and then organize the document properties form according to our requirements.

In the first chapter, we discussed the basics of a document library and how to edit and save document properties. Let's dig a little deeper and look at creating a form that looks good and provides some validations for product data documents. The product data library is accessible through the "Site contents" interface. Upload your document into the Food folder in the library. Using the rightmost ... icon, select the document and choose Properties from the top menu. See Figure 3-1.

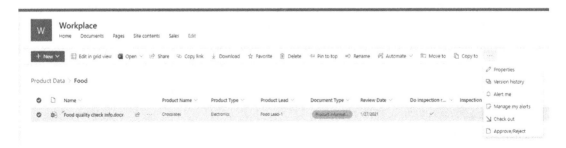

Figure 3-1. *Selecting the document properties*

You will see the properties window on the right. Select "Edit columns" from the drop-down menu, as shown in Figure 3-2.

Figure 3-2. *Edit columns item*

We will arrange the form as shown in Figure 3-3. Fields can be arranged by dragging them to their desired positions. Instead of dragging, you can also select Move Up or Move Down. You can hide a column by unchecking the box on the left. Once you have finished, click Save.

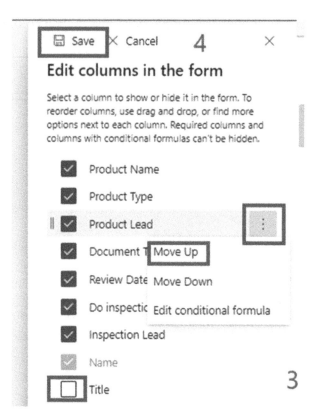

Figure 3-3. *Column order*

To meet the requirements, we want the Inspection Lead column to appear only when the "Do inspection required" option is selected. (See Chapter 2 for more information.) Let's do this using "Edit conditional formula," as shown in Figure 3-3.

Let's see how conditional formulas can be used to show or hide a column. Select "Edit conditional formula" next to the Inspection Lead column. Inside the pop-up, enter the condition.

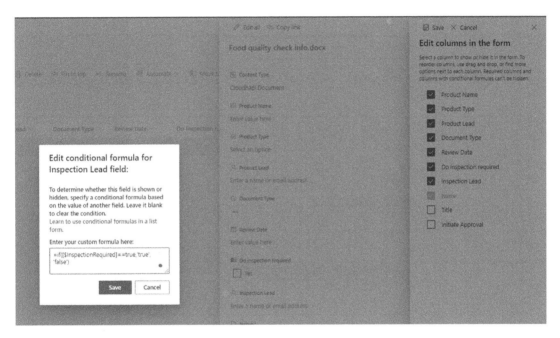

Figure 3-4. *Conditional formula for columns*

The condition =if([$InspectionRequired]==true,'true', 'false') specifies that if "Do inspection required" is set to Yes, the Inspection Lead column will be visible. It is important to note that we are using the internal name of the column here. Once the formula has been entered, save the pop-up and the form.

Note   The Content Type column can be hidden from the form by going to Library Settings ➤ Advanced Settings and selecting No for the "Allow management of content types" option. Since this library uses only a single type of content, it is OK to do this.

You can now enter the document's properties and save them. In the same way as before, select the document and then select Properties. When you enter data into each field, it will be saved. In this case, we are talking about *quick editing*. Refer to Figure 3-5.

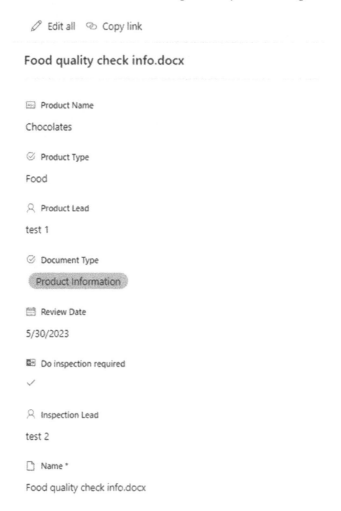

Figure 3-5. *Document properties quick edit*

The Inspection Lead column is hidden, as you can see. Upon selecting Yes for "Do inspections require?," the Inspection Lead column will appear. For now, you can enter any person for the Product Lead and Inspection Lead columns. I have entered **test 1** and **test 2** as the users. Make sure there are at least five users in the Microsoft 365 admin center that can be used in SharePoint groups and Person fields.

Alternatively, you can click "Edit all" and enter the properties. After entering the data, click the Save button at the top or bottom.

Using conditional formulas, you can do several other types of validation, such as validating a date range, user emails, etc.

Now we have the out-of-the-box list form with field arrangements, validations, and visibility settings. You learned how to organize fields, how validation works, how to conditionally show or hide columns, and how to edit document properties.

Form Security: Restricting People Selection

Currently, you can select any user from the site as the Product Lead or Inspection Lead. You would like to restrict it to Food Leads, Electronics Leads, and Furniture Leads. Using the OOB form, we can restrict the lead field to only one SharePoint group. There are three groups in this case. Using the form, we cannot accomplish this.

The only way to accomplish this out of the box is to create a common SharePoint group, say Product Leads, to which all leads from the three groups can be added. You can then restrict the Person field to the Product Leads group.

The only way we could achieve this out of the box is to create a common SharePoint group, say Product Leads, where all leads from the three groups can be added. Then restrict the Person field to the Product Leads group.

Note   We can automate this process to avoid the rework of adding a user to two groups at the same time. When a user is added to any of the three lead groups, we can add them to the Product Leads group via a Power Automation flow. Once you have read Chapter 5, you may want to try that option.

Create a Product Leads group with Read access in Site Settings ➤ Site Permissions, just like you did for Food Leads and other lead groups. Make sure you add two or more users to the group using the New button. Refer to Figure 3-6.

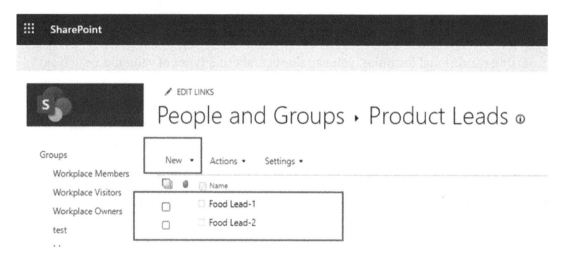

Figure 3-6. *Product Leads group*

Navigate to the library Product Data and select Library Settings ➤ More library settings. In the Columns section, click Product Lead. Under "Choose from," select SharePoint Group and select Product Leads. Refer to Figure 3-7.

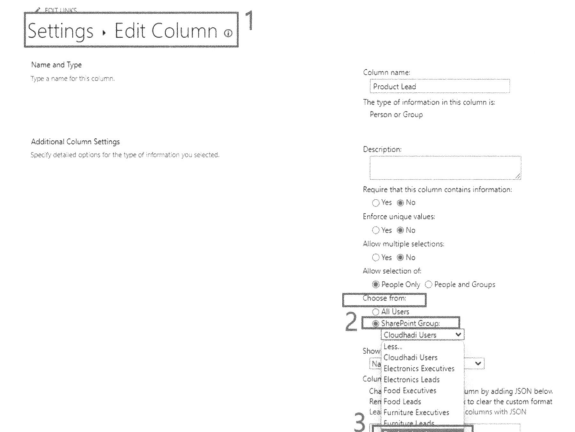

Figure 3-7. *Person field column settings*

For the Inspection Lead column, repeat the same steps. As a result, if you go back to the document we edited before, you will only be able to select members of Product Leads. In my case, only Food Lead-1 or Food Lead-2 can be selected since they are the only leads in the group. Refer to Figure 3-8.

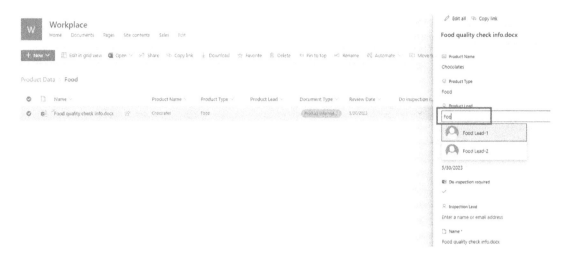

Figure 3-8. *Selecting value for Person field*

Note   Ensure that the users added to the Product Leads group are also added to the Food Leads group. Product Leads are a superset of the Food Lead, Electronics Lead, and Furniture Lead groups. You can add a few test users to the Microsoft 365 admin center if you don't have enough. See Chapter 1 for more information. When assigning the license, include the Microsoft 365 and Power Automate free licenses. It may take a few minutes for newly added users to be available in the SharePoint site.

Pros and Cons of Out-of-the-Box Forms

Although SharePoint out-of-the-box (OOB) forms have some limitations, they are quite powerful. You may find the following pros and cons helpful in choosing the best solution for a form.

The following are the pros:

- *Default branding*: The OOB form has the default modern look and feel that aligns well with the rest of the SharePoint site. Power Apps, SPFx, or other third-party forms must be explicitly styled to match the site theme. Using SharePoint OOB forms is easy and intuitive because they have a consistent design and look across the platform.

- *Built-in validation*: To ensure that data is entered in the correct format, OOB forms have a built-in validation feature. Custom coding is not required to validate mandatory columns, show/hide a column based on another, calculate column values from another, etc.

- *Column organization*: The option to move fields and show or hide columns using the Edit Columns option is very useful.

- *Integration*: A SharePoint OOB form can be easily integrated with other SharePoint features, such as workflows, to improve productivity and automate processes.

The following is a con:

- *Limited customization*: SharePoint OOB forms have limited customization options; for example, they may not support cascading drop-downs or complicated form layouts. For some requirements, this can be a deal-breaker.

In short, SharePoint OOB forms are a quick and easy way to create forms in SharePoint, but they have some limitations in terms of customization. It is important that organizations carefully evaluate their requirements before they use OOB forms or consider custom form solutions if these forms do not meet their needs.

Views

A *view* represents a virtual representation of a list or library of content. Different views may display different columns and have different sorting and filtering options, groupings, and styles. The first chapter touched on views. My goal here is to show you how you can quickly edit the columns in a view from the modern interface without having to go to the list or library settings.

Upload a few documents to the Product Data library and update their properties. You can view a document's properties by selecting and clicking them.

We rely on the library interface view to view multiple documents' properties together. Currently, the library's view is the "All items" view, which is the default view. Refer to Figure 3-9. The product details we are looking for are the name of the product, the type of product, etc. Also, we need to select an order to see how it appears.

Let's see how this works. As shown in Figure 3-9, click Add Column in the library interface and then "Show or hide columns."

Figure 3-9. *Library default view*

In the sliding window that appears, you can drag and drop or click Move Up and Move Down to order them. You can also check or uncheck columns to show or hide them. Once done, click Apply to save the view. Refer to Figure 3-10.

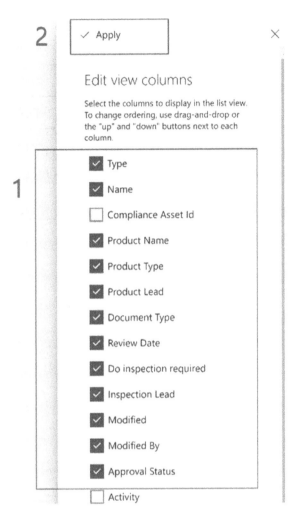

Figure 3-10. *Customizing a view*

After clicking Apply, the library view will be updated with the changes, and you can see all the columns in the view in the order you selected.

Column Formatting with JSON

SharePoint has column formatting and view formatting capabilities that allow you to customize columns and views with JavaScript Object Notation (JSON).

Column formatting is used to change how data in a column is displayed. You can apply conditional formatting, which highlights values that meet certain criteria, adds icons or progress bars, and more. To make data more engaging and user-friendly, you can also add links, images, and other visual elements.

By using column formatting, we can add a custom button or custom text to a library view without developing an SPFx extension. Data in JSON is written as name-value pairs. With a simple example, let's understand the basics of column formatting and then move on to a view formatting example.

As mentioned in Chapter 2, use case UC-15 requires that product names be displayed in different colors based on the type of product. Let's customize product names based on product types. You can format the column by clicking the column and selecting Product Name ➤ Column Settings. See Figure 3-11.

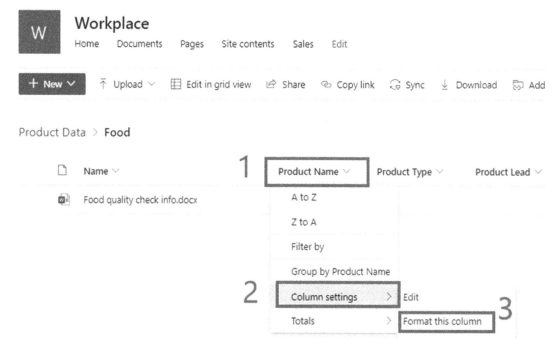

Figure 3-11. *Formatting a column*

As shown in Figure 3-12, select "Advanced mode" at the bottom.

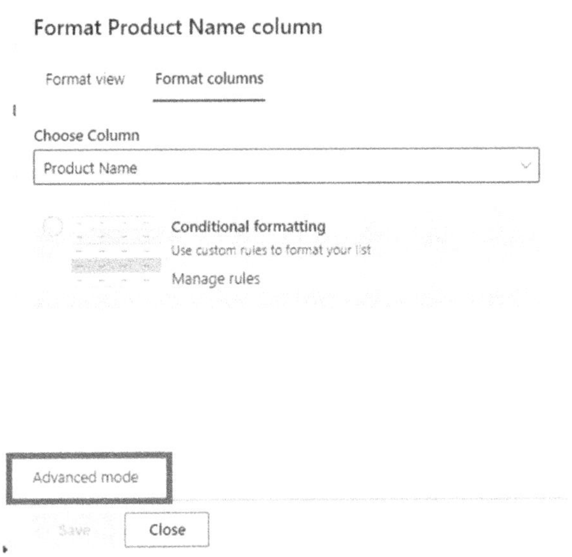

Figure 3-12. *Column formatting advanced mode*

Paste the code shown in Listing 3-1 into the box. The following explanation will help you understand it.

Listing 3-1. Column Formatting

```
{
   "$schema":"https://developer.microsoft.com/json-schemas/sp/column-
   formatting.schema.json",
   "elmType": "div",
   "txtContent": "[$ProductName]",
   "style": {
      "color": "=if([$ProductType] == 'Food', 'green', if([$ProductType]
      == 'Electronics', 'blue', 'yellow'))",
      "font-weight": "bold"
   }
}
```

Based on the value of the Product Type column, this JSON formatting displays the value of the Product Name column within a `div` element with a font color and weight. In the case of Food, the font color will be green; in the case of Electronics, it will be blue; and in the case of Furniture, it will be yellow.

The [$ProductName] refers to the ProductName field of the SharePoint list item displayed. We need to use the internal name of the column here. The square brackets, [], denote a SharePoint column or field. The same applies to the product type. To fit your needs, you can customize the color and font-weight styles.

"$schema" describes which schema version should be used when validating JSON formatting in SharePoint. For this example, we are using sp/v2/column-formatting. schema.json, the most recent schema version available at the time of writing. The schema version validates the JSON formatting syntax and ensures compatibility with SharePoint Online.

Note   You can find all the code sections used in this book on the book's product page in the GitHub repository. See Chapter 3 of the GitHub repository. Here is the direct link to access it: https://github.com/apress/building-modern-workplace-SharePoint-online-2e.

Close the dialog box by clicking Save. See Figure 3-13.

Figure 3-13. *Applying JSON formatting to a column*

The product name Chocolates now appears in bold green. The product name will appear in blue if you set Product Type to Electronics.

View Formatting

We can change the way the list or library view is presented by applying view formatting. It lets us change the layout, add custom headers and footers, and apply conditional formatting to the entire view. As part of view formatting, you can also create custom buttons, add tooltips, and change other aspects of the user interface.

Using JSON formatting, let's create an approval dashboard for our Product Data library. The goal is to have a good-looking dashboard for product leads to view their pending documents for approval and approve or reject them. This should satisfy the requirements in Chapter 2's UC -D16 use case.

Let's start by creating a few columns. As shown in Figure 3-9, select the Add Column option and create two choice columns for Product Status and Inspection Status. I created a Product Status column, as shown in Figure 3-14.

To enable the product executives to submit their documents for approval, it is important to configure the Product Status column with the appropriate values. Here are the recommended values for the column:

- *Draft*: This value should be set as the default when a document is uploaded, indicating that it is in the draft stage.

- *Pending*: When a product executive submits a document for approval, the status should be changed to Pending, indicating that it is awaiting review.

- *Approved*: If the product lead approves the document, the status should be changed to Approved, indicating that it has been approved.

- *Rejected*: If the product lead or inspection lead rejects the document, the status should be changed to Rejected, indicating that it has been rejected.

- *Completed*: If no inspection is required, when the product lead approves the document, the status should be changed to Completed. However, if an inspection is required, the status should change to Completed only after both the product lead and the inspection lead have approved it.

To configure these values, you can navigate to the Product Status column in the All Documents view, select "Column settings," and set the desired values accordingly. Additionally, make sure to set Draft to the default value for the column. This will ensure that the appropriate statuses are assigned to the documents throughout the approval process.

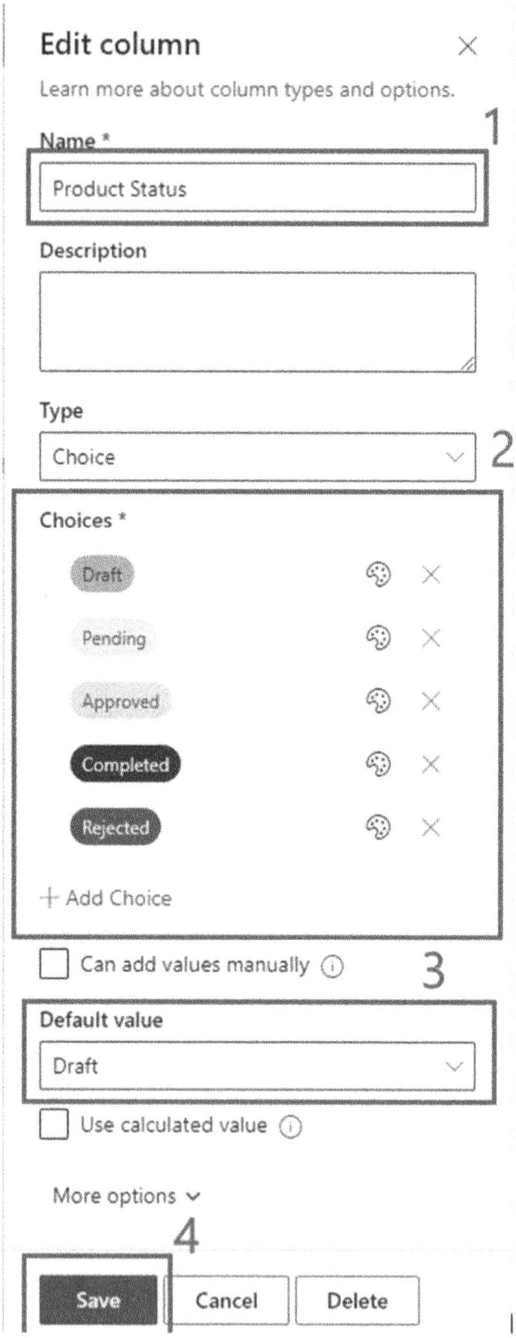

Figure 3-14. *Adding the Product Status column*

You can optionally create an Inspection Status column. Also create two multiple lines of text fields: Product Lead Comments and Inspection Lead Comments. We may not need these columns now. Next, let's create a view for product leads to approve documents. Choose "Create a new view" from the drop-down menu. Refer to Figure 3-15.

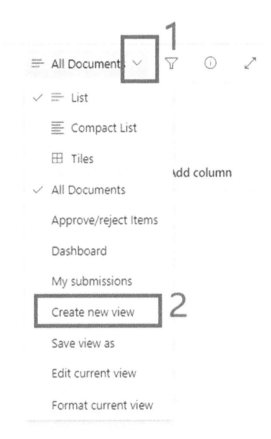

Figure 3-15. *Creating a view*

Enter **Product Lead Dashboard** as the name of the view and click Create. A view will be created, and you will be redirected to the view interface. Similarly, as shown in Figure 3-9, click the "Add column" and "Show or hide columns" buttons. Rearrange the newly created columns, as shown in Figure 3-16. Click Apply.

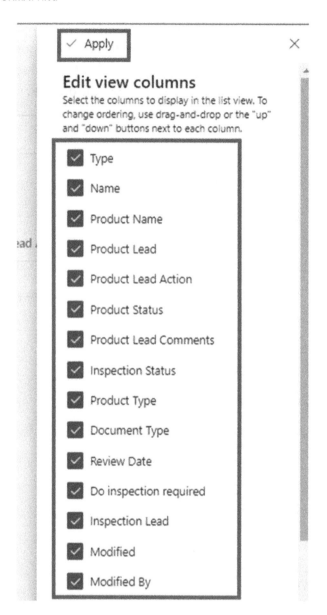

Figure 3-16. *Editing the Product Lead Dashboard view columns*

Note   By clicking "Edit current view" on the Product Lead Dashboard view page, you can hide folders from the Dashboard view. In the view edit interface, scroll down and expand the Folder option. Then, select the "Show all items without folders" option. This configuration ensures that items are displayed without folders in the Dashboard view. No additional filters are required for this view.

To enhance the display and filtering of folders in the Product Lead Dashboard view page, you can edit the view. Begin by clicking "Edit current view" on the Product Lead Dashboard view page to access the view editing interface. Once there, navigate to the Folder option and expand it to reveal additional settings. Selecting the "Show all items without folders" option will remove the folder structure and present the items directly in the dashboard view.

Additionally, expand the Filters option and add a filter for the Product Status column. Set the filter condition Product Status to Pending. This refinement ensures that only the documents in the Pending state will be displayed within the Product Lead dashboard.

Let's format the view. To have more documents to test, upload two or more documents inside the Food folder first. As shown in Figure 3-17, open the product Lead Dashboard view and click the "Format current view" button.

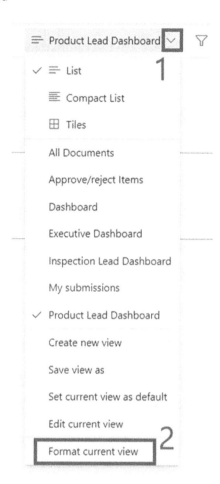

Figure 3-17. *Formatting the Product Lead dashboard view*

Click "Advanced mode," copy the code in Listing 3-2, and insert it into the "Format view" box. Refer to Figure 3-18.

Listing 3-2. View Formatting

```
{
  "$schema": "https://developer.microsoft.com/json-schemas/sp/v2/row-
  formatting.schema.json",
  "debugMode": true,
  "hideSelection": true,
  "hideColumnHeader": true,
  "rowFormatter": {
```

```
"elmType": "div",
"attributes": {
  "class": "ms-borderColor-neutralLight"
},
"style": {
  "display": "flex",
  "box-sizing": "border-box",
  "width": "100%",
  "border-width": "1px",
  "border-color": "#a9a9a9",
  "border-style": "solid",
  "padding": "0 0 0 20px",
  "margin-bottom": "10px",
  "align-items": "stretch",
  "padding-bottom": "3px",
  "overflow": "auto"
},
"children": [
  {
    "elmType": "div",
    "style": {
      "flex": "1 1 300px",
      "display": "flex",
      "flex-wrap": "wrap",
      "width": "100%"
    },
    "children": [
      {
        "elmType": "div",
        "style": {
          "flex": "1 1 300px",
          "box-sizing": "border-box",
          "padding-top": "10px"
        },
        "children": [
```

```
{
  "elmType": "span",
  "style": {
    "line-max-height": "1.5em",
    "margin-bottom": "1em",
    "color": "#fa8072",
    "background-color": "transparent",
    "cursor": "none",
    "text-decoration": "none",
    "font-size": "21px",
    "width": "80%"
  },
  "txtContent": "=[$FileLeafRef]"
},
{
  "elmType": "span",
  "attributes": {
    "iconName": "separator"
  },
  "style": {
    "font-size": "24px",
    "padding-left": "5px",
    "padding-top": "5px",
    "position": "absolute",
    "width": "20%",
    "color": "#fa8072",
    "font-weight": "500"
  }
},
{
  "elmType": "span",
  "style": {
    "line-max-height": "1.5em",
    "margin-bottom": "1em",
    "border": "0",
```

```
      "padding-left": "40px",
      "color": "#fa8072",
      "background-color": "transparent",
      "cursor": "pointer",
      "text-decoration": "none",
      "font-size": "21px",
      "width": "80%"
    },
    "txtContent": "[$ProductName]"
  },
  {
    "elmType": "span",
    "attributes": {
      "iconName": "separator"
    },
    "style": {
      "font-size": "24px",
      "padding-left": "5px",
      "padding-top": "5px",
      "position": "absolute",
      "width": "20%",
      "color": "#fa8072",
      "font-weight": "500"
    }
  },
  {
    "elmType": "span",
    "style": {
      "line-max-height": "1.5em",
      "margin-bottom": "1em",
      "border": "0",
      "padding-left": "40px",
      "color": "#fa8072",
      "background-color": "transparent",
      "cursor": "pointer",
```

```
        "text-decoration": "none",
        "font-size": "21px",
        "width": "80%"
    },
    "txtContent": "='Product Type: +[$ProductType]+  "
},
{
    "elmType": "span",
    "attributes": {
        "iconName": "separator"
    },
    "style": {
        "font-size": "24px",
        "padding-left": "5px",
        "padding-top": "5px",
        "position": "absolute",
        "width": "20%",
        "color": "#fa8072",
        "font-weight": "500"
    }
},
{
    "elmType": "span",
    "style": {
        "line-max-height": "1.5em",
        "margin-bottom": "1em",
        "border": "0",
        "padding-left": "40px",
        "color": "#fa8072",
        "background-color": "transparent",
        "cursor": "pointer",
        "text-decoration": "none",
        "font-size": "21px",
        "width": "80%"
    },
```

```
      "txtContent": "='Document Type: +[$DocumentType]"
  },
  {
    "elmType": "div",
    "attributes": {
      "class": "ms-fontSize-m"
    },
    "style": {
      "line-max-height": "1.5em",
      "padding-bottom": "8px",
      "padding-top": "20px"
    },
    "children": [
      {
        "elmType": "span",
        "style": {
          "font-style": "italic",
          "color": "#0078D4"
        },
        "txtContent": "Document Type: "
      },
      {
        "elmType": "span",
        "style": {},
        "txtContent": "[$DocumentType]"
      },
      {
        "elmType": "span",
        "style": {
          "font-style": "italic",
          "color": "#0078D4"
        },
        "txtContent": " Product Executive: "
      },
      {
```

```
              "elmType": "span",
              "attributes": {
                "class": "ms-fontColor-neutralPrimary"
              },
              "txtContent": "[$Author.Title]"
          },
          {
              "elmType": "span",
              "style": {
                "font-style": "italic",
                "color": "#0078D4"
              },
              "txtContent": " Review Date: "
          },
          {
              "elmType": "span",
              "txtContent": "= toLocaleDateString([$ReviewDate]) "
          }
        ]
      },
      {
        "elmType": "div",
        "attributes": {
          "class": "ms-fontSize-m"
        },
        "style": {
          "line-max-height": "1.5em",
          "margin-bottom": "8px"
        },
        "children": [
          {
            "elmType": "span",
            "style": {
              "font-style": "italic",
              "color": "#0078D4"
```

```
          },
          "txtContent": " Product Lead: "
        },
        {
          "elmType": "span",
          "attributes": {
            "class": "ms-fontColor-neutralPrimary"
          },
          "txtContent": "[$ProductLead.Title]"
        },
        {
          "elmType": "span",
          "style": {
            "font-style": "italic",
            "color": "#0078D4"
          },
          "txtContent": " Inspection Lead: "
        },
        {
          "elmType": "span",
          "txtContent": "[$InspectionLead.Title]"
        }
      ]
    }
  ]
}
},
{
  "elmType": "div",
  "style": {
    "flex-directon": "row",
    "display": "=if([$ProductStatus] == Pending || [$ProductStatus]
    == Approved || [$ProductStatus] == Rejected, inherit,'none')",
    "justify-content": "left",
```

```
          "align-items": "center",
          "flex-wrap": "nowrap",
          "padding-top": "50px",
          "padding-right": "10px"
      },          "children": [
        {
          "elmType": "div",
          "style": {
            "display": "=if([$ProductStatus] == 'Pending' ||
            [$ProductStatus] == '', 'inherit','none')",
            "flex-directon": "row",
            "justify-content": "left",
            "align-items": "center",
            "flex-wrap": "wrap"
          },
          "children": [
            {
              "elmType": "button",
              "customRowAction": {
                "action": "setValue",
                "actionInput": {
                  "ProductStatus": "Approved"
                }
              },
              "attributes": {
                "class": "ms-fontColor-themePrimary ms-fontColor-
                themeDarker--hover"
              },
              "style": {
                "background-color": "transparent",
                "border": "none",
                "width": "110px",
                "cursor": "pointer",
                "flex-directon": "row",
                "justify-content": "left",
```

```
      "align-items": "center",
      "flex-wrap": "wrap",
      "font-size": "18px",
      "color": "#008000"
    },
    "children": [
      {
        "elmType": "span",
        "attributes": {
          "iconName": "SkypeCircleCheck"
        },
        "style": {
          "padding": "4px"
        }
      },
      {
        "elmType": "span",
        "txtContent": "Approve",
        "style": {
          "word-break": "keep-all"
        }
      }
    ]
  },
  {
    "elmType": "button",
    "customRowAction": {
      "action": "setValue",
      "actionInput": {
        "ProductStatus": "Rejected"
      }
    },
    "attributes": {
      "class": "ms-fontColor-themePrimary ms-fontColor-
      themeDarker--hover"
```

```
        },
        "style": {
          "border": "none",
          "width": "110px",
          "background-color": "transparent",
          "cursor": "pointer",
          "flex-directon": "row",
          "justify-content": "left",
          "align-items": "center",
          "flex-wrap": "wrap",
          "font-size": "18px",
          "color": "#FF4500"
        },
        "children": [
          {
            "elmType": "span",
            "attributes": {
              "iconName": "Blocked"
            },
            "style": {
              "padding": "4px"
            }
          },
          {
            "elmType": "span",
            "txtContent": "Reject",
            "style": {
              "word-break": "keep-all"
            }
          }
        ]
      }
    ]
  },
  {
```

```
"elmType": "div",
"style": {
  "padding-right": "20px"
},
"children": [
  {
    "elmType": "span",
    "attributes": {
      "iconName": "tasklogo"
    },
    "style": {
      "display": "=if([$ProductStatus] == 'Pending'
      ||[$ProductStatus] == '' , 'none','inherit')",
      "padding-top": "4px",
      "padding-left": "20px",
      "font-size": "20px",
      "color": "=if([$ProductStatus] == 'Approved'
      ||[$ProductStatus] == '' , '#008000','#FF4500')",
      "float": "left"
    }
  },
  {
    "elmType": "span",
    "txtContent": "=if([$ProductStatus] == 'Rejected',
    'Rejected', 'Approved'",
    "style": {
      "display": "=if([$ProductStatus] == 'Pending'
      ||[$ProductStatus] == '' , 'none','inherit')",
      "padding-left": "5px",
      "color": "=if([$ProductStatus] == 'Approved'
      ||[$ProductStatus] == '' , '#008000','#FF4500')",
      "font-weight": "400",
      "font-size": "20px",
      "float": "left",
      "word-break": "keep-all"
```

```
                            }
                          }
                      ]
                    }
                  ]
                }
              ]
            }
          }
        }
```

You can collapse and expand the elements in the "Format view" box to see each section individually. To see how the view looks, click Preview. Refer to Figure 3-18.

Figure 3-18. *View formatting display*

The JSON object has the following properties:

> *$schema:* Specifies the JSON schema that should be used to validate this formatting rule.

> *debugMode:* If set to true, enables debugging information in the list view.

hideSelection: If set to true, hides the selection checkbox that appears next to each row in the list view.

hideColumnHeader: If set to true, hides the column headers in the list view.

rowFormatter: Specifies the formatting rule for the rows in the list view. The `rowFormatter` property is an object that specifies how the rows in the list view should be formatted. It has the following properties:

>   *elmType*: Specifies the type of HTML element to use for the row
>
>   *attributes*: Specifies the HTML attributes to apply to the row
>
>   *style*: Specifies the CSS styles to apply to the row
>
>   *children*: Specifies child elements to include in the row

The row formatting rule specified in this JSON object formats rows to display a file name, product name, product type, and document type in a specific format using HTML elements and CSS styles.

Let's look at the `rowFormatter` in detail. The `rowFormatter` property is the root of the schema and includes a `div` element. Within the `div` element, if you look at the `children` property, there are two `div` elements. The first `div` element (marked as green in Figure 3-18) defines the document properties. It contains several child elements, including three `span` elements that display values such as `Name(FileLeafRef)`, `ProductName, ProductType, Review Date`, etc. This information is displayed on two lines with one as the header and the remaining information at the bottom.

If you look at the second `div` element (marked as brown in Figure 3-18), here is where we defined the Approve and Reject areas. This section represents a row containing two buttons, one to approve and one to reject the document, and a status indicator hidden. The buttons and status indicator are conditionally displayed based on the value of the `ProductStatus` field. The product lead will view this section only if the document status is either pending, approved, or rejected.

The `children` property of this `div` element contains two `div` elements that define the layout and contents of the row. The first `div` element contains two button elements that have custom row actions associated with them. Clicking the Approve button sets the

ProductStatus field to Approved, and clicking the Reject button sets the ProductStatus field to Rejected. The second div element contains a span element that displays the status of the product.

The styling of the elements is defined using CSS properties, and some of them are conditional based on the value of the ProductStatus field. For example, the display property of the span element that displays the status is set to none if the status is Pending or empty and set to visible otherwise. Similarly, the color of the status indicator is set to green if the status is Approved or an empty string and set to red if the status is Rejected.

Click Save and try to approve or reject documents. You can see "Approved" or "Rejected" once you click the buttons. See Figure 3-19 where I approved one and rejected another.

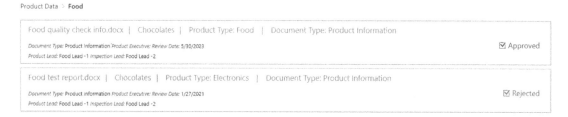

Figure 3-19. *Updating field values using JSON formatting*

The Product Status column has now been updated. It is a powerful feature of JSON formatting that you can update values from the SharePoint interface. This dashboard can be beautified further with custom styling. By using simple JSON coding, you can set up the view and execute the action.

To meet the requirements, we need to create two additional views: one for executives to submit documents for approval and another for inspection leads to complete the final approval.

To create the Executive Dashboard view, follow these steps:

1. Go to the library settings and click "More library settings." Scroll to the bottom and under the Views section, click "Create view."

2. Select "Start from an existing view" and choose "Product Lead Dashboard" to ensure all the required columns are included. Name the view **Executive Dashboard**.

3. Expand the Filters option and update the filter for the Product
    Status column. Set the filter condition Product Status to Draft.
    This refinement ensures that only the documents in the Draft state
    will be displayed within the Executive Dashboard.

4. Now, navigate to the Executive Dashboard view and click the
    drop-down next to the view name at the top right. Select "Format
    current view" and paste the provided JSON code from Listing 3-2.

5. Replace the bottom-most div element with the new JSON
    code from Listing 3-3. Make any necessary adjustments to the
    formatting, and then save the view.

Listing 3-3. View Formatting, Executive Dashboard Submit section

```
{
  "elmType": "div",
  "style": {
    "flex-direction": "row",
    "justify-content": "left",
    "align-items": "center",
    "flex-wrap": "nowrap",
    "padding-top": "30px",
    "padding-right": "10px"
  },
  "children": [
    {
      "elmType": "div",
      "style": {
        "display": "=if([$ProductStatus] == Draft || [$ProductStatus]
        == '', 'inherit','none')",
        "flex-direction": "row",
        "justify-content": "left",
        "align-items": "center",
        "flex-wrap": "wrap"
      },
      "children": [
```

```
{
    "elmType": "button",
    "customRowAction": {
      "action": "setValue",
      "actionInput": {
        "ProductStatus": "Pending"
      }
    },
    "attributes": {
      "class": "ms-fontColor-themePrimary ms-fontColor-
      themeDarker--hover"
    },
    "style": {
      "background-color": "transparent",
      "border": "none",
      "width": "110px",
      "cursor": "pointer",
      "flex-direction": "row",
      "justify-content": "left",
      "align-items": "center",
      "flex-wrap": "wrap",
      "font-size": "18px",
      "color": "#008000"
    },
    "children": [
      {
        "elmType": "span",
        "attributes": {
          "iconName": "SkypeCircleCheck"
        },
        "style": {
          "padding": "4px"
        }
      },
      {
```

```
          "elmType": "span",
          "txtContent": "Submit",
          "style": {
            "word-break": "keep-all"
          }
        }
      ]
    }
  ]
},
{
  "elmType": "div",
  "style": {
    "padding-right": "20px"
  },
  "children": [
    {
      "elmType": "span",
      "txtContent": "='Current Status: '+[$ProductStatus]",
      "style": {
        "display": "inherit",
        "padding-left": "5px",
        "padding-top": "15px",
        "color": "#a8072",
        "font-weight": "400",
        "font-size": "16px",
        "float": "left",
        "word-break": "keep-all"
      }
    }
  ]
}
]
}
```

Let's look at the changes. In Listing 3-3, the bottommost div is modified to set the formatting for the Executive Dashboard view. It is designed for executives to submit documents for approval. The code includes a button only for executives to submit documents and a label that displays the current status of each document.

On the other hand, in Listing 3-2, the bottom div element represents the formatting for the Production Lead Dashboard view. This view is intended for production leads to complete the approval of documents. The code includes two buttons for production leads to approve or reject documents.

The main difference between the two is in the conditions and actions associated with the buttons. The displayed status and styling also differ between the two listings to align with the respective roles and actions.

Note   The complete listing for all the views is available in the Chapter 3 section of the GitHub repo. You can access it here: `https://github.com/apress/building-modern-workplace-SharePoint-online-2e`.

By following these steps, you will create the Executive Dashboard view and apply the required formatting for executives to submit documents for approval.

Repeat the same steps to create another view for Inspection Leads, but name it **Inspection Dashboard**. While creating the view, expand the Filters option and update the filter for the Product Status column. Set the filter condition Product Status equal to Approved. This refinement ensures that only the documents approved by the product lead will appear in the Inspection Dashboard view.

Use the code in Listing 3-4 for the bottommost div. Refer to the GitHub repository for the full code for the view formatting.

Listing 3-4. View Formatting, Inspection Lead Dashboard Approval Section

```
{
    "elmType": "div",
    "style": {
      "flex-directon": "row",
      "display": "=if([$ProductStatus] == 'Completed' ||
      [$ProductStatus] == 'Approved' || [$ProductStatus] == 'Rejected',
      'inherit','none')",
      "justify-content": "left",
```

```
      "align-items": "center",
    "flex-wrap": "nowrap",
    "padding-top": "50px",
    "padding-right": "10px"
  },
  "children": [
    {
      "elmType": "div",
      "style": {
        "display": "=if([$ProductStatus] == 'Approved'
        || [$ProductStatus] == '', 'inherit','none')",
        "flex-directon": "row",
        "justify-content": "left",
        "align-items": "center",
        "flex-wrap": "wrap"
      },
      "children": [
        {
          "elmType": "button",
          "customRowAction": {
            "action": "setValue",
            "actionInput": {
              "ProductStatus": "Completed"
            }
          },
          "attributes": {
            "class": "ms-fontColor-themePrimary ms-fontColor-
            themeDarker--hover"
          },
          "style": {
            "background-color": "transparent",
            "border": "none",
            "width": "120px",
            "cursor": "pointer",
            "flex-directon": "row",
            "justify-content": "left",
```

111

```
        "align-items": "center",
        "flex-wrap": "wrap",
        "font-size": "18px",
        "color": "#008000"
      },
      "children": [
        {
          "elmType": "span",
          "attributes": {
            "iconName": "SkypeCircleCheck"
          },
          "style": {
            "padding": "4px"
          }
        },
        {
          "elmType": "span",
          "txtContent": "Complete",
          "style": {
            "word-break": "keep-all"
          }
        }
      ]
    },
    {
      "elmType": "button",
      "customRowAction": {
        "action": "setValue",
        "actionInput": {
          "ProductStatus": "Rejected"
        }
      },
      "attributes": {
        "class": "ms-fontColor-themePrimary ms-fontColor-
        themeDarker--hover"
      },
```

```json
    "style": {
      "border": "none",
      "width": "110px",
      "background-color": "transparent",
      "cursor": "pointer",
      "flex-directon": "row",
      "justify-content": "left",
      "align-items": "center",
      "flex-wrap": "wrap",
      "font-size": "18px",
      "color": "#FF4500"
    },
    "children": [
      {
        "elmType": "span",
        "attributes": {
          "iconName": "Blocked"
        },
        "style": {
          "padding": "4px"
        }
      },
      {
        "elmType": "span",
        "txtContent": "Reject",
        "style": {
          "word-break": "keep-all"
        }
      }
    ]
  }
],
},
```

```
{
  "elmType": "div",
  "style": {
    "padding-right": "20px"
  },
  "children": [
    {
      "elmType": "span",
      "attributes": {
        "iconName": "tasklogo"
      },
      "style": {
        "display": "=if([$ProductStatus] == 'Approved'
        ||[$ProductStatus] == '' , 'none','inherit')",
        "padding-top": "4px",
        "padding-left": "20px",
        "font-size": "20px",
        "color": "=if([$ProductStatus] == 'Completed'
        ||[$ProductStatus] == '' , '#008000','#FF4500')",
        "float": "left"
      }
    },
    {
      "elmType": "span",
      "txtContent": "=if([$ProductStatus] == 'Rejected',
      'Rejected', 'Approved'",
      "style": {
        "display": "=if([$ProductStatus] == 'Approved'
        ||[$ProductStatus] == '' , 'none','inherit')",
        "padding-left": "5px",
        "color": "=if([$ProductStatus] == 'Completed'
        ||[$ProductStatus] == '' , '#008000','#FF4500')",
        "font-weight": "400",
        "font-size": "20px",
        "float": "left",
```

```
        "word-break": "keep-all"
      }
    }
  ]
}
]
}
```

In Listing 3-4, the formatting for the Inspection Lead Dashboard view is adjusted to cater to the needs of inspection leads completing the approval process. Conversely, in Listing 3-2, the formatting is for the Production Lead Dashboard view. Notable differences between the two include the conditions for displaying buttons and the button text itself. In the Inspection Lead Dashboard view, buttons are displayed based on the Approved status, while in the Production Lead Dashboard view, they are based on the Pending status. Additionally, the button text is updated to Complete from Approve to reflect the action required by the Inspection Leads. These modifications ensure that each dashboard view is tailored to the specific roles and tasks of the respective leads, while adhering to the given requirements.

Try uploading a few documents and submit them for approval from the Executive Dashboard. Then you can see them on the Product Lead Dashboard for approval. Approving from there will take you to the Inspection Lead Dashboard; there you can complete the approval process.

Note   As part of the Cloudhadi requirements, the document submission dashboard and the approval dashboards have now been set up. Product Status can now be set to Approved or Rejected or Completed. Power Automate can handle the rest of the process, such as the role-based access at each stage and email notifications, by setting up a trigger on the Product Status column update. In Chapter 5, we will see how this works.

To simulate the document submission and approval process at this stage and ensure the formatting works as expected, you can proceed as follows. First, upload the desired documents to the system. Then, navigate to the Executive Dashboard view and select the documents you want to submit for approval. Utilize the provided Submit button to initiate the approval process for those documents.

Once the documents have been submitted, they will become visible in the Product Lead Dashboard view. This is where the product leads can review the submitted documents and proceed with the approval process. From the Product Lead Dashboard, you can use the Approve button to approve the documents, signaling their approval of the content.

Upon approval by the product leads, the documents will be transferred to the Inspection Lead Dashboard. In this dashboard view, you can carry out the final stages of the approval process.

Forms and Formatting

We have formatted the library columns and view. Now let's look at the product list and see if we can input some data there. We are dealing with the solution for use case UC-PL1 from Chapter 2.

From Site Contents, navigate to the Products list. Select "Show or hide more columns" from the view, just as we did for the library. Click Apply after selecting the columns highlighted in Figure 3-20.

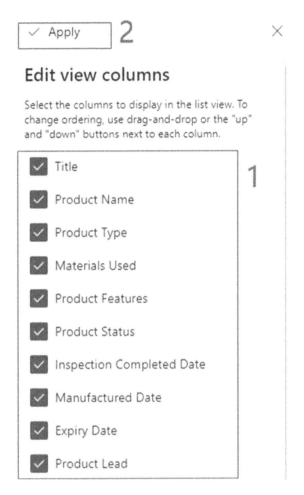

Figure 3-20. *Products list, setting columns for the default view*

The new product form opens when you click the New button. Using JSON formatting, let's arrange the columns and validate them. Refer to Figure 3-21.

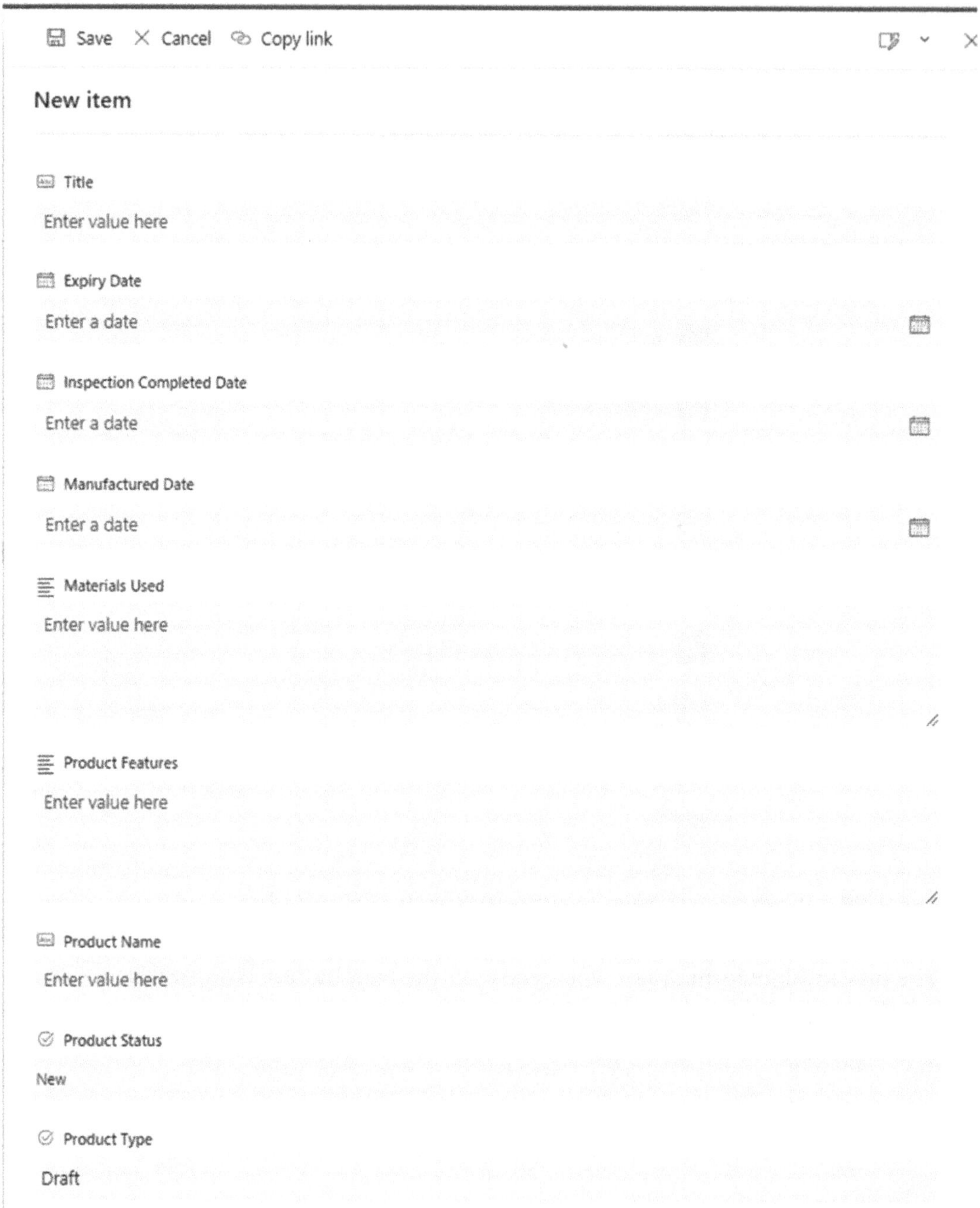

💾 Save   ✕ Cancel   🔗 Copy link   ☐ ⌄   ✕

New item

🔤 Title

Enter value here

📅 Expiry Date

Enter a date   📅

📅 Inspection Completed Date

Enter a date   📅

📅 Manufactured Date

Enter a date   📅

☰ Materials Used

Enter value here

                                                                                ⁄⁄

☰ Product Features

Enter value here

                                                                                ⁄⁄

🔤 Product Name

Enter value here

⊘ Product Status

New

⊘ Product Type

Draft

Figure 3-21. *New product form*

Click the Edit form icon on the right and then click Configure Layout. See
Figure 3-22.

Figure 3-22. *Configuring the form layout*

You can apply formatting to the body by selecting it from the "Apply formatting to" drop-down. Refer to Figure 3-23.

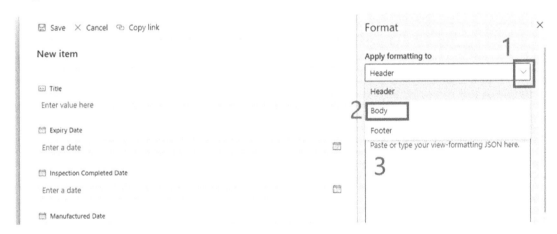

Figure 3-23. *Applying the formatting*

Now copy the code in Listing 3-5 into the "Formatting code" box and save.

Listing 3-5. Form Body Formatting

```
{
    "sections": [
        {
            "displayname": "Product Details",
            "fields": [
                "Title",
                "Product Name",
                "Product Type"
            ]
```

119

```
        },
        {
            "displayname": "",
            "fields": [
                "Product Features"
            ]
        },
        {
            "displayname": "Manufacturing",
            "fields": [
                "Manufactured Date",
                "Materials Used",
                "Expiry Date"
            ]
        },
        {
            "displayname": "Product Workflow",
            "fields": [
                "Product Status",
                "Product Lead",
                "Inspection Completed Date"
            ]
        }
    ]
}
```

We added JSON code to customize the display of a SharePoint list form, allowing the user to select which fields appear in which sections. This JSON code defines an array, called *sections*, that contains four objects. Each object represents a section of a list form and includes a display name and a fields array that lists the names of the fields to be displayed in that section.

The four sections are as follows:

- The Product Details section, which includes the fields Title, Product Name, and Product Type

- An unnamed section, which includes the fields Title and Product Features

- The Manufacturing section, which includes the fields Manufactured Date, Materials Used, and Expiry Date

- The Product Workflow section, which includes the fields Product Status, Product Lead, and Inspection Completed Date

Let's customize the header section next. Use the Edit Columns button to uncheck any additional columns in the form before proceeding.

Click the "Configure layout" button again, this time selecting the Header option from the "Apply formatting" drop-down menu. The code in Listing 3-6 should be placed inside that. I will explain the code after the listing.

Listing 3-6. Form Header Formatting

```
{
    "elmType": "div",
    "style": {
        "width": "99%",
        "background-color": "#0078D4",
        "margin-bottom": "20px",
        "height": "80px"
    },
    "children": [
        {
            "elmType": "div",
            "txtContent": "=if([$ProductName] == , New Product,
            Product -  + [$ProductName])",
            "style": {
                "display": "flex",
                "color": "white",
                "font-size": "28px",
                "padding-left": "20px"
            }
        }
    ]
}
```

Overall, this code creates a header section for the list form that displays a title with a background color like our site theme. The logic to display the header text is in the children `div`.

```
=if([$ProductName] == '', 'New Product', 'Product - ' + [$ProductName])
```

The previous expression uses the `if` function to check if the `ProductName` field is empty or not. If it is empty, then the text content of the `div` element is set to New Product. If the `ProductName` field has a value, then the text content of the `div` element is set to `Product` followed by the value of the `ProductName` field.

So, in summary, this part of the code sets the text content of a `div` element to display the name of the product, with a prefix of `Product`, if the `ProductName` field is not empty. For a new form, this means when there is no value for Product Name, it displays "New Product."

Finally, the new form will look like Figure 3-24.

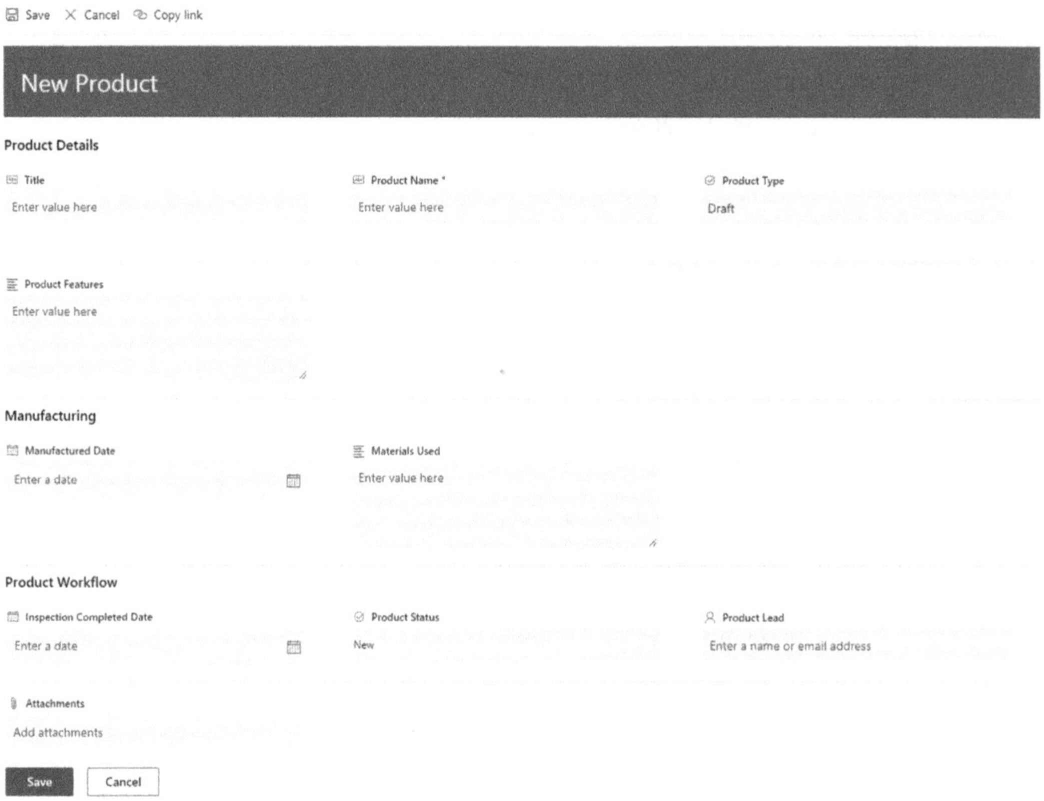

Figure 3-24. *Formatted form*

Fill out the form and save it. Note that I made Product Name mandatory. You can do this by clicking the column from the view, selecting the column settings, and selecting Edit and more options from the pane.

You can see the header gets updated as soon as you enter the product name. For my example, see Figure 3-25. Use the New button to create five or more items. In the default view, you can see the items that have been created. By selecting an item and clicking Edit from the top, you can edit or view it in the same form.

Figure 3-25. *Saving the product data*

Create 5 to 10 items in the list that will be handy in upcoming chapters. Figure 3-26 shows the three items I created in the product list.

Figure 3-26. *Product items*

There are several customizations you can make with JSON formatting, such as displaying a progress bar in columns, setting text as a hyperlink, setting a hover display on a column, etc. Play around with different scenarios. JSON formatting enables interactive experiences for SharePoint users. For example, you can create clickable buttons to perform specific actions or display pop-up boxes to provide additional information.

JSON Formatting Capabilities and Limitations

The capabilities of JSON formatting are summarized here:

- *Conditional formatting*: You can use JSON to apply conditional formatting to columns in a list or library. For example, you can highlight overdue tasks or show a progress bar based on the completion percentage.

- *Customized forms*: With JSON formatting, you can create customized forms for SharePoint lists and libraries. This allows you to tailor the user experience for specific use cases, including hiding or showing specific fields, changing field labels, or adding custom validation.

- *Customized views*: You can use JSON formatting to customize the display of data in SharePoint list views. For example, you can group data, add custom icons, and apply conditional formatting.

- *Interactive experiences*: JSON formatting enables the creation of interactive experiences for users in SharePoint. For example, you can create clickable buttons to perform specific actions or display pop-up dialog boxes to provide additional information. JSON formatting can greatly improve the user experience of SharePoint, making it easier and more intuitive for users to interact with data.

- *Consistency*: JSON formatting enables the creation of consistent user experiences across SharePoint sites and pages.

- *Integration with external data sources*: You can use JSON formatting to integrate external data sources into SharePoint. For example, you can display data from a weather API, stock prices, or social media feeds in a SharePoint list or library.

- *Cost-effective*: JSON formatting is a cost-effective way to create custom views and forms in SharePoint, as it requires no additional licensing or software.

While SharePoint JSON formatting is a powerful tool for customizing the appearance and behavior of list views, forms, and fields, there are some limitations to what it can do. Here are a few of the limitations you may face:

- *Complexity*: JSON formatting can become quite complex and difficult to manage when dealing with nested objects or multiple conditional statements.

- *Performance*: Using JSON formatting can impact the performance of SharePoint lists and libraries, especially when working with large datasets. Complex formatting can slow down the rendering of the view and the overall page performance.

- *Limited branding*: While JSON formatting can customize the appearance of list views, forms, and fields, it has some limitations when it comes to layout and styling. For example, you can't use CSS to style elements or change the position of fields on a form.

- *Limited functionality*: While JSON formatting allows for a lot of customization, there are still some limitations to what can be achieved with logic and dynamic content. For example, there are certain actions that cannot be performed using JSON formatting, such as cascading drop-downs, for example. JSON formatting supports some conditional logic, such as the ability to show or hide elements based on another field value or logged-in user, but it doesn't have the full range of conditional logic capabilities that other tools such as Power Apps, Power Automate, or SPFx can provide.

Project Development Review

Let's look at where we stand regarding building a modern workplace for Cloudhadi. For us, each chapter is treated like a sprint where we develop functionality along with learning.

In the previous chapter, we created the basic artifacts. We developed a dashboard view for Product Data documents in this chapter. Users can now upload documents to the Product Data library and set its properties, as well as view them in the dashboard. The Product Lead and Inspection Lead columns have been restricted to the Product Lead group. It is not possible for product executives to select a random person for approval. The Inspection Lead field is also conditionally validated so that if Do Inspection Required is true, the Inspection Lead will be displayed. The color of the product name is also set based on the type of product.

The dashboard is set up with document properties. The product lead can now approve or reject a document from the dashboard. A status update will be made accordingly.

We entered data using a new form and saw how to edit it with the product name displayed on the header.

Summary

The purpose of this chapter was to introduce you to the world of JSON formatting. The chapter began with a discussion of OOB forms in SharePoint. You learned how to use a default SharePoint form for validating and saving data. We discussed how conditional formulas can be used to show and hide columns based on other columns. A look at the advantages and disadvantages of using an out-of-the-box form followed.

Furthermore, we discussed how to customize columns and views with JSON formatting. Following a quick look at column formatting, we created a dashboard view using view formatting. As we explored JSON formatting with approvals, we learned about its interactive side.

Next, you learned how to customize a list form using JSON. A custom form has been created with filed arrangements and a custom header. Using that form, we inserted data.

Before catching up on our project progress in the last section, we looked at JSON formatting capabilities and limitations. We have seen, with examples, how powerful it can be. JSON formatting is without a doubt the king of low code when it comes to SharePoint Online customization.

We will begin developing custom forms in the next chapter. Power Apps form development will be the focus of this chapter. We will discuss how the Power Platform can be integrated with SharePoint Online to achieve various business goals. As part of this process, we will develop a few custom Power Apps solutions for Cloudhadi.

CHAPTER 4

Power Apps

In the previous chapter, you learned how to customize forms using JSON formatting. In this chapter, we explore one of the most modern solutions for customizing list or library forms and creating interactive web parts. This approach does not require extensive coding.

Power Apps is a powerful, low-code app development solution that enables businesses to quickly meet their specific requirements. With Power Apps, you can easily access and interact with your business data, including SharePoint Online as our chosen data source. It offers the flexibility to integrate with various other data sources as well.

In this chapter, we will delve into the world of Power Apps by exploring canvas and model-driven apps. Our primary focus will be on creating a stand-alone canvas app that allows users to efficiently manage products in the Cloudhadi Products list. Throughout the chapter, we will cover the essential aspects of building a canvas app in Power Apps, including configuring the user interface, implementing business logic, and seamlessly integrating with SharePoint Online.

You will gain a solid understanding of Power Apps forms, their components, and the wide range of properties available to customize their behavior. We will explore important concepts such as managing data, working with variables, leveraging context, utilizing the patch function, and modifying data card properties to ensure a comprehensive learning experience.

It's important to note that Power Apps is a vast and versatile toolset, and this chapter serves as an introductory overview specifically focused on its integration within SharePoint Online. This chapter will lay a strong foundation for you to further explore and expand your Power Apps knowledge and capabilities beyond the basics.

© Hari Narayn 2023
H. Narayn, *Building the Modern Workplace with SharePoint Online*,
https://doi.org/10.1007/978-1-4842-9726-1_4

Canvas and Model-Driven Apps

In Power Apps, there are two types of apps: model-driven and canvas apps. Model-driven apps and canvas apps differ in how they're built and designed.

Canvas apps are as follows:

- A canvas app lets you drag and drop elements onto a blank canvas to create custom user interfaces.

- You have complete control over the app's layout, design, and functionality, making it ideal for building visually appealing and highly tailored applications.

- You can directly interact with the app's interface, adding and configuring elements such as buttons, forms, galleries, and data sources.

- Canvas apps are built to adapt to different screen sizes and orientations, allowing users to access them on various devices such as desktops, tablets, and mobile phones. The app's layout and controls automatically adjust to fit the available screen space.

- Canvas apps offer a variety of layout options, such as fluid layouts, which automatically resize and reflow controls based on the screen size, as well as fixed layouts, where controls maintain their relative positioning but adjust their sizes to fit the screen.

- If you need a custom app from scratch and want more control over the user experience, canvas apps are the way to go.

Model-driven apps are as follows:

- Model-driven apps are built around a predefined data model, known as Microsoft Dataverse (formerly known as the Common Data Service [CDS]). Based on the data model, the app's interface and functionality are automatically generated.

- Model-driven apps are more structured, with standardized layouts and components. The overall structure is predefined, but you can customize themes and branding.

- The app's functionality is driven by the underlying data model. Features such as forms, views, and navigation are automatically generated based on the data entities and relationships defined in Dataverse.

- A model-driven app is great for scenarios where you want to quickly build something that leverages existing data models.

Canvas apps are highly customizable and visually flexible, while model-driven apps are structured and data-driven. Which one you choose depends on your specific requirements, level of customization, and data model.

Model-driven apps are well-suited to scenarios where you need to quickly create data-driven applications, such as customer relationship management (CRM) systems or line-of-business applications. They provide a consistent and standardized user experience across devices.

Regarding SharePoint, canvas apps are often used because they're more flexible in design and integration. You can extend and enhance SharePoint's customization capabilities through canvas apps. This is done by creating custom user interfaces, integrating with external systems, or embedding them within SharePoint pages.

However, it's worth noting that you can also use model-driven apps with SharePoint by integrating Power Apps. You can build model-driven apps that use SharePoint as a data source or integrate with SharePoint lists and libraries. Choosing canvas apps or model-driven apps in SharePoint depends on your application requirements and complexity. Model-driven apps aren't covered in this book.

Get Online with Power Apps Designer

First, let's familiarize ourselves with Power Apps Designer to create an app. Join Power Apps by going to `https://make.powerapps.com` and following the prompts. There is no need for a separate license since you already have the Microsoft 365 developer trial license. When you follow the steps for signing up, a window will appear, as shown in Figure 4-1.

Note Create 5 to 10 items in the Products list before creating the app to ensure you have few items to test. Refer to Chapter 3, specifically Figure 3-26, for the items I created for my example. This will be reflected in the app that I am going to show how to create in the next steps.

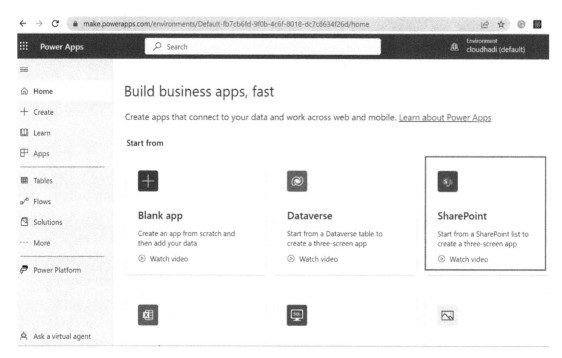

Figure 4-1. *Power Apps Designer*

The data source options include Dataverse, Excel, SQL, etc. Click SharePoint as the data source. Next, enter the SharePoint site URL, select the Connection option using your SharePoint credentials, click Go. Select Products from the list and click Connect. Check out Figure 4-2.

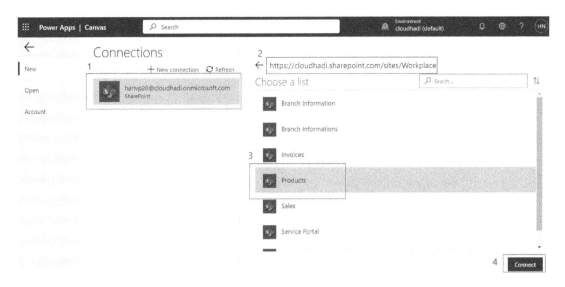

Figure 4-2. *Connecting to SharePoint Online data source*

After clicking Connect, the canvas will load in a few seconds. A welcome dialog box will appear. You can skip it. You can now see your product list items on the canvas. See Figure 4-3.

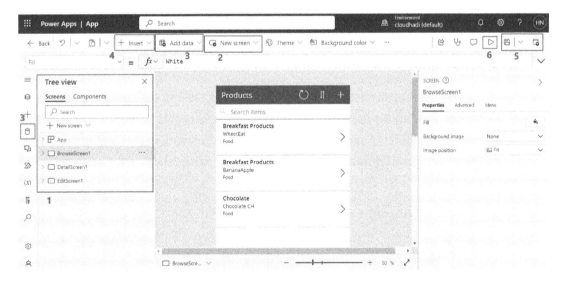

Figure 4-3. *Browse screen, products*

In Figure 4-3, you'll notice a Power Apps screen displaying all the product items. Let's look at each of the highlighted elements in Figure 4-3. The numbering corresponds to that in Figure 4-3.

1) *Tree view:* On the left side, there is a tree view that shows the app's structure. It consists of three screens: BrowseScreen1, DetailScreen1, and EditScreen1.

   - *BrowseScreen1*: This screen is the default view that presents a list of products, as shown in Figure 4-3. It allows users to scroll through the products and select specific items for further information. If you expand BrowseScreen1, you can see a BrowseGallery1. Within a browse screen, the browse Gallery control is typically used to present a list of items. Each item in the gallery is represented as a separate card or container that contains information about the item, such as its title, description, or image.

   - *DetailScreen1*: Clicking this screen will display detailed information about the selected product. It provides a comprehensive view of all the details associated with a particular product.

   - *EditScreen1*: When navigating to this screen, users can view the same product details but in an editable mode. It allows users to modify the information and make changes to the selected product.

   To explore the app, click each screen in the tree view to see how the app appears and functions. This will provide a better understanding of the different screens and their purposes within the app. Each screen serves a specific role in presenting and managing the product data, enhancing the overall user experience.

2) *New screen:* The "New screen" option provides the flexibility to create additional screens in addition to the default three screens mentioned earlier. It allows you to design and customize new screens based on your specific requirements. By selecting the "New screen" option, you can create a fresh screen from scratch or choose from predesigned templates available in Power Apps. This new screen can serve various purposes, such as displaying specific subsets of data, incorporating additional functionalities, or providing alternative user interfaces.

When creating a new screen, you have the freedom to define its layout, add controls and components, and configure interactions and behaviors. Whether you want to showcase different views of data, introduce advanced search capabilities, create custom reports, or implement specialized forms, the "New screen" option allows you to extend the app's capabilities beyond the initial set of screens.

3) *Data:* The Data option on the left side of the tree view in Power Apps refers to the section where you can manage and configure data connections and data sources for your app.

When you click the Data option, it opens a panel or view that allows you to perform various actions related to data. You can view and manage the data sources connected to your app, such as SharePoint lists, SQL databases, Excel files, or other external data sources. You can add new data sources, modify existing ones, or remove connections to data sources.

The "Add data" option in a Power Apps screen refers to the ability to add new data source to the app, such as a SharePoint list, or from another data source.

4) *Insert:* When you click the Insert button, it opens a panel with a range of options for inserting different types of elements into your app. The Insert button in Power Apps allows you to add new controls, components, or elements to enhance your app's functionality and design. It provides a range of options for inserting controls, media, layouts, data-related elements, charts, and custom components. You can either use the top insert option or use the + icon on the left to insert elements.

5) *Save & Publish:* As highlighted on the top right of Figure 4-3, you have saved and publish options for your app. When you click the Save button, any modifications you have made to the app's design, functionality, or data connections are saved. This ensures that your progress is preserved and can be accessed later. The app is saved in a draft mode, meaning that the changes are not immediately visible or accessible to other users.

The Publish option is used to make your app available for usage by other users. Once published, the app becomes accessible to the intended users or audience. The published app can be shared with others, allowing them to collaborate, use, and interact with the app's functionality and data. Also, when you publish the app, it creates a new version that can be tracked and managed.

6) *Preview:* To experience the app's functionality, click the Preview app button, as highlighted in Figure 4-3. Alternatively, you can use the F5 key from your keyboard to load the app in preview mode.

Once the app is loaded, you can perform several operations within the preview. Start by clicking each item in the list to view its details. On the view page, you'll notice a pencil icon that allows you to edit the field values. Clicking the pencil icon will enable you to modify any of the displayed fields. Additionally, there will be a delete icon that allows you to remove an item if needed.

To view or edit more fields, use the vertical scroll bar to navigate through the content. Once you have made the desired edits, use the tick mark icon located at the top to save the changes. This will update the data back into SharePoint, ensuring that your modifications are persisted.

If you navigate back to the home screen, you'll find a + icon. Clicking this icon enables you to add a new item to the list. Enter the relevant details for the new item and save the changes, like how you would edit existing items. Moreover, the browse screen provides additional functionality. You can utilize the search feature to find specific items based on your search query. Sorting options are available to arrange the items in ascending or descending order based on selected fields. Lastly, the refresh option allows you to update the list of items, ensuring that you have the latest data.

By exploring these features during the app preview, you'll gain a better understanding of the app's capabilities and how it enables efficient data management and interaction with the SharePoint list. Try adding more items using the preview.

You can close the preview, and once you navigate back to the designer, ensure you click respective screen from the tree view to edit Screens and Components such as BrowseScreen1.

Let's save the current form. Click the Save icon, provide a name, and click Save, as highlighted in Figure 4-4.

Figure 4-4. *Saving the app*

You can also save changes to the canvas anytime during the development using the keyboard shortcut Ctrl+S.

Delving into Data in Canvas Apps

By leveraging the products' data source, we can create a dynamic and responsive app that reflects the real-time state of the Products list, enabling users to browse, view, and edit product information seamlessly within the app's screens. Let's look at this in detail.

In our previous discussion, we established that our app consists of three screens: the browse screen for displaying the list of products and the detail and edit screens for displaying and editing the product details.

To gain a thorough understanding, let's delve into the data options available within canvas apps and explore their functionalities in greater detail. Refer to Figure 4-5 and the explanation following.

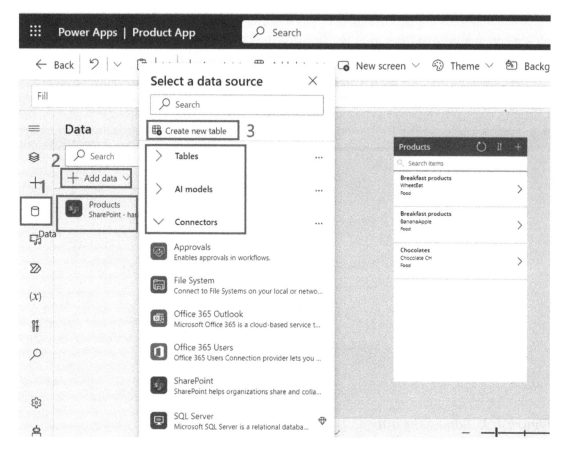

Figure 4-5. *Data source*

To view the existing data connection and options to add new data, you can click the data icon located on the left side of the designer interface. Let's look at those options highlighted in Figure 4-5.

The "Add data" option allows you to connect external data sources to your app. It involves selecting a data source, configuring the connection, mapping data fields, and then retrieving and manipulating the data within your app. This feature expands the capabilities of your app by integrating real-time or stored data from various systems and services. By selecting the "Add data" option, you can access a range of data connectors provided by Power Apps. These connectors allow you to establish connections to different types of data sources such as SharePoint, SQL databases, Excel files, Dataverse, cloud services like Microsoft Azure, and many more.

The "Create table" option allows you to create a new table or data source within your app. It's useful for storing and managing data internally, without relying on external sources. You can define the table structure, including column names, data types, and constraints. This feature enables you to handle app-specific data, such as user preferences or local settings, independently from external databases or SharePoint lists. With the "Create table" option, you can design a self-contained data storage solution within your app for efficient organization and interaction with data.

You can also connect to AI models and Dataverse tables using the respective options under Data.

Now, let's explore the source of data for the screens in our app. During the app creation process, we established a connection to the Products list, which serves as our data source. Figure 4-5 highlights the data icon and the existing connection of products data source for your reference.

By connecting to the Products list, our app establishes a link to the underlying data, allowing us to retrieve and manipulate the product information within our app's screens. This connection enables us to seamlessly display the list of products in the browse screen and access their details for viewing and editing in the respective form screens. It ensures that our app remains synchronized with the latest updates and changes made to the Products list in the underlying SharePoint environment.

Now let's look at how this data is displayed in the canvas. Click the Tree view icon on the top to return to the tree view, as shown in Figure 4-6. By selecting a value from the tree view, such as "Breakfast products," you can access the properties associated with the selected field on the right side. From there, you have the flexibility to configure these properties based on your specific requirements. Refer to Figure 4-6.

Figure 4-6. *Properties and expressions*

Within the canvas, select a specific value such as "Breakfast products." At the top of the screen, locate the Text property that currently holds the expression ThisItem.Title. To display the product name instead, modify the expression to ThisItem.'Product Name'.

Each field value displayed on the screen is associated with an expression. For instance, when clicking Food, the expression ThisItem.'Product Type'.Value is visible. The addition of Value is specific to the choice fields.

On the right side, you will find various properties for the selected field. These properties can be customized to suit your specific requirements. Notably, the properties you set will apply to all items displayed. For example, if you set the font size to 24 for the title, it will be applied to all cards representing the items on the canvas.

Additionally, properties can also be configured from the top section. By clicking the drop-down next to Text, you can access additional properties for customization.

When you click the > sign located on the right side of any card in the browse screen, you will find the OnSelect property both at the top and within the Advanced section of the right side properties. By default, this property is set to the expression Select(Parent). Refer to Figure 4-7.

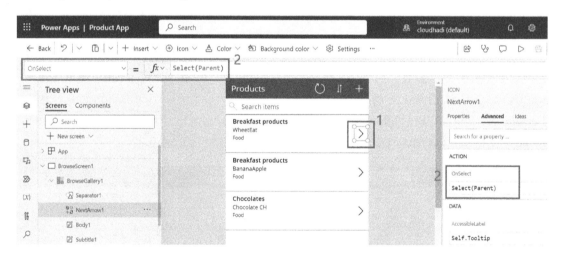

Figure 4-7. *Navigation to view item*

The Select(Parent) expression is used to reference the parent item of a control or element within a data-driven control, such as a gallery or a form. In our BrowseGallery1, each item in the gallery represents a record or entity from a data source, and the controls within that item are considered child elements.

When you click an icon within the browse screen that has an OnSelect expression set to Select(Parent), it triggers the navigation to the detail screen associated with the selected item. The detail screen then retrieves and displays the comprehensive information of the selected item, including various fields, properties, or related data associated with it.

The detail screen association to DetailScreen1 is set on the OnSelect property of the BrowserGallery itself. We will see this in Figure 4-8 and its explanation.

This mechanism ensures a smooth transition from the browse screen to the detail screen, presenting the relevant item details based on the item clicked within the browse screen. This allows users to easily explore and access in-depth information about specific items from the collection displayed in the browse gallery.

You have the flexibility to customize the remaining two screens, DetailScreen1 and EditScreen1, in a similar manner. Take a moment to explore and modify their properties according to your preferences.

Unlike the browse screen, the properties you configure for each field in the Detail and Edit screens will apply only to that specific field. This is because these screens represent individual items, whereas the browse screen represents a collection of multiple items.

By customizing the properties of each field in the Detail and Edit screens, you can tailor the appearance and behavior of the screens to meet your specific requirements. This allows you to create a cohesive and intuitive user experience when viewing or modifying the details of a particular item.

By selecting BrowseGallery1 in the designer, you can access and modify the properties of the Gallery control on the right side of the screen. This allows you to customize the behavior and appearance of the gallery according to your needs. Refer to Figure 4-8 for a visual reference.

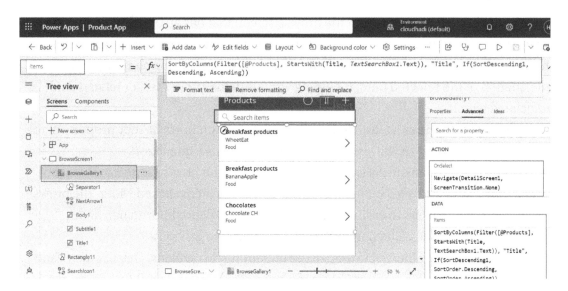

Figure 4-8. *Browse gallery items, sort and search*

In the OnSelect property of the gallery, you will find the expression Navigate(DetailScreen1, ScreenTransition.None). As discussed earlier, this expression is responsible for defining the destination screen when an item in the gallery is selected.

By default, DetailScreen1 is set as the target screen for navigation. However, if you have created an additional detail screen and want to navigate to that screen instead, you can modify the OnSelect property to specify the desired screen.

This flexibility allows you to easily switch between different detail screens based on your app's requirements. By updating the OnSelect property, you can ensure that the appropriate screen is displayed when an item in the gallery is selected, providing access to the relevant details of the chosen item.

Next, look at the Items property, as highlighted Figure 4-8. The Items property of a gallery in Power Apps specifies what data is shown in the gallery and how it is presented. By combining filtering and sorting operations within the Items property, you can control which records are displayed in the gallery and in what order during search and sort. This allows you to create dynamic galleries that adapt to user input or specific search criteria, presenting the filtered and sorted results accordingly. Let's go through the expression in details.

```
SortByColumns(Filter([@Products], StartsWith(Title, TextSearchBox1.Text)),
"Title", If(SortDescending1, SortOrder.Descending, SortOrder.Ascending))
```

The expression part `Filter([@Products], StartsWith(Title, TextSearchBox1.Text))` within the `Items` property enables search functionality in the gallery. When a search is performed, it filters the products based on the condition that the `Title` column starts with the text entered in the TextSearchBox1 search box. It retrieves a subset of records that match the filter condition. The TextSearchBox1 is the search box control highlighted in Figure 4-8. You can preview the app and search for a `Title`, and the results will dynamically update to display the relevant items based on the searched title.

As an example, when you search for *Breakfast*, the search will return the first two products that have titles starting with *Breakfast*. You can experiment the search behavior by replacing `StartsWith` with `EndsWith` in the expression. This change will return the products whose titles end with the entered keyword. By making this adjustment, you can customize the search functionality to suit your specific requirements.

The expression part `SortByColumns(..., "Title", If(SortDescending1, SortOrder.Descending, SortOrder.Ascending))` within the `Items` property enables sorting functionality in the gallery. It sorts the filtered data based on the `Title` column. The sorting order, whether ascending or descending, is determined by the value of the Power Apps variable `SortDescending1`. This variable toggles its value when the sort icon is clicked. You can experience this functionality by previewing the app and interacting with the sort icon. Further details about variables and their workings will be discussed in a subsequent section.

You have the flexibility to modify the `SortByColumns` expression to sort by any other field in the gallery. For example, to sort by the `Product Name` field, you can replace `Title` with `ProductName` in the expression. Remember to use an internal name. The modified expression would look like this:

```
SortByColumns(Filter([@Products], StartsWith(Title, TextSearchBox1.
Text)), "ProductName", If(SortDescending1, SortOrder.Descending, SortOrder.
Ascending))
```

By making this change, the gallery will be sorted based on the `Product Name` field, and the search functionality will still filter data based on `Title` as we haven't modified it.

Now that we have gained a basic understanding of the canvas app designer and how it works with SharePoint data, let's proceed to customize the Edit and Details screens according to the specific requirements of our Cloudhadi project.

Context and Variables

In Power Apps, *context* refers to the current state or environment in which an app is running. It includes various pieces of information and data that can be accessed and used within the app. The context provides valuable context-specific information to the app, such as user details, device information, and app settings.

The UpdateContext function is used to update the value of a context variable within the app. It allows you to modify the context and store information that can be accessed and used throughout the app.

In the app designer, when you click the sort icon, you will notice that the onSelect property is set to UpdateContext({SortDescending1: !SortDescending1}) by default. Refer to Figure 4-9.

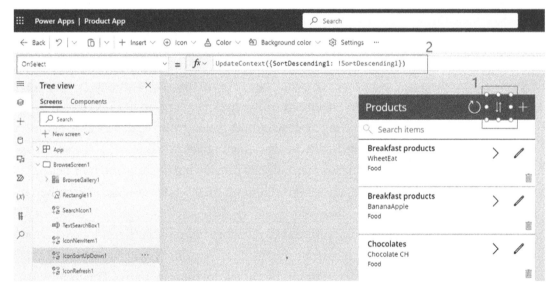

Figure 4-9. *Updating the context*

In this specific case, the UpdateContext function is being used to update the value of a variable called SortDescending1. The exclamation mark (!) in front of SortDescending1 is a logical operator that negates the current value of the variable.

Essentially, when the sort icon is clicked, the UpdateContext function is triggered, and it updates the value of SortDescending1 to be the opposite of its current value. This allows for toggling between ascending and descending sorting based on the current state of the variable.

Overall, the `UpdateContext` function helps in managing and updating variables or contexts within Power Apps, providing dynamic behavior and interactivity.

What exactly is a variable? In Power Apps, a variable is a named storage location that holds a value or a collection of values. Variables are used to store and manipulate data within an app. They can be used to store user inputs, perform calculations, control app behavior, and more.

Variables in Power Apps are dynamically typed, which means they can hold different types of values such as text, numbers, dates, Boolean values, and collections. The value of a variable can be changed throughout the execution of the app based on user interactions or app logic.

Variables can be created and initialized in different ways, such as by using the Set function or by assigning a value directly. For example, you can create a variable called `cloud1` and set its initial value to a number like 4.

```
Set(cloud1, 4)
```

Once a variable is created, its value can be referenced and manipulated using its name in formulas and expressions throughout the app. Variables are local to the app and are not stored persistently, which means their values are reset when the app is closed or refreshed.

Variables provide a flexible way to store and manage data within Power Apps, enabling dynamic behavior and interactions with the user and other app components.

Multiple Edit Screens

During app preview, you may have noticed a vertical scroll bar on the Edit screen when editing an item. To enhance the user experience, we can create two separate screens and distribute the columns between them. This will help in providing a more organized and user-friendly interface for editing items in our app.

So, we have an Edit screen, and we need to create another one and link it together. To start with click ... on the right EditScreen1 and click Duplicate Screen to create a copy of the screen. Refer to Figure 4-10.

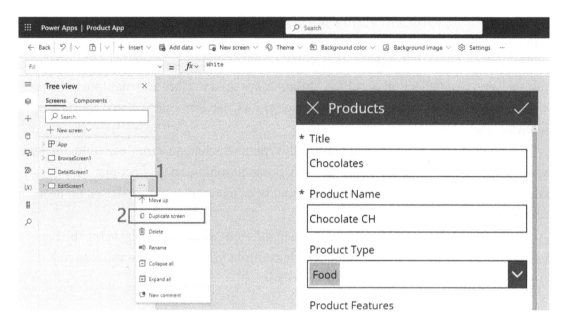

Figure 4-10. *Duplicating a screen*

An additional screen called EditScreen1_1 will be created. In the first screen, EditScreen1, let's choose to retain the fields Title, Product Name, Product Type, Materials Used, and Product Status. To do this, expand the EditForm1 control under EditScreen1 in the tree view. From there, you can select the data cards that are not associated with the mentioned fields and delete them. This can be done by selecting multiple data cards using the Ctrl key and clicking each card. Then click .. against any of the cards and click Delete, or use the keyboard's Delete key. Refer to Figure 4-11. By removing the unwanted data cards like this, we can customize the layout of EditScreen1 and keep only the desired fields displayed.

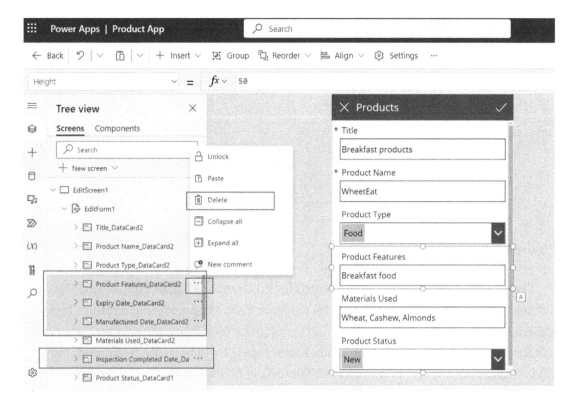

Figure 4-11. *Deleting data cards*

Additionally, the "Edit fields" option allows you to manage the list fields within the Power Apps Designer. By navigating to EditScreen1 ➤ EditForm1 ➤ Properties ➤ Edit fields, you can access a fields pane where you have the flexibility to add, remove, or rearrange fields from the available data source, which in this case is the product list. This feature enables you to customize the form by selecting the specific fields you want to include or exclude, ensuring that the app captures and displays the relevant data from the list. Refer to Figure 4-12.

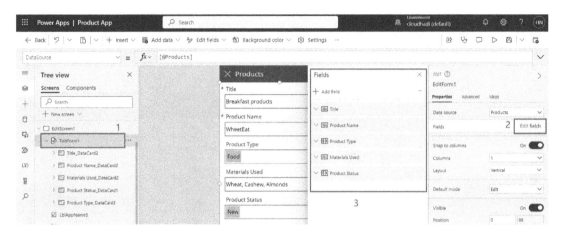

Figure 4-12. *Editing fields*

Perform the same deletion of data cards for EditForm1_1 under EditScreen1_1 as we did before. However, this time, delete the cards for Title, Product Name, Product Type, Materials Used, and Product Status, while keeping the remaining cards intact. As a result, EditScreen1 will contain five fields, while EditScreen1_1 will have the remaining four fields. This customization allows us to distribute the fields across two screens, providing a more organized and user-friendly editing experience. The resulting EditScreen1_1 will look like Figure 4-13.

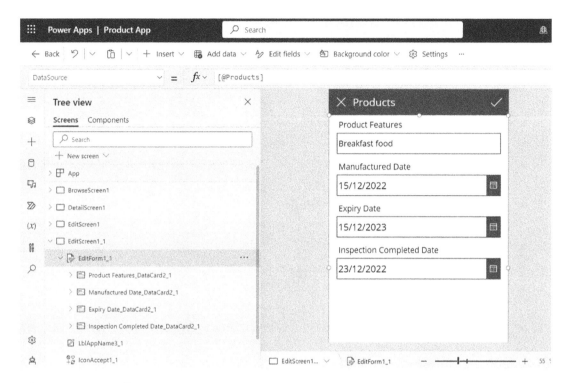

Figure 4-13. *Edit screen 2*

Next, we will add a heading to both edit forms. To do this, select EditForm1 and move it downward to create space for the heading. You can use the top circle on the line to drag it into position. Refer to Figure 4-14.

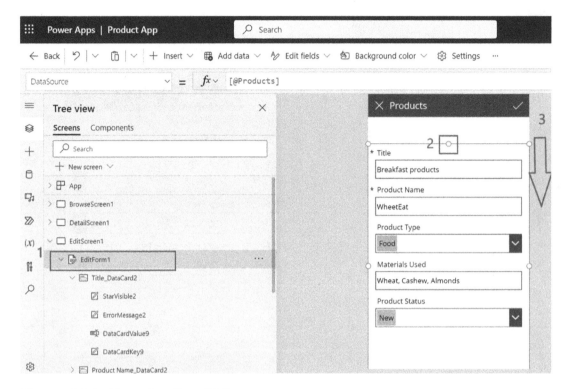

Figure 4-14. *Dragging the edit form*

Next, let's add a text label for the heading. Click the + icon to insert a text label, and position it in the space we created earlier. Refer to Figure 4-15 for visual guidance. By default, the label will have the text *Text*. Edit the text to Product Info by clicking it, and adjust its position to align with the edit form. You can configure the style of the label using the top control or using the properties window according to your preference. In Figure 4-15, you can see the styling that has been applied as an example.

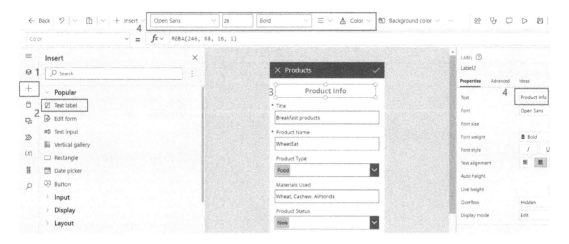

Figure 4-15. *Inserting and styling a heading*

Go back to the tree view and perform a similar exercise for EditScreen1-1. Add a text label as a heading and name it **Quality Info**. Make sure to adjust its position and style it as desired. Once you have made the changes, click the Save button to save your progress.

To establish a link between both screens, we'll add an arrow icon on EditScreen1 to navigate to EditScreen1_1. Click the tree view and go to EditScreen1. Select EditForm1. Using the + icon, expand Shapes and choose "Next arrow." The "Next arrow" component will be inserted onto the screen. Position it at the bottom of EditForm1, as shown in Figure 4-16. As highlighted in Figure 4-16, set the `OnSelect` property of the arrow icon to `Navigate(EditScreen1_1)`. This will ensure that when the icon is clicked, it will take us to the next screen. Customize the color and other styles of the icon as desired.

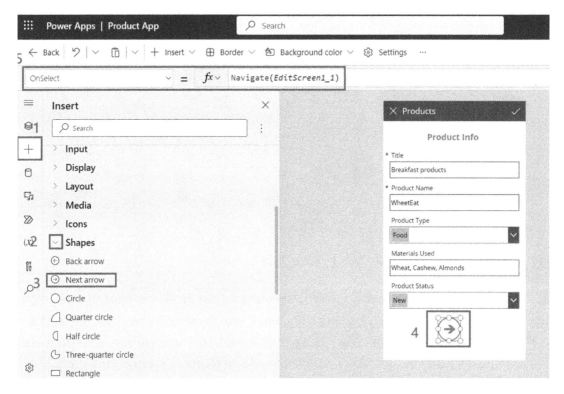

Figure 4-16. *Setting the navigation and style for the Next arrow*

We need to ensure that the form is submitted only from the second edit form, that is, the Quality Info screen, after filling in the details on both screens. You can hide the submit icon from the first edit screen. This prevents users from mistakenly submitting the form prematurely. So, in EditScreen1, let's hide the submit icon (tick) from the top. First, select the submit icon on the first edit screen. Then, in the properties pane, locate the Visible property. Set the toggle for Visible to off. This action will hide the submit icon from the screen. Refer to Figure 4-17.

Figure 4-17. *Hiding the tick icon from EditForm1*

To create a similar navigation experience on the Quality Info screen, repeat similar steps in EditForm1_1. Insert a back arrow icon and configure its `OnSelect` property to `Navigate(EditScreen1)` to navigate back to the EditScreen1. This allows users to easily navigate between the screens and provides a consistent user experience. Additionally, you can apply similar styles to the Quality Info screen to maintain visual consistency across the app.

After completing the previous steps, you can press F5 to preview the app and test the navigation between the screens. Ensure that the navigation is working as expected and that you can move back and forth between the Product and Quality Info screens. Once you have tested the functionality, close the preview, and save your changes.

Next, let's explore how to set up some basic form validations.

Validation

On the Product Info screen, all fields except Materials Used should be mandatory.

Furthermore, it's important to note that the validation should specifically occur within the Product Info screen when clicking the "Next arrow" button, rather than during the submission process on the Quality Info page.

To make a field mandatory, in the Properties pane's Advanced section, unlock the data card and set the "Required" property to "true" at the top or in the Properties pane. Repeat this for all data cards where the fields need to be mandatory. Some fields like Product Name will be required by default as we set this in a SharePoint list. Refer to Figure 4-18 where I make Product Status mandatory.

Figure 4-18. *Making a field required*

Once you change the required to true, the * icon will be visible on the left of Product Status. Repeat the same steps for the remaining fields.

Next, we need to implement validation to prevent the user from proceeding to the next screen unless all the mandatory fields are filled in.

To ensure a better user experience and prevent users from navigating to the next screen without filling in the required fields, we can disable the arrow icon when the necessary information is missing.

To implement this functionality, first select the arrow icon on the Product Info screen. In the Advanced section of the Properties pane, locate the `DisplayMode` property. This property determines the mode in which the icon will be displayed. To set the DisplayMode property correctly, use the following formula: `If(EditForm1.Valid, DisplayMode.Edit, DisplayMode.Disabled)`. Refer to Figure 4-19, which highlights the steps.

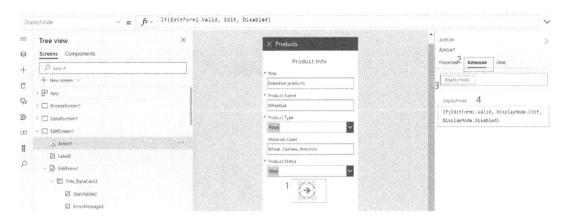

Figure 4-19. *Display mode validation*

This formula checks if the EditForm1, which contains the mandatory fields, is valid. If it is valid, the `DisplayMode` will be set to `Edit`, allowing the user to interact with the icon. However, if the form is not valid, indicating that some required fields are empty, the `DisplayMode` will be set to Disabled, effectively disabling the icon.

By implementing this logic, the arrow icon will be enabled only when all the necessary fields are filled in on the Product Info screen. This helps enforce data completeness before proceeding to the next screen.

To test the implemented functionality, first navigate to the browse screen in the Power Apps designer. Next, press the F5 key to preview the app. In the preview mode, click the + button to create a new product. Pay attention to the arrow icon, which represents the navigation to the next screen. You will notice that the arrow icon remains disabled until you enter values for the Title, Product Name, Product Type, and Product Status fields. This means that the arrow will be enabled only when all the mandatory fields are filled in. By enforcing this validation, the app ensures that users provide the necessary information before proceeding to the next screen. This validation step helps maintain the integrity and completeness of the data entered the app.

Close the preview, and from the tree view, go to EditScreen1_1. Make all three date fields required in the Quality Info screen using similar steps we did for Product Info.

Next, let's add a submit button in the Quality Info screen (EditScreen1_1). We already have a tick icon on the top, but let's have an additional one on the bottom of the screen. Use the + icon to add the button and then update its text and apply some styles. Refer to Figure 4-20 for visual guidance.

Figure 4-20. *Submit button*

Now that we have completed the user interface for the new/edit form and implemented the necessary validation, it's important to connect the data in both screens and establish a formula for submitting the data. Without these steps, the form will not be able to effectively create or edit items. In the next section, we will explore how to connect the data and implement the submission formula, enabling the form to function properly.

Interacting with SharePoint Data

In this section, our focus will be on enhancing the user interface (UI) of the app to facilitate easy editing of product properties. Additionally, we will complete the submit functionality, enabling users to create or edit products.

Currently, in the browse screen, we can view the properties of a product by clicking it and accessing the detail screen. However, to edit the properties, we need to click the pencil icon from the detail screen. To improve usability, we will add a pencil icon directly to the browse screen. This way, users can navigate from the browse screen to edit a product without the need to access the detail screen.

To enhance the browse screen, we will adjust accommodate an edit icon. Begin by selecting the right arrow icon and moving it toward the left, creating space on the right side. Then, copy the right arrow icon using keyboard shortcuts and paste it in the same location. Drag the copied icon to the right of the existing icons, resulting in two right arrow icons on the screen.

Next, click the copied icon and navigate to the Advanced section of the Properties pane. Look for the icon property and change it from ChevronRight to Edit. This modification will replace the icon with an Edit icon. For a visual reference, you can refer to Figure 4-21.

Figure 4-21. *Enabling Edit on the browse screen*

By adding the Edit icon to the browse screen, we enable users to quickly access the edit functionality directly from the browsing view.

Select the Edit icon again to configure additional properties to enhance its functionality. Begin by setting the `OnSelect` property to `Navigate(EditScreen1, ScreenTransition.None)`. This ensures that when a user clicks the Edit icon, they will be navigated to EditScreen1, which represents our Product Info screen.

Next, search for the Tooltip property and set it to "Edit product." This allows a tooltip to be displayed when hovering over the icon, providing users with a descriptive hint that they can edit the product by clicking it.

Now let's configure the new item functionality. To configure the + icon for creating a new item, follow these steps:

1. Click the + icon located at the top of the screen.

2. Set the `OnSelect` property of the + icon to the following expression:

    ```
    Set(varProductsInfo, Defaults(Products)); NewForm(EditForm1);
    Set(varMode, FormMode.Edit); Navigate(EditScreen1)
    ```

This expression performs the following actions:

- Sets the selected item of the Products list to the variable `varProductsInfo`.

157

- Resets the EditForm1 to a new form for data entry. This is done to ensure that any previous data is cleared before starting a new product item submission.

- Sets the variable varMode to FormMode.Edit, indicating that it is in edit mode.

- Navigates to the EditScreen1, allowing users to enter new product information.

By configuring the + icon with this expression, you enable users to create a new product by clicking the icon, which triggers the necessary actions for initiating the creation process.

Refer to Figure 4-22 for visual guidance.

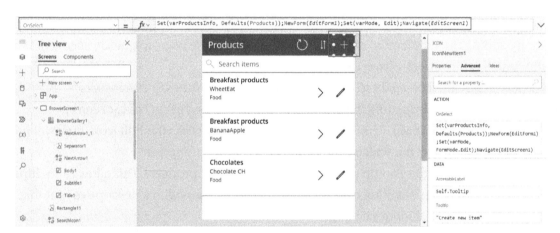

Figure 4-22. *Enabling Edit on the browse screen*

Overall, when the OnSelect property is triggered, the current state of the selected product item is stored into a variable, the form is emptied for data entry, and the user is navigated to the Product Info screen.

Next, set the same property for the Edit and View (right arrow) icons also.

To configure the icons for edit and view functionality, follow these steps:

For the Edit icon:

1. Click the Edit icon that you added earlier.

2. Set the OnSelect property of the Edit icon to the following expression:

```
Set(varProductsInfo, ThisItem); Set(varMode, FormMode.Edit);
Navigate(EditScreen1)
```

This expression sets the variable varProductsInfo to the current item, indicating that it is being edited. It also sets the varMode variable to FormMode.Edit and navigates to EditScreen1.

For the View icon:

1. Click the View (right arrow) icon.

2. Set the OnSelect property of the view icon to the following expression:

```
Set(varProductsInfo, ThisItem); Set(varMode, FormMode.View);
Navigate(EditScreen1)
```

This expression sets the variable varProductsInfo to the current item, indicating that it is being viewed. It also sets the varMode variable to FormMode.View and navigates to EditScreen1.

By configuring the icons with these expressions, you ensure that the correct item and mode are passed to the EditScreen1 when the icons are clicked. This allows users to either edit or view the selected item based on the chosen icon.

Now, navigate to EditScreen1 ➤ EditForm1 and set the DefaultMode property of EditForm1 to varMode. This ensures the form is displayed in the appropriate mode based on the value of the varMode variable.

By configuring this, EditForm1 is effectively synchronized with the selected mode, ensuring a smooth and uninterrupted editing or viewing experience for the user. Refer Figure 4-23 for a visual representation.

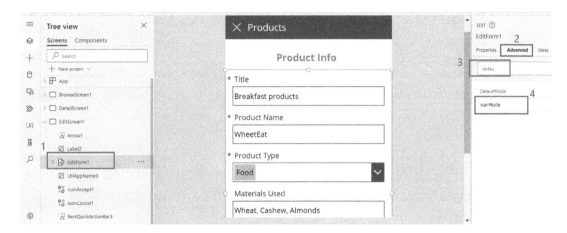

Figure 4-23. *Setting the item and mode*

Apply the same step for the EditScreen1_1 ➤ EditForm1_1 configuration. This is for the Quality info screen. This will ensure that the mode for both screens is dynamically set based on the user's selection.

As a final step, let's update the submit button properties. Go to EditScreen1_1 ➤ EditForm1_1 . Select the submit button in EditForm1_1 and set the OnSelect property to the following:

```
Patch(Products, varProductsInfo, EditForm1.Updates, EditForm1_1.Updates);
If(
    IsEmpty(Errors(Products)),    Notify("Products data updated",
    NotificationType.Success); Navigate(BrowseScreen1),
    Notify(First(Errors(Products)).Message, NotificationType.Error)
)
```

Refer to Figure 4-24. We will go through the code after that.

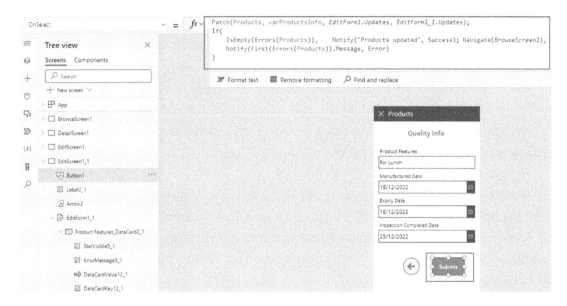

Figure 4-24. *Patch*

Let's break down the code:

1. `Patch(Products, varProductsInfo, EditForm1.Updates, EditForm1_1.Updates)`

   The `Patch()` function is used to update the Products data source with the changes made in both the EditForm1 and EditForm1_1 forms. Products refers to the data source, which is our Products list that is being updated.

   `varProductsInfo` is a variable that contains the record or item being edited or created.

   `EditForm1.Updates` represents the changes made in the EditForm1 form and `EditForm1_1.Updates` represents the changes made in the `EditForm1_1` form.

   So, this line essentially updates the Products list with the combined changes from both forms.

2. `If(IsEmpty(Errors(Products)), Notify("Products data updated", NotificationType.Success); Navigate(BrowseScreen1), Notify(First(Errors(Products)).Message, NotificationType.Error)):`

161

This is an `If` statement that checks if there are any errors in updating the Products list. `IsEmpty(Errors(Products))` checks if there are no errors in the data update.

If there are no errors:

`Notify("Products data updated", NotificationType.Success)` displays a success notification to indicate that the data was successfully updated.

`Navigate(BrowseScreen1)` navigates the user back to the BrowseScreen1, which is the screen displaying the list of products.

If there are errors:

`Notify(First(Errors(Products)).Message, NotificationType.Error)` displays an error notification with the message from the first error that occurred during the data update.

In summary, this code snippet updates the Products list with the changes from both forms and provides appropriate notifications based on the success or failure of the data update process.

To ensure that the submit button is visible in the EditForm1_1 (Quality Info screen) when the form is in Edit mode, you can update its `Visible` property using the following expression:

```
If(EditForm1_1.Valid && varMode = FormMode.Edit, true, false)
```

This condition ensures that the button will be visible only if both the Quality Info details are valid (`EditForm1_1.Valid`) and the form is in Edit mode (`varMode = FormMode.Edit`). By setting the `Visible` property in this way, the icon will not be displayed in View mode or if the Quality Info details are invalid.

By applying this visibility rule, we maintain consistency in the user interface, allowing the submit button to be displayed only when the necessary conditions are met, providing a better user experience and preventing unintended actions in the form.

Additionally, remove the tick icon on the top if you haven't already done it so as it is redundant. This completes the setup of submit button and the edit forms.

You can remove the DetailScreen1 from your app as it is not being used. Since you have implemented the edit functionality on the BrowseScreen1, you can directly edit the product properties from there.

To add the delete functionality to the BrowseScreen1, you can follow these steps:

1. Select the item template or the container that represents each product in the Browse screen.

2. Add a delete icon to the right bottom of the product card. I used the cancel badge icon for this (Highlighted as 1-4 in Figure 4-25)

3. Set the OnSelect property of the delete icon or button to the following formula (Highlighted as 5 in Figure 4-25)

Remove(Products, BrowseGallery1.Selected)

The Selected property of the gallery or container refers to the currently selected products, which will be removed from the Products list when the Delete icon is clicked.

4. Add a tooltip to the icon that says "Delete Product." (Highlighted as 6-8 in Figure 4-25)

By adding the delete functionality to the BrowseScreen1, users will have the option to delete a product directly from the browse screen, providing a more comprehensive and efficient user experience. Refer to Figure 4-25 where the steps are highlighted in detail.

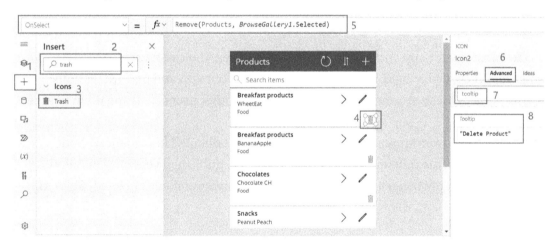

Figure 4-25. *Delete option*

To complete the process, make sure to save all the changes you've made to the app. Afterward, navigate to the BrowseScreen. You can then preview the app and thoroughly test the create, edit, view, delete, and validation features to ensure they work as intended. Take your time to verify that all aspects of the app are functioning correctly.

Once you are satisfied with the app's performance and functionality, you can proceed with the final step: publishing the form. To do this, click the "Publish" icon located at the top of the screen. A pop-up window will appear, and you should select "Publish this version" to finalize the publishing process.

Refer to Figure 4-26.

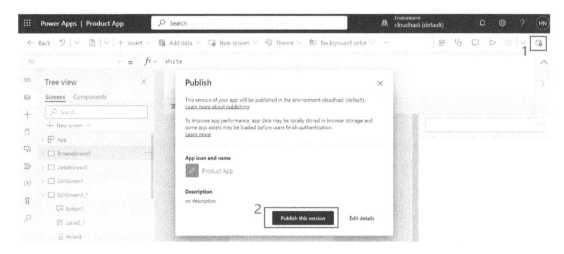

Figure 4-26. *Publishing the app*

To manage your app and access additional features, you can navigate to make. powerapps.com. Once there, you will be able to view your app and perform various actions. One of these actions is sharing the app with other users, allowing them to access and use it.

Within the Power Apps portal, you can also access detailed information about your app, such as the different saved versions and the published version. This allows you to keep track of changes and easily revert to previous versions if needed. Refer to Figure 4-27.

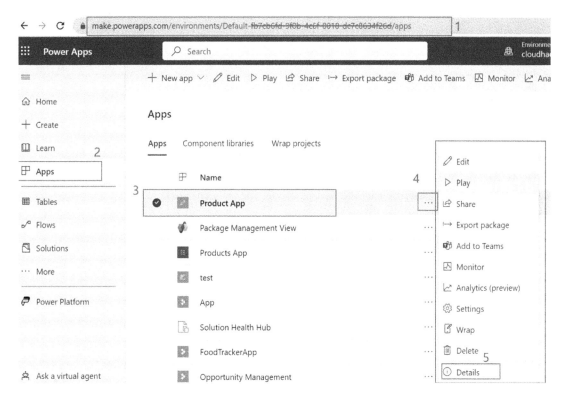

Figure 4-27. *Viewing the app*

Furthermore, if you click Details, you will find a web link for your app, which you can use to create or edit products directly in the SharePoint list through Power Apps. This provides a convenient way to manage and update your data. Refer to Figure 4-28.

Figure 4-28. *App details*

Copy the URL under web link and keep it for further use when we embed this app in SharePoint.

Also, you can see different app versions if you click the Versions tab, and you will be able to restore to another version.

By utilizing the features and options available in the Power Apps portal, you can efficiently manage, share, and utilize your app for collaboration and data management.

Adding Power to Your SharePoint Site

Now that we have published the app, let's explore how we can add it to a SharePoint site. Start by navigating to the home page of the SharePoint site where you want to add the app. From there, click the Edit option available in the top menu. This will allow you to make changes to the site's content and layout.

Follow these steps to add your app to the home page. I am adding it to the top left of the page.

1. Click Edit page from the top right. Once the page is loaded in edit mode, click to add a new section at the top left. Add a "one-third right" section to the page. Refer to Figure 4-29.

Figure 4-29. *Adding a section to a page*

2. Click the "Add a web part" option from the second column, which is the right most column. Search for *powerapps* and click Microsoft PowerApps to add to the section. Refer to Figure 4-30.

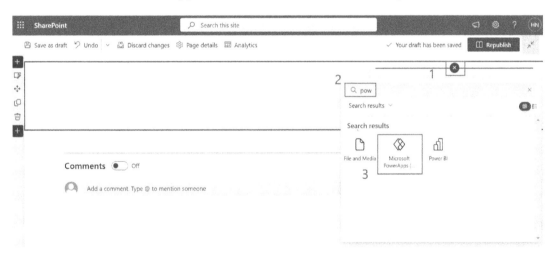

Figure 4-30. *Adding Power Apps*

3. Now click the Edit icon of the web part and add your app link (copied in the previous section) to the web part's "App web link" property. Refer to Figure 4-31.

Figure 4-31. *Adding and configuring Power Apps*

4. Let's add a Text web part above our app in the same section and give it a heading of "Manage products." Refer to Figure 4-32.

Figure 4-32. *Adding a Text web part*

5. Republish the page, and now your home page will look like Figure 4-33.

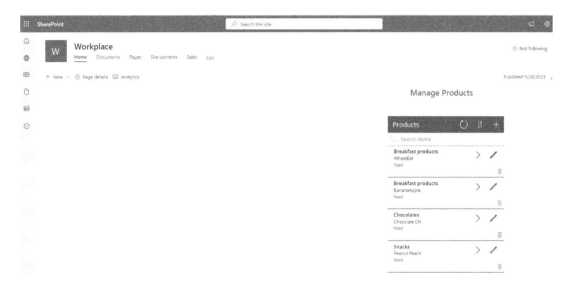

Figure 4-33. *SharePoint page with Power Apps*

Now, you can create, edit, view, or delete products directly from the Products app that is configured on your home page. If you need to make any changes to the app, you can do so using Power Apps Studio and then publish the updated version. These changes will be automatically reflected on the SharePoint page where the app is embedded.

Project Development Review

Let's look at where we stand regarding building a modern workplace for Cloudhadi.

We created a stand-alone app to manage products in this chapter. This will satisfy one of the requirements for Products list (UC-PL2 in Chapter 2).

The home page now provides product leads with a visual overview of their products, presenting them as a set of cards for easy reference. This allows product leads to quickly assess their product portfolio at a glance. Moreover, they have the convenience of performing essential actions directly from the home page, including creating new products, viewing and editing product information, and efficiently deleting products. This streamlined approach empowers product leads to manage their products effectively from a single, visually appealing interface.

Summary

In this chapter, we delved into creating a stand-alone canvas app using Power Apps. We familiarized ourselves with the Power Apps designer and its various components. By creating multiple screens and establishing connections between them, we learned how to build a cohesive app flow. Form validations and customization of component properties were also explored in detail.

In addition, we discussed the integration of data sources with Power Apps. We explored the capability of adding a data source to a canvas app, allowing for a comprehensive and unified data management experience.

Furthermore, we discussed the usage of variables, updateContext, and the Patch functions. Variables enable us to store and manipulate data within the app, while updateContext allows for the dynamic updating of variable values. The Patch function proved to be a powerful tool, as it enables the simultaneous update of multiple SharePoint lists, streamlining data management processes. We used it to update a single list in this chapter.

By leveraging these features and functions, Power Apps provides a versatile platform for integrating, manipulating, and managing data from various sources, allowing for more efficient and comprehensive app development.

Lastly, we explored the integration of Power Apps with SharePoint, fulfilling the specific requirements of the Cloudhadi project by developing a dedicated app for managing product data.

While this chapter provided a foundational understanding of Power Apps, it is important to note that the scope of Power Apps is vast and extends beyond the contents covered here. To further enhance your expertise with Power Apps, I encourage you to engage in practical exercises and explore different aspects of the platform. By doing so, you can continue to expand your knowledge and become proficient in utilizing Power Apps to its full potential.

In the upcoming chapter, we will explore the next segment of the Power platform, which is Power Automate. We will delve into SharePoint workflows and discover how Power Automate empowers us with advanced automation capabilities, enabling modern and efficient workflows.

CHAPTER 5

Power Automate

In this chapter, we will delve into the topic of business process automation using Power Automate with SharePoint Online. While previous chapters focused on creating and customizing SharePoint Online forms, our attention now shifts to building automated workflows using Power Automate. Workflows are essentially preprogrammed sets of tasks that can be executed automatically.

Power Automate is a powerful service that allows us to create these automated workflows. It provides seamless integration with a wide range of data sources, allowing us to connect to and interact with various systems. With Power Automate, we can automate processes such as sending automatic reminders based on due dates, triggering actions based on specific conditions, and much more.

In this chapter, we will be using SharePoint Online as the primary data source for Power Automate. However, it's important to note that Power Automate offers connectivity to numerous other data sources as well. It has gained popularity as a go-to tool for automating business processes, thanks to its versatility and ease of use.

Throughout this chapter, we will focus on creating a flow within Power Automate and how to effectively communicate with SharePoint. We will explore different triggers and actions available in Power Automate and learn about expressions and variables to enhance our workflows. We will discuss error handling and a few additional features. We'll also emphasize the significance of analyzing and monitoring flows to ensure their effectiveness.

It's worth mentioning that the scope of Power Automate extends far beyond the confines of this chapter. It encompasses a wide range of capabilities and features. However, our goal here is to provide you with a solid foundation in Power Automate within the context of SharePoint Online. We will focus on learning by designing a solution that covers key concepts and workflows relevant to our project.

© Hari Narayn 2023
H. Narayn, *Building the Modern Workplace with SharePoint Online*,
https://doi.org/10.1007/978-1-4842-9726-1_5

By the end of this chapter, you will gain a comprehensive understanding of Power Automate and its application to various business requirements. Moreover, we will complete the development of the Product Data Approval flow, which will fulfill a significant requirement in our project.

Recap of Requirements and Setting the Stage

Let's embark on implementing an enhanced solution for product document approval. Building upon the existing document dashboards, as showcased in Chapter 3, we will now incorporate additional functionality to fulfill the requirements outlined in Chapter 2.

Before proceeding with the implementation of the Product Data Approval logic, it is advisable to review the Executive Dashboard view of the Product Data library on your site. Make sure that you have uploaded a few documents for testing purposes. You can refer to Figure 5-1 as an example, which showcases the Executive Dashboard view, displaying few documents that are pending approval.

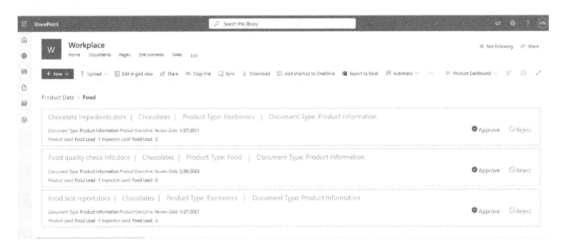

Figure 5-1. *Executive Dashboard view*

Even though we already have a few documents in the pending stage, we haven't yet fully set the stage for product documents approval and publishing. To fulfill the Product Data documents Approval requirement using Power Automate, we have two main aspects to address. The first aspect is implementing role-based access for documents at each stage of the approval process. The second one is the email notifications.

Let's define stages from document creation to final publishing.

Stage 1: Product Document Upload/Create

During the document upload stage, only the respective product executive should have access to the documents.

For example, in the case of the Food folder, only the "Food executives" should be able to view or edit the documents. Similar access restrictions apply to the Electronics and Furniture folders. Throughout this implementation, we will focus on the Food product as an example.

To achieve this, we can set the default permissions at the folder level to Food Executives and remove the permissions of all other groups. To do this, navigate to the Product Data library, right-click the Food folder, select "Manage access," and then click Advanced Settings. Refer to Figure 5-2 for visual guidance.

Figure 5-2. *Managing access at the folder level*

In the Advanced Settings page, stop inheriting permissions if you have not already done so. Refer to the "Permissions in SharePoint" section of Chapter 1, and see Figure 1-37 for detailed steps on how to stop inheriting permissions.

Next, you need to select all the groups except the Food Executives group and remove them. Set the Food Executives permission to Contribute. This ensures that only the Food executives have the Contribute permission to upload documents to the Food folder and set their properties. This process should be repeated for the other two folders as well, namely, Electronics and Furniture. Refer to Figure 5-3 for a visual representation of these steps. By following this approach, you can enforce access restrictions and ensure that only the relevant product executives have control over their respective folders and documents.

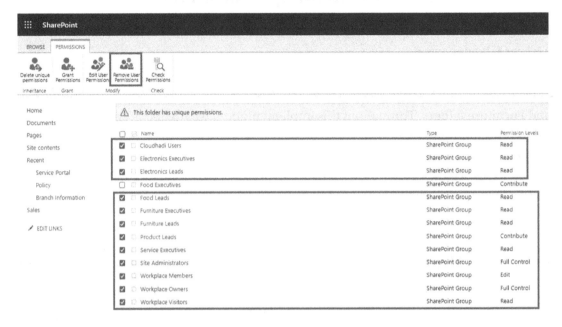

Figure 5-3. *Setting unique permissions for the upload stage*

With the implementation described, the product executives now have the ability to upload and create documents specifically within their respective folders. They can also set the necessary document properties, including assigning a product lead and document lead. By configuring the access permissions in this manner, we have successfully restricted other users from uploading or creating documents in these folders, as well as viewing any uploaded documents during this initial stage. This ensures that the document creation process is limited to the designated product executives, allowing for the proper control and management of the documents within the Product Data library.

Stage 2: Product Document Submission

Now the product documents have been uploaded and their properties set. We need to implement a notification to inform the respective product lead when an executive submits a document for approval from their dashboard. Additionally, the document permissions need to be set so that the product lead can approve the document, while the product executives can only read it and no longer have editing privileges. At this point, no other users should have access to the documents.

Stage 3: Product Lead Approval

At this stage, the product lead will have the authority to review and act on the document request from their dashboard. Depending on whether an inspection is required, different actions and notifications will take place.

If an inspection is required and the product lead approves the document, both the inspection lead and the product executive will be notified. The inspection lead will be granted contribute permission, allowing them to approve or reject. Meanwhile, the product executives and the product lead will have read-only access to the document.

Alternatively, if an inspection is not required and the product lead approves the document, the product executives will be notified. The respective product executives' group will be granted Contribute permission, enabling them to make further edits to the document. Meanwhile, the document will become accessible for all users to read, although only the respective product executives group will retain editing capabilities.

In addition, it is essential to set the content approval status of the document to Approved, indicating that it has been published. Initially, the content approval status will be Pending when the document is created. However, it will become visible to users with read access only once the status is changed to Approved. This ensures that the document is properly reviewed and deemed suitable for public viewing before it is made available to users.

This marks the completion of a round in the publishing process, where the document has undergone review and approval and is now available for reading by all users.

In both cases, if the product lead rejects the document, the product executive will be notified, and access to the document will be restricted to Contribute permissions for the respective executive's group, ensuring they can only make changes and resubmit if required.

Stage 4: Inspection Lead Approval

During this stage, the designated inspection lead will have the responsibility to review and act on the document request from their dashboard. If the inspection lead approves the document, both the product lead and the product executive will receive notifications.

The respective product executives' group will be granted Contribute permission, enabling them to make further edits to the document. Meanwhile, the document will become accessible for all users to read, although only the respective product executives' group will retain editing capabilities. Also, the content approval status of the document needs to be set to Approved.

This marks the completion of a round in the publishing process, where the document has undergone review and approval and is now available for reading by all users.

If rejected by the inspection lead, the product executive and the product lead will be notified, and access to the document will be restricted to Contribute permissions for the respective executive's group, ensuring they can only make changes and resubmit if required.

Stage 4.1: Resubmission of a Rejected Document

If a product executive wants to resubmit a rejected document, they can edit the document or its properties and resubmit it to the selected leads to get it approved and published.

Stage 4.2: Resubmission of a Published Document

If a product executive wants to resubmit a document, they can edit the document or its properties. This action will create a published version for them, and they can submit it further to the leads to get it approved and published.

This summarizes the requirement design for the approval process. Next, let's get online with Power Automate and see how it can automate this process.

Flow Design

To accomplish the discussed requirement, we will leverage the power of Power Automate. Before proceeding to Power Automate and creating a flow, let's outline the necessary design to meet the requirements. We will follow a design-first approach here. In a design-first approach in development, the design and planning of a solution take precedence before the actual implementation. Instead of diving directly into development, this approach emphasizes the importance of thoroughly designing and visualizing the solution before proceeding.

These steps will act as a useful reference and provide clarity throughout the flow creation process. If any step appears unclear, you can revisit it while building the flow to gain a better understanding. Now, let's delve into a detailed examination of the defined steps necessary to create a flow that fulfills the requirements.

Stage 0

1) Trigger the flow when document properties are modified.

2) Initialize static (constant) variables.

3) Get changes to the document from the previous version.

4) Initialize the dynamic variable Executives and set its value based on the document path. For example, for documents inside the Food folder, the value of this variable should be Food Executives.

5) Check if the Product Status column is modified. If yes, proceed to step 6; otherwise, terminate the flow.

6) Check the value of the Product Status column:

   a. If Pending, proceed to step 7 (stage 1).

   b. If Approved, proceed to step 10 (stage 2).

   c. If Completed, proceed to step 16 (stage 3).

   d. If Rejected, proceed to step 14 (stage 4).

Stage 1

7) Break the permission inheritance of the document and remove all the existing permissions.

8) Assign the Read permission to the product lead. Also, assign the Contribute permission to the selected product lead.

9) Notify the product lead via email, informing them that a document is pending their approval. Provide a link to the product dashboard and the specific document for approval. Add the product executive as a CC recipient. Stage 1 of the flow ends here.

Stage 2

10) Remove all the permissions of the document. Then check the value of the Do Inspection Required? column:

   a. If Yes, go to step 11 (stage 2.1).

   b. If No, go to step 11 (stage 2.2).

Stage 2.1

11) Update the permissions of the document, setting the product lead's permission to Read and the inspection lead's permission to Contribute.

12) Notify the inspection lead via email, notifying them that a document is pending their approval. Provide a link to the inspection dashboard for approval. Add the product executive and product lead as CC recipients.

Stage 2.2

13) Update the permissions of the document, setting the Workplace Visitors group Read permissions and the product executive group's permission to Contribute. The Workplace Visitors group represents all organization users. The product executive group is set in step 4 based on the folder the document is in.

14) Set the content approval status of the document to Approved, marking it as published.

15) Notify the product executive via email, informing them that the document has been approved by all parties and is now published. CC the product lead.

Stage 3

16) Remove all permissions on the document. Then perform exactly the steps of stage 2.2 (13, 14, and 15) here, with one difference being the CC in email step is now both the product lead and the inspection lead.

Stage 4

17) Remove all permissions on the document. And then grant Edit access to the product executive.

18) Send a notification to the product executive stating that the document has been rejected. Include the username and email of the user who modified the document in the email body and CC field. This will help differentiate between whether the document was rejected by the product lead or inspection lead.

This flow design defines systematic process for document submission, approval, and publication. By defining specific conditions and permissions based on the document status and roles, it ensures efficient collaboration and seamless progression through the approval stages. The notifications and permission adjustments are tailored to the respective individuals involved, streamlining the workflow and facilitating effective communication. Use this as a reference while developing the flow.

For a visual representation of the process, refer to Figure 5-4.

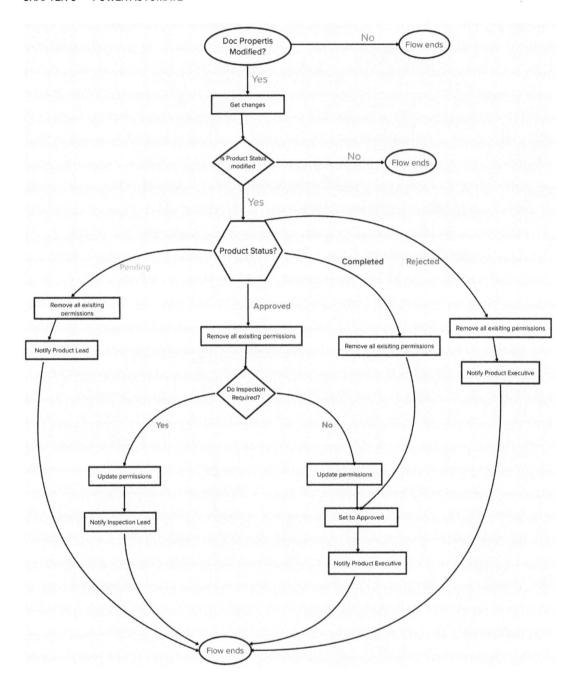

Figure 5-4. *Flow diagram*

Now, let's begin by getting acquainted with the Power Automate portal and creating a flow. This initial step will help us become familiar with the platform and its capabilities. Once we have created the flow, we can proceed with implementing the designed steps to meet our requirements effectively.

Coping with the Power

Let's start learning to navigate and handle the capabilities and features of Power Automate by creating your first flow. To get started, open your preferred browser, and navigate to `https://make.powerautomate.com/`. Since you already have a Microsoft 365 license, you have everything you need to proceed. While some premium connectors will be used later in this chapter, you can make use of the trial license for them.

Once the Power Automate home page is loaded, locate the Create option from the left navigation or the welcome page, as illustrated in Figure 5-5.

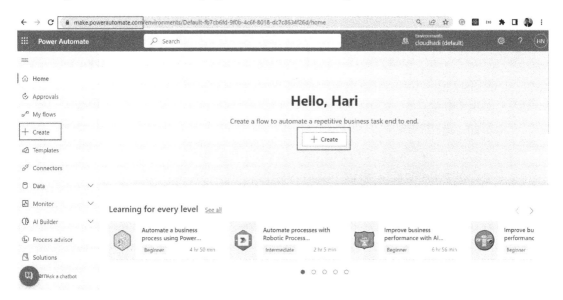

Figure 5-5. *Power Automate welcome page*

When you click Create in Power Automate, you are presented with several ways/options to create a flow. Refer to Figure 5-6.

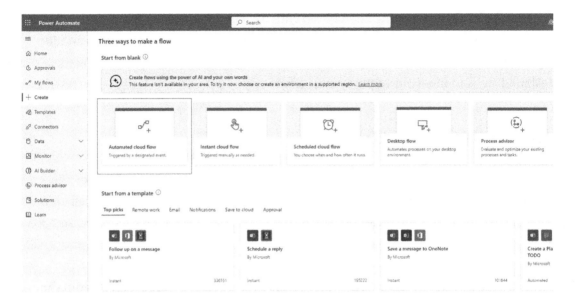

Figure 5-6. *Choosing the Automated Cloud flow*

Let's look at each way and options. First, look at "Start from blank" options.

- *Automated cloud flow*: This option allows you to create a flow that is triggered automatically based on predefined events or conditions. You can choose from a wide range of connectors and actions to build your automated workflow.

- *Instant cloud flow*: With this option, you can quickly create a flow to perform specific tasks or actions. It provides prebuilt templates and connectors to simplify the process of creating and configuring flows.

- *Scheduled cloud flow*: This option enables you to create a flow that runs on a predefined schedule, such as daily, weekly, or monthly. You can set the frequency and specific times for the flow to execute.

- *Desktop flow*: This option allows you to create flows that automate tasks on your computer. You can interact with applications, perform UI automation, and streamline desktop processes using the Power Automate Desktop app.

- *Process advisor*: This option leverages AI capabilities to analyze your existing business processes and provide recommendations for automation. It helps you identify areas where automation can improve efficiency and provides guidance on creating flows.

- *Create flows using the power of AI and your own words*: This option allows you to use natural language processing and AI to create flows by describing the desired outcome in plain language. Power Automate will interpret your words and suggest actions and connectors to build the flow.

There are two more ways to make a flow. You can see this at the bottom when you scroll down.

- *Start from a template*: With this way, you can choose from a wide range of prebuilt templates for common use cases. These templates provide a starting point for creating your own flows and can be customized to fit your specific needs.

- *Start from a connector*: By starting with the SharePoint connector and configuring the appropriate trigger, we establish the connection to SharePoint Online and specify the event that will trigger the flow. This allows us to build the subsequent actions and conditions to automate the product approval process effectively.

These options offer flexibility and a variety of approaches to create flows based on your requirements and preferences. Automated cloud flow, Instant cloud flow, and Scheduled cloud flow are commonly used in conjunction with SharePoint Online.

Now, let's move on to selecting the appropriate flow type for our product approval process. Since we want the flow to be triggered automatically when the approval status changes to either approved or rejected, we should choose the "Automated Cloud flow" option. You can find and select this option as highlighted in Figure 5-6.

A pop-up will appear, where you can enter a name for the flow and choose your flow's trigger. Refer to Figure 5-7.

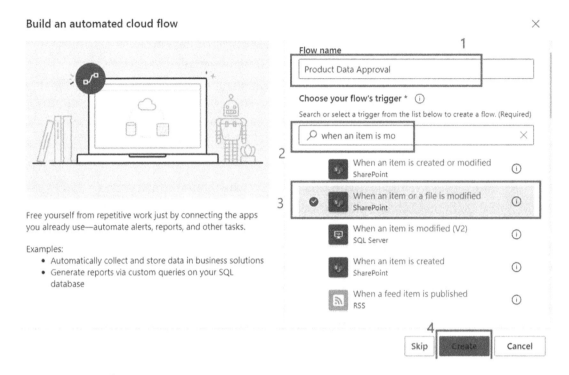

Figure 5-7. *Choosomg a trigger*

You can search for the trigger labeled "when an item is modified" and choose it from the available results, ensuring that the data source selected is SharePoint. It's important to note that there might be similar triggers available for other data sources as well, so be cautious while selecting. After selecting the trigger, click the Create button, which will initiate the creation of the flow and redirect you to the flow edit screen.

Triggers and Actions

In a flow, triggers and actions are fundamental components that define the workflow and behavior of the automation.

Triggers are the events that initiate the flow. They act as the starting point for the automation and can be based on various events such as receiving an email, creating a new item in a SharePoint list, or hitting a scheduled time. Triggers define when the flow should start executing.

Actions, on the other hand, are the steps or operations performed within the flow. They specify what actions should be taken once the flow is triggered. Actions can include activities such as sending an email, creating a file, updating or creating a SharePoint list item, or performing custom operations using code or connectors. Actions define the specific tasks or operations that need to be executed as part of the workflow.

Together, triggers and actions form the building blocks of a flow, allowing you to automate processes, integrate systems, and streamline tasks by defining the trigger event and the subsequent actions to be performed.

Let's get back to the flow edit screen. Once you are in the flow edit screen, you will notice that only the default trigger has been added. Now, let's examine this trigger to understand its functionality. You can refer to Figure 5-8 for a visual representation.

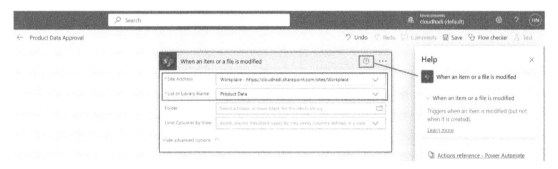

Figure 5-8. *A trigger*

The "When an item or file is modified" trigger in Power Automate is designed to initiate a flow when any item or file within a SharePoint list or library undergoes modification. This trigger enables you to automate actions based on changes made to items or files in a specific SharePoint location.

Let's examine the available options within this trigger:

- *Site Address*: This option requires you to provide the URL of the SharePoint site where the list or library is located. It specifies the location from which the trigger will monitor modifications.

- *List or Library Name*: In this field, you need to enter the name of the SharePoint list or library that you want to monitor for modifications. The available options in the drop-down list are populated based on the selected site address.

- *Folder*: If you want to focus on changes occurring within a specific folder within the selected list or library, you can specify the folder path here. By default, the trigger monitors modifications across the entire list or library.

- *Limit Columns by View*: This option allows you to narrow down the data returned by the trigger to only the columns specified in a particular view. By selecting a view from the drop-down list, the trigger will activate only when changes occur in the columns included within that view.

The help section located at the top of the trigger typically provides contextual guidance and explanations to assist you in understanding and configuring the trigger. It may offer additional details, examples, or links to relevant documentation, which can be valuable in making informed decisions while setting up the trigger.

Note   Try exploring the various trigger options available in Power Automate when using SharePoint as the data source. There are numerous triggers tailored to different scenarios and requirements within SharePoint, allowing you to automate workflows based on specific events, conditions, or changes in your SharePoint environment. Take some time to navigate through the trigger options and discover the ones that best suit your needs and objectives.

Developing the Flow: Stage 0

Our next step is to create a JSON object variable that will store all the constant values we need for the upcoming flow steps. This approach allows us to manage and update all the constants in a single place, making it easier to maintain and modify them in the future.

For instance, we can declare constants for commonly used values like the site address and library name. By storing these values in a JSON object variable, we can easily refer to them in multiple steps throughout the flow. This provides a centralized and efficient way to manage these constants. If any changes need to be made in the future, we can simply update the values in the JSON object variable instead of searching and modifying each individual step.

Click "New step," search for "Initialize variable," and add that action to the flow. Refer to Figure 5-9.

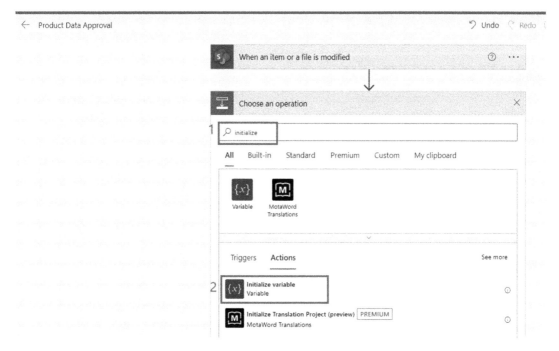

Figure 5-9. *Adding an action step to flow*

Click the ... (ellipsis) icon in the action and choose Rename. Rename the action to "Initialize constants." Set the variable name as Constants, and Type as Object. In the value field, provide the following JSON structure, replacing the SiteAddress with your site URL:

```
{
  "SiteAddress": "https://cloudhadi.sharepoint.com/sites/Workplace",
  "ListName": "Product Data"
}
```

Next, include a Parse JSON step in your flow. To configure this step, select the Constants variable as the Content parameter. As for the Schema field, you can copy the value of the Constants variable. Then, under the Parse JSON step, click the "Generate from sample" button. Paste the copied value into the provided field and click OK. This action will automatically generate the schema based on the provided sample data. The Parse JSON step is helpful as it enables you to easily select the constant variables in subsequent steps of your flow.

Refer to Figure 5-10 for visual guidance. Note that you can click the action/trigger header to collapse/expand it.

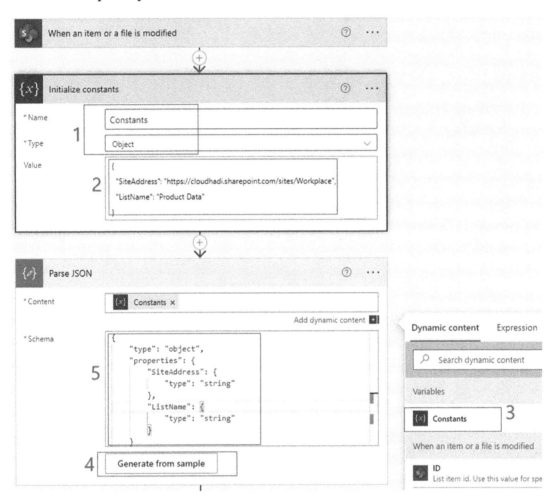

Figure 5-10. *Initializing and parsing the object variable for constants*

The next step is that we need to check if the Product Status column has been modified. If there are no changes, we can terminate the flow. However, if modifications are detected, we can proceed with the next steps. Let's implement this functionality by adding a new step in Power Automate.

To begin, click New Step in the flow designer interface. Then, search for the "Get changes for an item or a file (properties only)" action. You can find this action by referring to Figure 5-11, which provides a visual guide for easy navigation.

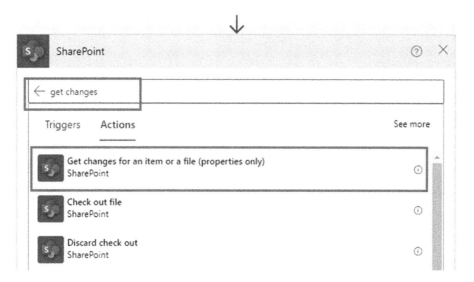

Figure 5-11. *Getting changes for an item or file*

The "Get changes for an item or a file (properties only)" action in Power Automate allows you to retrieve the changes made to specific properties of an item or a file within a SharePoint list or library. It enables you to track and capture the modifications that occurred to the selected item or file.

When you use this action, you specify the item or file you want to monitor, and the action returns the changes that have been made to its properties since the last trigger or action. This information can be valuable for tracking changes, auditing purposes, or triggering subsequent actions based on specific modifications.

By utilizing this, we can effectively check if the Product Status column has been modified and proceed accordingly in your workflow.

To configure the mandatory fields for the "Get changes for an item or a file (properties only)" action, follow these steps:

1) For the Site Address field, click the drop-down and scroll to the bottom. Choose the option "Enter custom value."

2) In the pop-up window, search dynamic content and select the SiteAddress tab under the Parse JSON head. This retrieves the value from the constants variable that we have set.

3) Repeat the same steps for the List or Library Name field; here choose ListName instead.

Refer to Figure 5-12 for visual guidance.

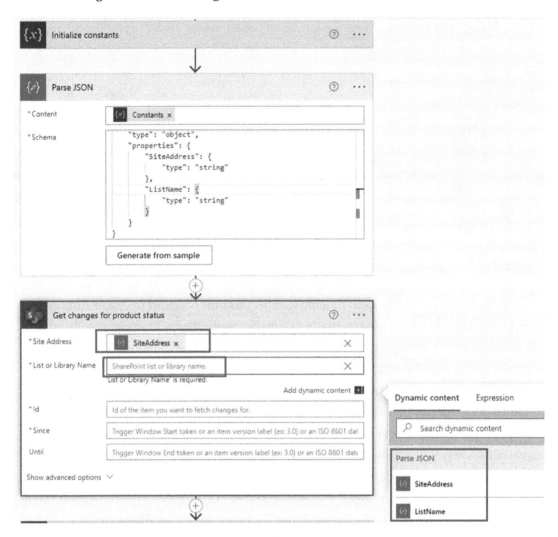

Figure 5-12. *Entering dynamic content from parsing JSON*

Now, for the ID column, click the Dynamic content tab. From the available options, select the ID field. This will fetch the ID of the current list item or document. By selecting the ID dynamic content, you ensure that the flow captures the specific ID value for the current document. Refer to Figure 5-13.

Figure 5-13. *Entering dynamic content from the trigger*

To track what columns has been modified from the last version of the document, we need to provide a value for the Since field in the "Get changes for an item or a file (properties only)" action.

Let's enter the expression `sub(int(triggerOutputs()?['body/{VersionNumber}']),1)` as the value for the Since field.

This expression calculates the previous version number by subtracting 1 from the current version number of the document. It retrieves the current version number using the `triggerOutputs()` function and the `body/{VersionNumber}` property. The `sub()` function performs the subtraction operation, and the `int()` function ensures that the version number is treated as an integer.

Additionally, click "advanced options" and set Include Minor Versions to true. By enabling this option, the action will retrieve all changes, including both major and minor versions. In Figure 5-14, you can see that we have successfully completed the entry for the action. Additionally, I have renamed the action to make it more readable and descriptive. The new name is now "Get changes for product status," which provides a clear indication of what this action is intended to do. By using the ellipsis (…) on the right side, you can easily rename the action.

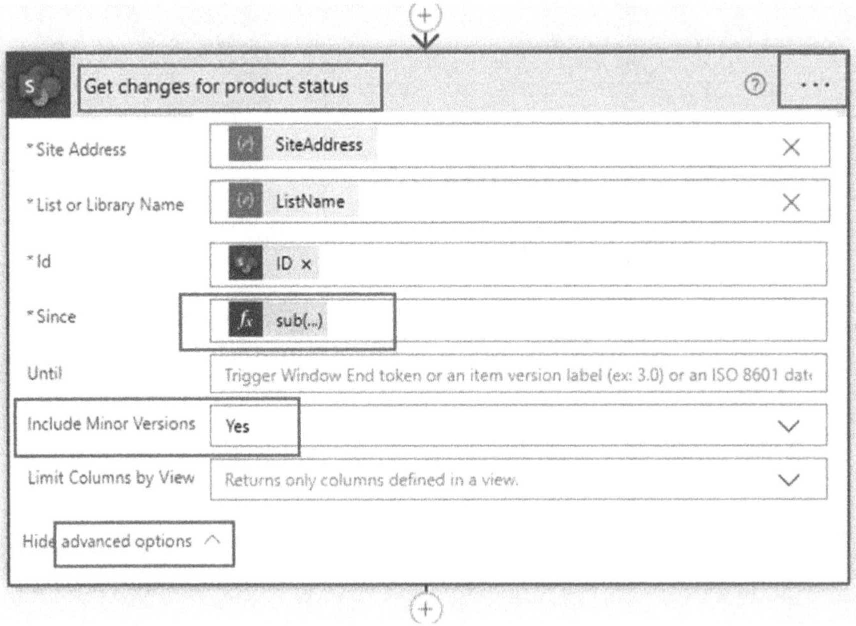

Figure 5-14. *Configured "Get changes" action*

By using this expression, we are instructing the flow to track changes in the current item starting from the previous version of the document. This allows us to capture any modifications made to all the columns since the previous modification.

Before checking if the Product Status column is modified, let's initiate the dynamic variables for this flow. To ensure a smooth execution of our flow, it is essential to initialize dynamic variables that will be utilized to store and manipulate data. To initiate these variables, we begin by adding a new step in the flow and searching for the "Initialize variable" action. Once added, we name the first variable Executives and set its type as a string and set the value with an expression. To do that, click the Value column, and click the Expression tab from the pop-up, enter the following expression, and click OK:

```
concat(split(triggerOutputs()?['body/{Path}'],'/')[1],' Executives')
```

Refer to Figure 5-15.

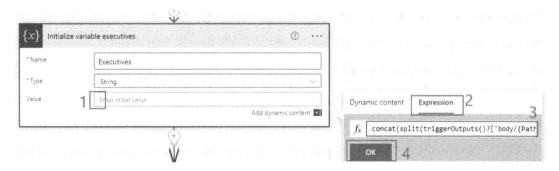

Figure 5-15. *Setting a variable to an expression*

Now, let's break down the expression.

- `triggerOutputs()?['body/{Path}']`: This retrieves the value of the {Path} property from the trigger outputs. It represents the path of the current item or document. For example, if the document is inside Food folder, the value of this will be `/ProductData/Food/`.

- `split(triggerOutputs()?['body/{Path}'], '/')`: This splits the path into elements using the forward slash (/) as the delimiter. It returns an array of elements. In the previous example, the result will be "Product Data" and "Food."

- `split(triggerOutputs()?['body/{Path}'], '/')[1]`: This selects the second element from the array of elements. In our example, it will be "Food," so we got the folder name here.

- `Executives'`: This specified the text "Executives" with a space next to the folder.

- `concat(...)` function: The `concat` function in the expression is used to combine two values: the element obtained from splitting the array using the / separator and the "Executives" string with a space before it. This concatenation results in the corresponding Executives group name. In our example, the folder name is Food, so when we concatenate it with a space and Executives, we get the value "Food Executives. This represents the executive group associated with the specific product.

Moving on to the next step, we need to add a condition to check if the Product Status column is modified. If it is not modified, we want to terminate the flow. If it is modified, we will proceed with the next steps. To implement this, click Next Step and search for the Condition action in the actions list and add it.

Once the Condition block is added, you can add the expression `outputs('Get_changes_for_product_status')?['body/ColumnHasChanged/ProductStatus']` to the left side of the condition. Select the condition "is equal to" from the drop-down and add true on the right side.

Let's break down the expression `outputs('Get_changes_for_product_status')?['body/ColumnHasChanged/ProductStatus']` and understand its components:

- `outputs('Get_changes_for_product_status')`: This part refers to the output of the previous action, which is the "Get changes for an item or a file" action that we discussed earlier. It retrieves the changes made to the item or file properties.

- `?`: The question mark represents optional chaining in the expression. It ensures that the expression handles scenarios where the previous action may not have returned any output.

- `['body/ColumnHasChanged/ProductStatus']`: This part specifies the path to the specific property we want to retrieve from the output. In this case, we are looking for the ProductStatus column and checking if it has changed.

So, putting it all together, the expression retrieves the value indicating whether the ProductStatus column has changed or not. It will return "true" if there has been a change and "false" if there hasn't been any change. By using this expression in the condition, we can determine whether the Product Status column has been modified and proceed accordingly in the flow.

At this stage, we need to add a termination step to the flow in case the expression evaluates to "false." To do this, we can click New Step inside the no block and search for and add a Terminate action. This action allows us to cancel the flow's execution if the condition is not met. By setting the status of the Terminate action to Cancelled, we ensure that the flow stops and does not proceed further. This termination step provides a way to exit the flow when the Product Status column has not been modified, preventing unnecessary processing of subsequent steps. Refer to 5.16 for visual guidance of the condition and termination steps. I have renamed both steps so they have more meaningful names. See Figure 5-16.

Figure 5-16. *Adding the Terminate action*

Now, let's move forward and add the necessary steps within the yes block of the condition.

Note   Refer to the "Flow Design" section if you encounter any confusion during the development of this flow. The design section provides a detailed explanation of the flow's steps and their purposes, which can serve as a helpful reference throughout the implementation process.

Developing the Flow: Stage 1

To handle different product statuses, we can add a Switch control in our flow. In the Switch control, we need to select the dynamic content Product Status Value for the On field. It's important to note that we should select Product Status Value and not Product Status. The Product Status represents the choice field object, whereas Product Status Value represents the actual value of the choice field.

By using the Switch control, we can create different cases based on the value of Product Status. This allows us to perform different actions or execute different branches of the flow based on the specific product status.

Refer to Figure 5-17 for a visual representation of how to configure the Switch control in your flow.

Figure 5-17. *Switch*

In the case, set the Equals field to Pending. Then, search and add the action Send an HTTP request to SharePoint. This action is used to break permission inheritance on the document and remove all existing permissions.

Set the Site Address field to the dynamic content SiteAddress from the Parse JSON action. Set the method to POST. For the Uri field, enter the following expression:

```
/_api/web/lists/getByTitle(")/items()/breakroleinheritance(copyRoleAssignme
nts=false, clearSubscopes=true)
```

Inside the getByTitle brackets, choose the dynamic content ListName from the Parse JSON action. Inside the items brackets, choose the dynamic content ID from the trigger.

Refer to Figure 5-18 for a visual reference. Note that I renamed the steps as usual. Let's break down the expression and understand its components after that.

Figure 5-18. *Sending an HTTP request to SharePoint*

The expression we added is a REST API call to break role inheritance for a specific item in a SharePoint list. Let's break it down:

- `/_api/web/lists/getByTitle()`: This part retrieves the SharePoint API endpoint for the specific list identified by the ListName dynamic content.

- `/items()`: This section appends the /items endpoint to the list URL and specifies the ID of the item. We used dynamic content for ID here.

- `/breakroleinheritance(copyRoleAssignments=false, clearSubscopes=true)`: This is the specific API call to break role inheritance for the item. The `copyRoleAssignments` parameter is set to false, indicating that the existing role assignments should not be copied. The `clearSubscopes` parameter is set to true, which means that role assignments on any child objects or subscopes of the item will also be removed.

197

To modify the permissions of the document, we use the POST method to make the appropriate changes in SharePoint. The Send an HTTP request to SharePoint action in this case is set to use the POST method because we are making a request to break permission inheritance on the document and remove all existing permissions. This operation requires modifying the underlying SharePoint list item and making changes to the permissions associated with it.

The POST method is commonly used for creating or updating resources in RESTful APIs, and in this case, it is used to update the permission settings of the document. By using the POST method, we can send the necessary data and instructions to SharePoint to perform the desired operation, which is breaking the permission inheritance.

Next, let's proceed to set the necessary permissions for the product lead and the product executive. To achieve this, we will use the "Grant access to an item or a folder" action in Power Automate. This action is used to assign specific permissions to users or groups for a particular item or folder in SharePoint. This action allows you to grant access to users or groups and define their level of permissions, such as read or edit, or a custom permission level.

Add the "Grant access to an item or a folder" action and select the appropriate dynamic content for the Site Address, List or Library Name, and Id fields, as we have done previously. In the Recipients field, choose the dynamic content Product Lead Email to grant permissions to the product lead. From the drop-down menu in the Roles field, select "Can edit" to provide edit permissions to the product lead.

Repeat these steps by adding the "Grant access to an item or a folder" action again. This time, select the dynamic content Created By Email for the Recipients field, which represents the product executive. In the Roles field, choose "Can view" to assign read-only access to the product executive.

Refer to Figure 5-19 for visual guidance.

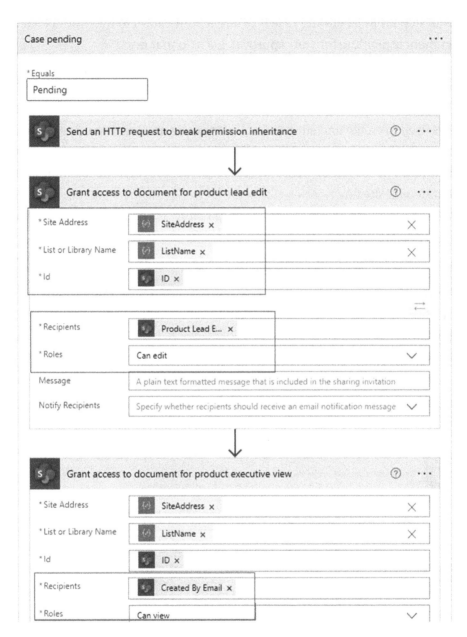

Figure 5-19. *Granting access to a document*

By using these actions, we can ensure that the product lead has the necessary permissions to approve items with edit access, while the product executive has read-only access to view the items. This helps maintain the appropriate level of access control and security for the document management process.

The final step for this Pending case is to add a notification to the product lead, saying that a document is pending for your approval. Let's do that next.

First, add two Compose actions one by one to create a link to the product lead dashboard and another link filtered by the current document. We will use these links in the next step while sending email to the product lead. The Compose action in Power Automate is used to create and store variables or expressions within a flow. It allows you to combine multiple values, concatenate strings, or perform calculations to generate a desired output. The output of the Compose action can be referenced and used in subsequent steps of the flow.

Rename both to meaningful names. Refer to Figure 5-20 for the Inputs provided for each of the Compose actions.

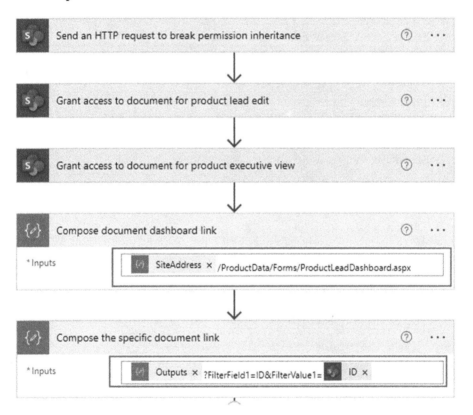

Figure 5-20. *Composing the document dashboard links*

As shown in Figure 5-20, the first Compose action involves providing a link to the Product Lead Dashboard view. This link allows the lead to access the dashboard directly from the email. By clicking this link, the lead is redirected to the dashboard where they can review and act on all the documents pending for their approval. Navigate to your SharePoint site and verify that the path to your product dashboard view is accurate in your case.

In the second compose action, the output from the first compose action is used and appended with a filter. Use dynamic content to select the output from the previous compose action. The query parameter `"?FilterField1=ID&FilterValue1={ID}"` is employed to filter the items or documents within the dashboard view based on a specific field value, which in this case is the ID of the current document. This filtering ensures that only the document that requires the lead's attention is displayed in the dashboard view.

This approach is particularly useful when the product lead has multiple items pending for their approval. By applying the filter, the dashboard view is tailored to show only the current document, allowing the lead to focus solely on the relevant item. Clicking the link from the email directs the lead to the dashboard where they can conveniently review and take appropriate action on the specific document without being overwhelmed by unrelated items.

Now, let's proceed with setting up the email notification for the product lead. To do this, add a new step and search for the "Send an email (V2)" action. Please note that it may take a few seconds for the action to load as it will first log you into the Outlook connector.

In the To field of the email action, provide the dynamic content Product Lead Email. Set the subject and body of the email, as shown in Figure 5-21. It's worth mentioning that I have included various dynamic content items such as "File name with Extension" and "Product Lead DisplayName" in the email body and subject.

Furthermore, click "Show advanced options" and add the dynamic content Created By Email in the CC field. This ensures that the product executive also receives a notification regarding the document update.

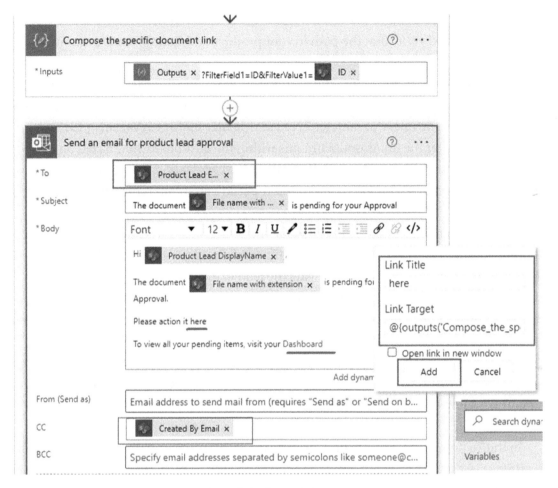

Figure 5-21. *Sendign an email with links*

In Figure 5-21, I have highlighted the inclusion of the outputs from the previous two compose actions as links. To set the link title and link target, you can click the link icon and a pop-up will appear. For the Dashboard link, use the first compose output as the link target. Similarly, for the here link, use the second compose output as the link target.

By configuring the email in this manner, the product lead will receive a notification with relevant details and the document link, allowing them to easily review and take necessary actions. The product executive is also included in the CC field to ensure they are informed about the document update.

You can now save the flow by clicking the Save button located at the top of the page. After clicking the Save button, you will see a message confirming that the flow has been successfully saved. You can refer to Figure 5-22 for a visual representation.

Figure 5-22. *Saving the flow*

This completes the development for the document submission stage. Now, the Product Lead will receive a notification with the link to approve or reject whenever the product executive submits a document. The Edit permission is also now only available for the product lead, leaving no permission to others except a view permission for the product executive.

Testing the Flow: Stage 1

To ensure the smooth functioning of the flow, let's test it before proceeding further with the development.

Stage 1: The product executive submits the document and the product lead receives notification.

Go to the executive dashboard and select a document that is in the Draft status for approval.

Wait for a few seconds, and then log in as the product lead. Check your email for the approval request, which should also include the dashboard links. Click the links and ensure that they are working as expected. Confirm that you can see the Approve and Reject buttons for the specific document in the dashboard.

Log in using the site admin account, and verify that the permissions are set correctly. The product executive should have Read access, the product lead should have Edit access, and others should have no access to the document. Click the document's "Manage access" option, and then select Advanced Settings for checking the document permissions.

Note   Ensure you have set up enough users in the admin center. Use one designated account each for site admin, the product executive, the product lead, and the inspection lead roles. The test users will need to have a mailbox license for logging into Outlook and checking emails. You can manage licenses, reset passwords, etc., of a particular user from the Microsoft 365 admin center. (https://admin.microsoft.com/AdminPortal/Home#/users)

By following these steps, you can validate the functionality of the flow and ensure that the email notifications, dashboard links, and document permissions are working as expected. This testing focuses on stage 1 of the flow, that is, the case pending block, where the executive can submit a document and the product lead receives the notification.

Analyzing the Flow: Stage 1

If you go to make.powerautomate.com, select "my flows" on the left, and click Product Data Approval. You can see the flow details interface and see if the flow ran successfully. Refer to Figure 5-23.

Figure 5-23. *Flow details*

From the flow detail page in Power Automate, there are several actions and options available to manage and interact with the flow, such as Share, Export, Turn On/Off the flow, etc. The Share option allows you to share the flow with other users or groups within your organization. The Export option enables you to export the flow as a package or template. This allows you to save a copy of the flow and share it with others or import it into another environment.

If you click the Flow Checker option, Power Automate performs a comprehensive scan of your flow and checks for common issues, best practices, and optimization opportunities. The Flow Checker examines various aspects of your flow, including actions, conditions, expressions, and connectors, to ensure they are configured correctly and efficiently.

The Edit Columns option in the instance section allows you to customize the columns displayed in the instance detail's view. When you click the Edit Columns option, a slider will appear, showing a list of available columns that you can include or exclude from the instance detail's view. These columns represent different data and information related to the flow instance.

Clicking an individual flow run in the run history opens the instance details page. This page displays the detailed information about that specific flow run, including its inputs, outputs, and the execution flow diagram. From there, you have the option to expand each step and examine the inputs and outputs for each step. You can inspect the step-by-step execution, review the data passed between actions, and analyze any errors or warnings.

Figure 5-24 shows one of my instances where I highlighted the Switch expression result and compose action output.

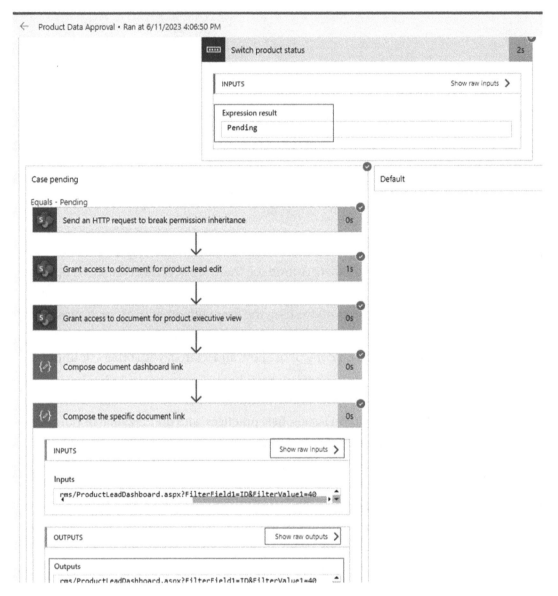

Figure 5-24. *Flow instance inputs and outputs*

By expanding the steps, you can review the details, inputs, and outputs such as expression results. This allows you to analyze the specific values and data being processed at each stage of the flow. To delve even further, you can use the "Show raw inputs" and "Show raw outputs" options, which provide more detailed information about the inputs and outputs of each step.

Exploring the inputs and outputs of each step gives you valuable insights into the flow's execution, enabling you to verify the data being passed between actions and troubleshoot any issues that may arise. It's a useful approach to understand the flow's behavior and ensure its proper functioning.

Up until now, we have covered the initial steps of creating a flow based on specific requirements. We have successfully implemented and tested part of the functionality. Additionally, we explored the various options and actions available on the flow detail page for analysis and management.

Moving forward, let's proceed with completing the remaining functionality for the product approval process. This will involve incorporating additional steps and actions to handle different scenarios and complete automating the approval workflow.

Developing the Flow: Stage 2

To handle the Approve action from the product lead, you can follow these steps.

Go back to the flow details page and click Edit to make changes to the flow. Then, expand the "Condition on product status change" action, which is responsible for checking the product status. Inside this action, expand the "Switch product status" control. Click the + button to add a new case in the switch control. Set Approved for the Equals field.

By adding this new case, you create a specific branch in the flow to handle the scenario when the product status is changed to Approved by the product lead. This allows you to define the necessary actions and logic to be executed when the approval is given. Refer Figure 5-25 where I added the new case for Approved.

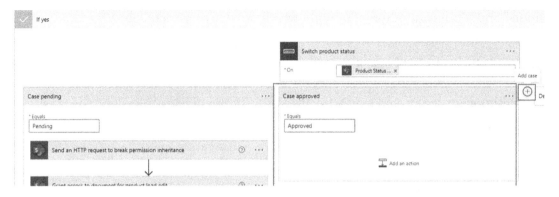

Figure 5-25. *Adding a new case*

Search and add a new step "Stop sharing an item or file." The action "Stop sharing an item or file" in Power Automate is used to revoke the sharing permissions for a specific item or file in SharePoint. When this action is triggered, it removes the access granted to users or groups, effectively stopping them from accessing the item or file.

This action is useful in scenarios where we need to restrict access to a document or item after a certain condition or event occurs. For example, in our approval process, we now want to stop sharing this document as it has been approved to ensure that the product lead can no longer access it.

Fill in Site Address, List Name, and Id to this action. The action fields are highlighted in Figure 5-25.

With the document access revoked for both the product lead and product executive, we now need to consider two scenarios. In the first scenario, if there is an inspection lead assigned, we will proceed to grant edit access to the inspection lead and read access to the product executive. In the second scenario, if there is no inspection lead assigned, we will proceed to grant edit access to the product executive and read access to all users. Also, we will need to set content approval status as Approved to make the document published.

So, we will incorporate a condition to handle the case when an inspection lead is involved. To do this, we need to ensure that two conditions are met. First, we will check if the Do Inspection Required field is set to true. This indicates whether an inspection is required for the document. Second, we will verify that Inspection Lead Email is not null, indicating that an inspection lead has been assigned.

To implement this logic, we will add a Condition block in the flow. Inside the block, we will set the conditions to be evaluated using the logical operator And. By doing so, we ensure that both conditions must be true for the subsequent actions to be executed.

Refer to Figure 5-26 for a visual reference on how the conditions should be configured. Then, we will proceed to add the necessary actions within the condition block.

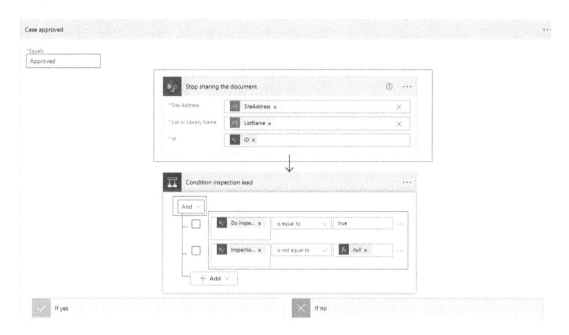

Figure 5-26. *Stopping sharing and checking inspection*

Inside the yes block, we will add two "Grant access" actions to manage permissions. To simplify this process, we can make use of the "Copy to clipboard" feature in Power Automate.

To do this, navigate to the Pending case and locate the action titled "Grant access to document for product lead edit." Click the ellipsis icon ('...') next to the action and select "Copy to my clipboard." This feature allows us to easily copy the action configuration for later use. Repeat the same things for "Grant access to document for product executive view."

By using this feature, we can quickly replicate the action and make the necessary modifications without having to manually re-create the entire action from scratch. Refer to Figure 5-27.

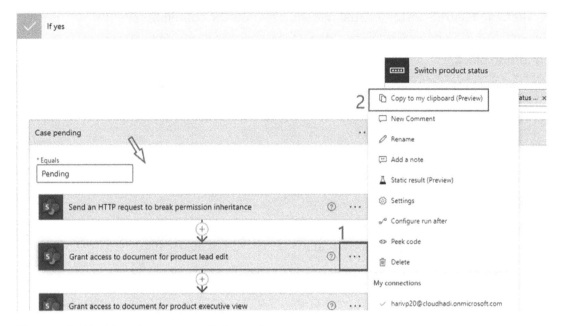

Figure 5-27. *Copying to my clipboard*

Now, let's navigate back to the "If yes" block inside the approved case and add a new step. Click the copied action from the "My clipboard" tab, which will enable us to insert the first copied action. Repeat the same process for the second copied action. By doing this, we will include the necessary "Grant access" actions within the "If yes" block. For a visual reference, consult Figure 5-28.

Note Since the "Copy to clipboard" feature is still in preview, there are certain limitations to its usage. One such limitation is that pasting the copied action inside a switch case block directly may result in an error. In such cases you can add the copied action outside of the control blocks and then drag it to the desired location

---

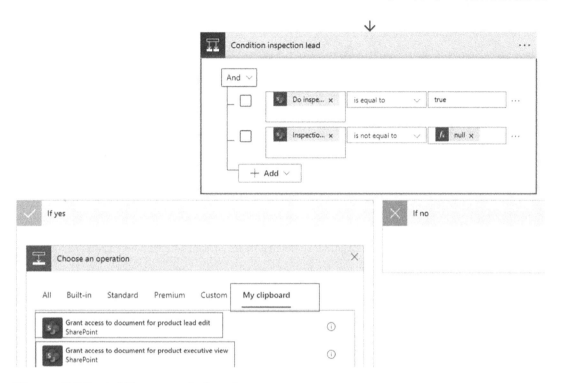

Figure 5-28. *Adding a copied action*

Now, let's rename the first copied action to "Grant access to document for inspection lead edit" to accurately reflect its purpose. Additionally, modify the Recipients field of this action by setting it to Inspection Lead Email instead of Product Lead Email. The second copied action does not require any changes, as it remains the same in this scenario. Refer to Figure 5-29.

Figure 5-29. *Updated copied actions*

In a similar manner, you can both copy the compose actions and send email action from the Pending case block to the "If yes" section in our approved case. However, there are a few modifications that need to be made.

For the first compose action, update the link to point to the inspection lead dashboard view. This ensures that the inspection lead is directed to the correct dashboard.

For the second compose action, you need to update the output to point to the current parent. When you copy, it will be still pointing to the compose action inside the Pending case block.

Next, modify the send email action to suit the inspection lead approval scenario. Adjust the action name to reflect the inspection lead approval. Modify the email subject, body, links, and the recipients in the To and CC fields to align with the inspection lead approval scenario. For CC, in addition to the current Created By Email, add Product Lead Email separated by ;.

Refer to Figure 5-30 for a visual representation of these changes. The modified sections are highlighted for your reference. Lines are drawn to denote the respective compose outputs.

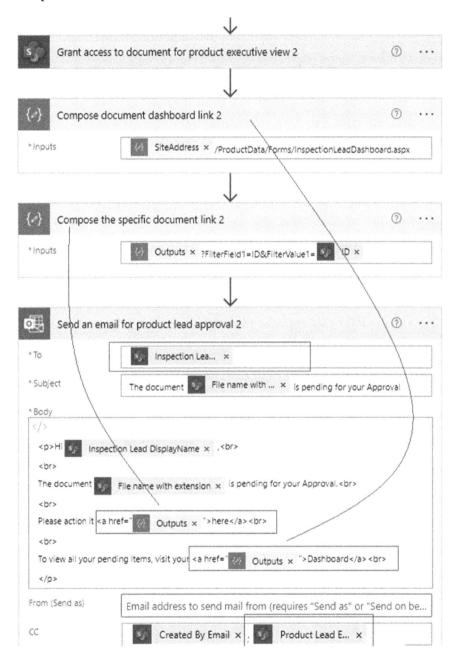

Figure 5-30. *Composing and sending an email*

This completes the scenario if the inspection lead is present. Next, let's handle the "If no" block where there is no inspection lead present.

In the "If no" block, first let's add a Scope block. The Scope block in Power Automate is used to group a set of actions together and define the boundaries of the actions within the block. It allows you to encapsulate a sequence of actions and define the error handling behavior for that specific set of actions. When the product status changes to Completed, we need to perform similar operation as in this no block. We can simply copy the entire Scope block containing the actions from the If No block and paste it into the appropriate location for handling the Completed status. And make minor changes. This saves time and effort by avoiding the need to re-create the actions from scratch.

Inside the scope block, add the following actions.

Note that the "Stop sharing the document" action is not required inside the scope block, as it has already been performed outside the scope block and is common to both the yes and no blocks.

Steps 1–3: Assign read permissions to workplace visitors group

1) *Get the Workplace Visitors group ID*: Add a Send an HTTP request action and name it "Get visitor group id." Set the method to GET and use the following expression in the Uri field to retrieve the group ID:

```
_api/web/siteGroups/getByName('Workplace Visitors')
```

2) *Add a compose action to extract the group ID*: Add a Compose action and use the following expression as the Input':

```
body('Get_visitor_group_id')['d']['Id']
```

The expression essentially extracts the ID of the Workplace Visitors group from the response body of the "Get visitor group id."

3) *Assign read access to the Workplace Visitors group*: Add a Send an HTTP request action and set the Site Address and Method to POST. Use the following expression in the Uri field to provide access to the group:

```
_api/web/lists/getbytitle('<list title>')/items(<ID>)/
roleassignments/addroleassignment(principalid=<compose output from
step 3>, roleDefId=1073741826)
```

Replace the placeholders marked with <> with the respective dynamic content.

Here, `principalid` is a parameter that should be replaced with the dynamic content that represents the ID of the SharePoint group or user you want to assign permissions to. So, this value should come from the Compose action in step 3. `roleDefId` is a parameter that represents the permission level you want to assign. In this case, the value 1073741826 corresponds to the Read permission level.

Overall, the endpoint is used to assign read access to the Workplace Visitors group for the current document.

Before continuing with further steps, refer to Figure 5-31 for visual guidance on these steps.

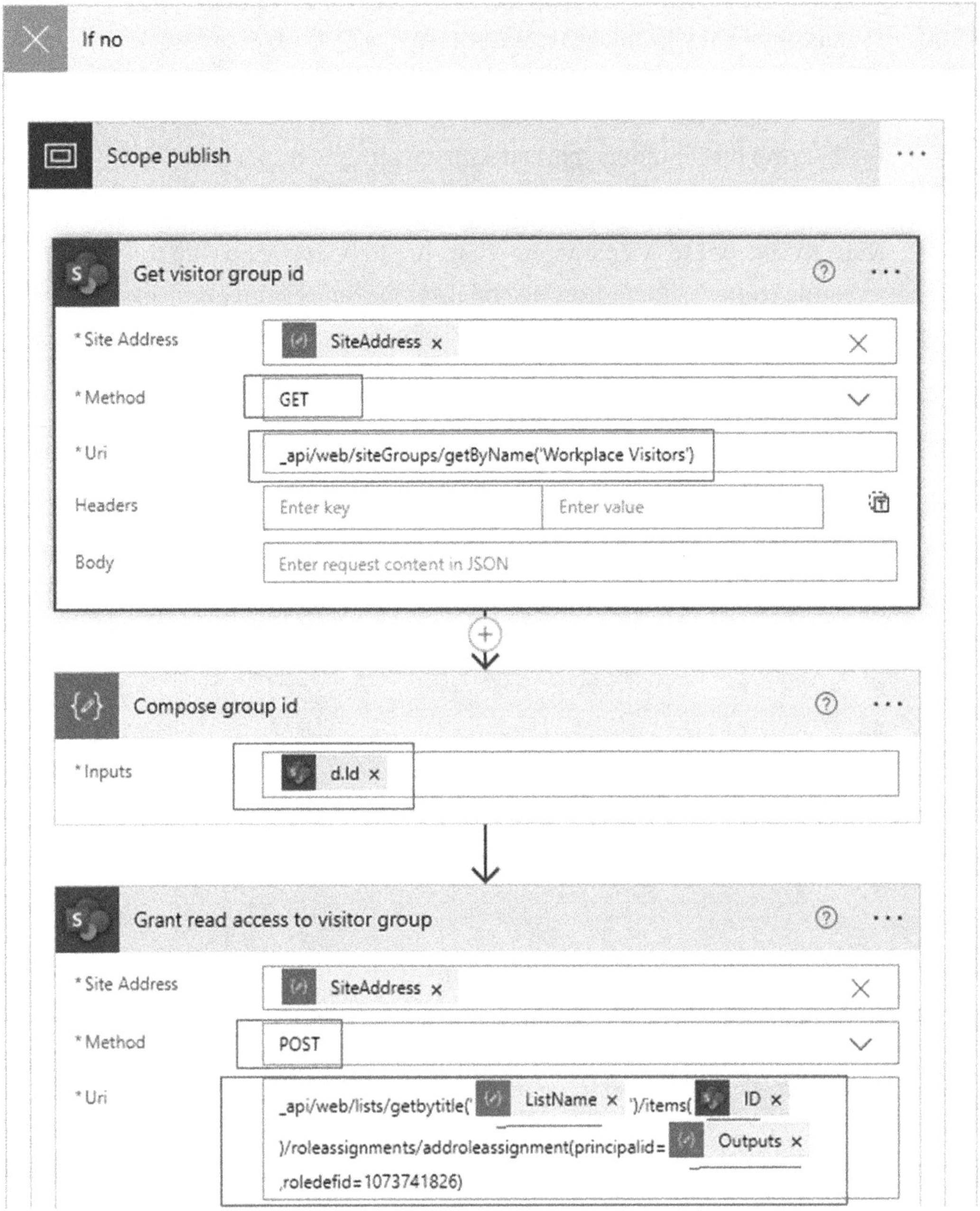

Figure 5-31. *Scope publish, steps 1-3*

Steps 4–6 involve assigning contribute permissions to the executive group. To accomplish this, you first copy the actions 1–3 and rename them accordingly.

4) In the first step, you need to use the group name as dynamic content from the variable Executives, which represents the executive group of the specific document. Make sure to update the group name accordingly.

5) In the second step, update the input of the compose action to reflect the output of the "Get executives group id" step.

6) In the third step, update the roledefid to 1073741827. This ID corresponds to the Contribute permission level, which allows users to edit and contribute to the document.

Before continuing with further steps, refer to Figure 5-32 for visual guidance on these steps. The changes from steps 1 are highlighted.

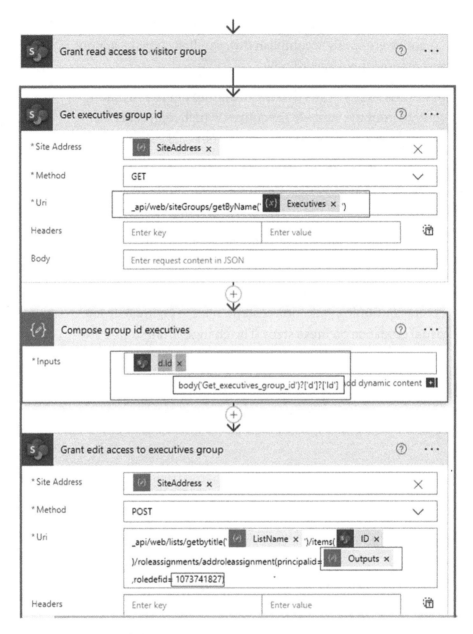

Figure 5-32. *Scope publish, steps 4–6*

7) *Add a "Get file metadata" action*: This action retrieves the ETag
    of the document. The ETag (Entity Tag) is an identifier that
    represents the current version or state of a document or resource
    in SharePoint. It is a string of characters that uniquely identifies

the document and its current state. The ETag is required to set the content approval status of a document because it serves as a mechanism to ensure that the document being modified is the most up-to-date version.

Add the Get file metadata action and provide the dynamic contents Site Address and Identifier. When you retrieve the ETag of a document using the "Get file metadata" action, it represents the version of the document at that moment.

8) *Set the content approval status to Approved'*: Use the "Set content approval status" action. Fill in the Site Address, List Name, ID, and ETag fields. ETag will be available as a dynamic content from the previous action. Select Approve from the Action drop-down. This action will set the content approval status of the document to Approved, publishing it to all users.

9) *Notify the product executive*: Add the :Send an email (V2)" action to notify the product executive that the document has been published. Set the To field to the dynamic content ExecutiveEmail and add the product lead email as CC recipients. Customize the email subject and body to indicate that the document has been published.

Refer to Figure 5-33 for a visual representation of steps 5–7 of the scope.

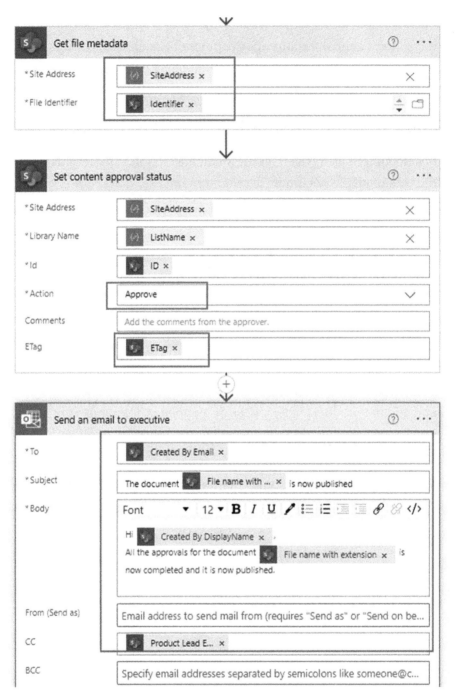

Figure 5-33. *Scope publish, steps 7–9*

This completes the setup for the Product Lead approval process, considering both the cases of having an inspection lead and not having an inspection lead. Make sure to save the flow before proceeding. You can now test this stage of the workflow to ensure that it functions as expected.

Testing the Flow: Stage 2

Here are the steps to test the flow for stage 2:

Note   Before testing this stage, ensure that you have enabled content approval for the Product Data library. You can do this by going to the library's settings and navigating to the versioning settings. Set the "Require content approval for submitted items?" option to Yes. Additionally, you can add the Approval Status column to the All Documents view of the library. This column will display the status of each document's approval process. By default, the column will show the value Pending; once a document is published, it will change to Approved. Make sure to complete these configuration steps before testing the workflow stage to ensure that the content approval feature works as expected.

`Stage 2.1: Inspection required: Inspection lead receives notification.` To test stage 2.1 of the workflow, follow these steps:

1) Go to the executive dashboard and select a document that is in the Draft status for approval. Before submitting, make sure that the document has the Do Inspection Required field set to true and an inspection lead assigned to it.

2) Wait for a few seconds, and then log in using the site admin account; verify that the permissions are set correctly. The product executive should have Read access, the product lead should have Edit access, and others should have no access to the document.

3) Now, log in as the product lead using a different browser profile. Check your email for the approval request, which should include the dashboard links. Click the specific document link and navigate to the dashboard. From the dashboard, click the Approve button for the document.

4) Wait for a few seconds, and then log in as the inspection lead. Check your email for the approval request, which should also include the dashboard links. Click the links and ensure that they are working as expected. Confirm that you can see the Complete and Reject buttons for the specific document in the dashboard.

5) Using site admin account and verify that the permissions are set correctly. The product executive should have Read access, the inspection lead should have Edit access, and others should have no access to the document.

By following these steps, you will be able to test stage 2.1 of the workflow, focusing on the "If yes" block in the case approved part.

Stage 2.2: Inspection not required: Document gets published.

To test stage 2.2 of the workflow, follow these steps:

1) Go to the executive dashboard and select a document that is in the Draft status for approval. Before submitting, make sure that the document has the Do Inspection Required field set to false and no inspection lead assigned to it.

2) Wait for a few seconds, and then log in using the site admin account; verify that the permissions are set correctly. The product executive should have Read access, the product lead should have Edit access, and others should have no access to the document.

3) Now, log in as the product lead using a different browser profile. Check your email for the approval request, which should include the dashboard links. Click the specific document link and navigate to the dashboard. From the dashboard, click the Approve button for the document.

4) Wait for a few seconds, and then log in as the product executive. Check your email for the final publishing notification. Go to the All documents view and ensure that the Approval Status column value for the document is now Approved.

5) Using the site admin account, verify that the permissions are set correctly. The product executive should have Edit access, and the Workplace Visitors group should have Read access.

By following these steps, you will be able to test stage 2.2 of the workflow, focusing on the "If no block in the case approved" part.

Navigate to the flow details page as done in stage 1 and analyze the different steps of the flow by accessing the instance run. Analyzing the flow in this way gives you a detailed understanding of how the data flows and is processed throughout the workflow. It helps you identify any issues or areas for improvement in the flow logic and configuration.

Now, let's proceed to develop the rest of the flow logic.

Developing the Flow: Stage 3

To handle the Complete action from the inspection lead, you can follow these steps.

Go back to the flow details page and click Edit to make changes to the flow. Then, expand the "Condition on product status change" action, which is responsible for checking the product status. Inside this action, expand the "Switch product status" control. Click the + button to add a new case in the switch control. Set Completed for the Equals field.

By adding this new case, you create a specific branch in the flow to handle the scenario when the product status is changed to Completed by the inspection lead. This allows you to define the necessary actions and logic to be executed when the approval is given by the inspection lead.

The first step is to copy the "Stop sharing the document" action from the case approved and then add to the case completed block. The second step is to copy and add the scope publish block. As I mentioned, you can reuse the "Scope publish" block from the "If no" section of the case approved ➤ Condition inspection lead section by using the "Copy to my clipboard" feature.

However, as mentioned, the "Copy to my clipboard" feature is still in preview, and you may encounter errors when adding both the copied block directly inside the case. To work around this, you can add a temporary condition block and add the copied action there from the clipboard. Then drag and drop each of the copied block outside of it and then delete the temporary condition block. Figure 5-34 depicts this workaround.

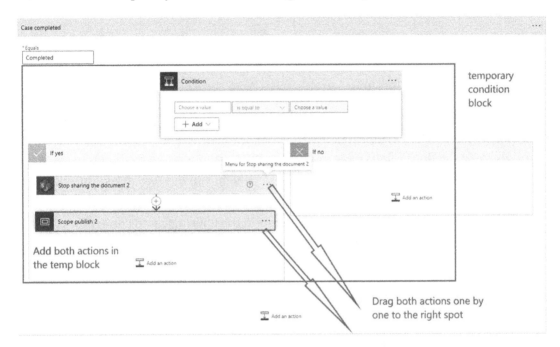

Figure 5-34. *Copying the "Scope publish" block through a workaround*

The process for the final approval by the Inspection Lead is the same as the Product Lead approval without an Inspection Lead. The only change required is to add the Inspection Lead email in the CC field of the last email step. This is illustrated in Figure 5-35. The figure shows the entire copied scope expanded.

Figure 5-35. *Scope publish, inspection lead approval*

This completes the Completed case where the Inspection Lead finally approves the document. Let's save the flow and test this part before proceeding to the Rejected cases.

Testing the Flow: Stage 3

Here are the steps to test stage 3 of the flow.

Stage 3: Inspection required: Inspection lead completes approval.

To test stage 3 of the workflow, follow these steps:

1) Go to the executive dashboard and select a document that is in the Draft status for approval. Before submitting, make sure that the document has the Do Inspection Required field set to true and an inspection lead assigned to it.

2) Wait for a few seconds, and then log in using site admin account; verify that the permissions are set correctly. The product executive should have Read access, the product lead should have Edit access, and others should have no access to the document.

3) Now, log in as the product lead using a different browser profile. Check your email for the approval request, which should include the dashboard links. Click the specific document link and navigate to the dashboard. From the dashboard, click the Approve button for the document.

4) Wait for a few seconds and then log in using the site admin account; verify that the permissions are set correctly. The product executive should have Read access, the inspection lead should have Edit access, and others should have no access to the document.

5) Wait for a few seconds, and then log in as the inspection lead. Check your email for the approval request, which should also include the dashboard links. Click the links and ensure that they are working as expected. Confirm that you can see the Complete and Reject buttons for the specific document in the dashboard. Click the Complete button.

6) Wait for a few seconds, and then log in as the product executive. Check your email for the final publishing notification. Go to the "All documents view" and ensure that the Approval Status column value for the document is now Approved.

7) Using the site admin account, verify that the permissions are set correctly. The product executive should have Edit access, and the Workplace Visitors group should have Read access.

By following these steps, you will be able to test stage 3 of the workflow, focusing on the "case completed" part. As before, analyze the flow instance and each step in detail before moving on to the next stage.

Developing the Flow: Stage 4

To handle the Reject scenarios where a product lead or inspection lead can reject a document, you can follow these steps:

Go back to the flow details page and click Edit to make changes to the flow. Then, expand the "Condition on product status change" action, which is responsible for checking the product status. Inside this action, expand the "Switch product status" control. Click the + button to add a new case in the switch control. Set the Rejected for the Equals field.

In the Rejected case, there are a few actions to be performed. We need to set edit permissions for the product executive, remove all other permissions, and notify the product executive about the rejection. Additionally, we need to indicate whether the document was rejected by the product lead or the inspection lead.

To implement this, first, copy the "Stop sharing the document 2" action from the case completed block and add it to the case rejected block. Then, copy the "Grant access to document for product executive edit 2" action from the Scope Publish 2 block under the "case completed" section. Use a workaround condition block to facilitate adding this action inside the "case rejected" block.

Finally, add a "Send an email" action and provide the necessary details such as the To field, Subject, Body, and CC. In the email body, you can use the Modified By dynamic content to identify whether the document was rejected by the product lead or the inspection lead. You can extract the display name and email from the Modified By dynamic content.

Refer to Figure 5-36 for a visual representation of the Rejected case.

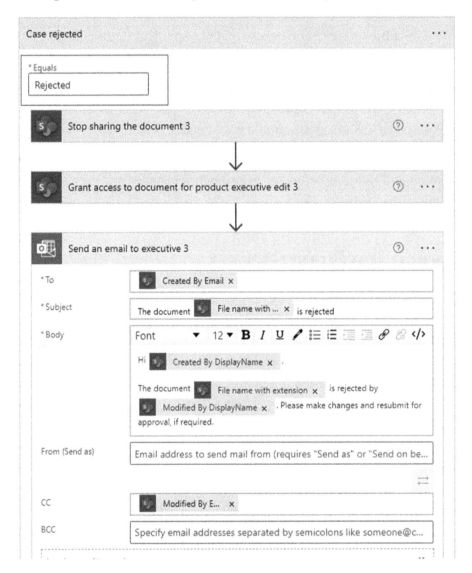

Figure 5-36. *Case rejected*

This completes the setup for the rejected case. Let's now test this final stage of the flow.

Testing the Flow: Stage 4

This is stage 4:

Stage 4.1: Product lead rejects a document.

To test stage 4.1 of the workflow, follow these steps:

1) Go to the executive dashboard and select a document that is in the Draft status for approval.

2) Wait for a few seconds, and then log in using site admin account. Verify that the permissions are set correctly. The product executive should have Read access, the product lead should have Edit access, and others should have no access to the document.

3) Now, log in as the product lead using a different browser profile. Check your email for the approval request, which should include the dashboard links. Click the specific document link and navigate to the dashboard. From the dashboard, click the Reject button for the document.

4) Wait for a few seconds, and then log in as the product executive. Check your email for the rejection notification.

5) Log in using the site admin account and verify that the permissions are set correctly. The product executive should have Contribute access, and others should have no access to the document.

Stage 4.2: Inspection lead rejects a document.

To test stage 4.2 of the workflow, follow these steps:

1) Go to the executive dashboard and select a document that is in the Draft status for approval. Before submitting, make sure that the document has the Do Inspection Required field set to true and an inspection lead assigned to it.

2) Wait for a few seconds, and then log in using site admin account. Verify that the permissions are set correctly. The product executive should have Read access, the product lead should have Edit access, and others should have no access to the document.

3) Now, log in as the product lead using a different browser profile. Check your email for the approval request, which should include the dashboard links. Click the specific document link and navigate to the dashboard. From the dashboard, click the Approve button for the document.

4) Wait for a few seconds, and then log in using site admin account. Verify that the permissions are set correctly. The product executive should have Read access, the inspection lead should have Edit access, and others should have no access to the document.

5) Wait for a few seconds, and then log in as the inspection lead. Check your email for the approval request, which should also include the dashboard links. Click the links and ensure that they are working as expected. Confirm that you can see the Complete and Reject buttons for the specific document in the dashboard. Click the Reject button.

6) Wait for a few seconds, and then log in as the product executive. Check your email for the reject notification.

7) Using the site admin account, verify that the permissions are set correctly. The product executive should have Contribute access, and others should have no access to the document.

By following these steps, you will be able to test stage 4 of the workflow, focusing on the "case rejected" part. As before, analyze the flow instance and each step in detail.

With the completion of the Product Data Approval flow development, we have successfully followed a design-first approach, breaking down the flow into stages and testing each stage before progressing to the next. It is essential to analyze flow runs during each stage to ensure smooth execution and identify any potential issues.

Now, let's take a brief overview of some of the key features of Power Automate.

Note   The Product Data Approval flow developed in this chapter is available as a zip package in the Chapter 5 section of GitHub repo. You can import it to your environment for reference if required. How to export and import a flow is explained in the next section. You can access the repository at `https://github.com/apress/` `building-modern-workplace-SharePoint-online-2e`.

Export and Import a Flow

Exporting and importing a flow refers to the process of saving a workflow as a file from one Power Automate environment and then loading it into the same or another environment. This allows users to move, share, or duplicate workflows between different instances of Power Automate.

Exporting a Flow

When you export a flow, you are creating a file that contains all the configuration settings, actions, triggers, and logic that make up the workflow. The exported file acts as a self-contained package representing the entire flow.

Let's see how we can export our product data approval flow.

1. Go to your flow details page, click Export, and select the Package (.zip) option. Refer to Figure 5-37.

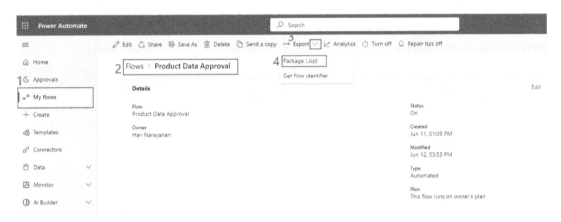

Figure 5-37. *Exporting a flow, step 1*

2. Provide a name for the export, and then click Export. Refer to Figure 5-38.

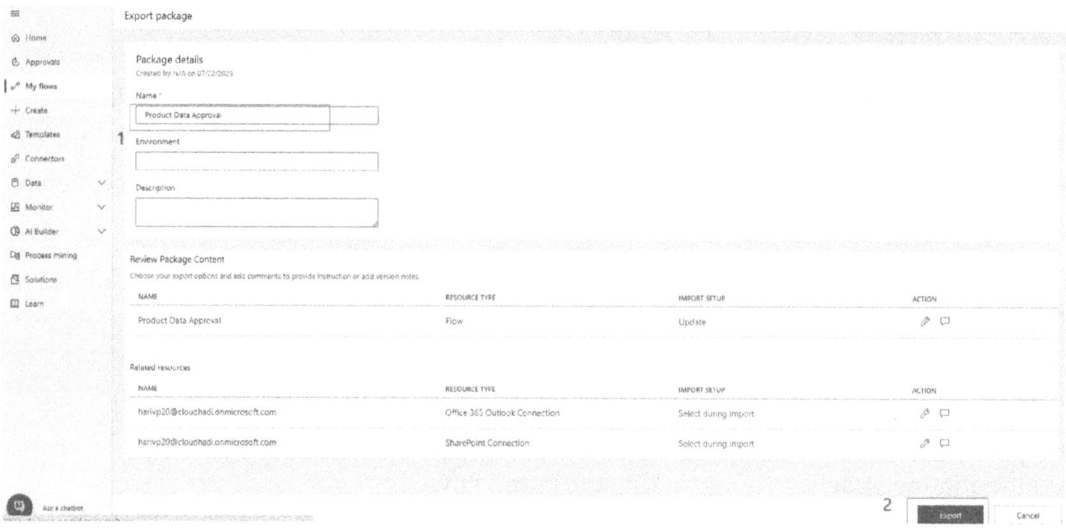

Figure 5-38. *Exporting a flow, step 2*

After a few seconds, the flow will be downloaded to your local drive.

Importing a Flow

Importing a flow is the process of taking the previously exported file and loading it into another Power Automate environment. This can be the same environment on a different account or a completely separate Power Automate instance. The import process reconstructs the flow based on the information contained in the exported file.

Let's see how you can import product data approval flow using zip from the GitHub repo for example. To import a flow, follow these steps:

1. Go to `make.powerautomate.com` and select Import ➤ Import Package . Refer to Figure 5-39.

Figure 5-39. *Importing a flow, step 1*

2. In the next page, click the Upload button and choose the zip file
    you want to import. Refer to Figure 5-40.

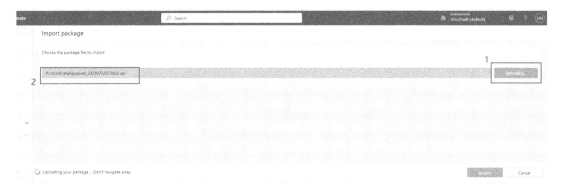

Figure 5-40. *Importing a flow, step 2*

3. After the package is automatically uploaded, you will be directed
    to the next page where you can review the contents of the package.
    To ensure proper connections for each resource, click the "Select
    during import" link. For our specific case, select your account
    connection for both SharePoint and Outlook. Click Import once
    connections are updated. You can refer to Figure 5-41 for a visual
    guide on how to proceed with these steps.

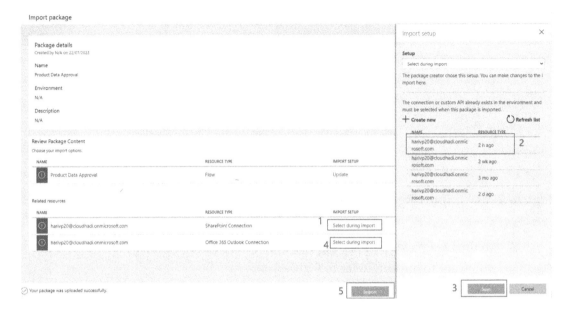

Figure 5-41. *Importing a flow, step 2*

The connections in Power Automate represent the authentication and authorization credentials required to access external services or data sources. When you import a flow package into a new environment or tenant, the existing connections in the package may not be valid or authorized to access resources in the new environment. Updating connections allows you to establish the necessary authentication for each resource within the new environment.

Once the flow is successfully imported into your environment, you'll have the flexibility to manage it according to your needs. You can navigate to the flow details page, where you'll be able to view and make any desired changes to the flow. This gives you full control over the flow's settings, configurations, and logic, allowing you to customize it to suit your specific requirements.

Exporting and importing flows in Power Automate is useful in various scenarios. Some of them are listed here:

- *Data Protection and Recovery*: When you export a flow, it creates a backup that safeguards your flow's design, settings, and configurations. This ensures that if any issues arise or if you need to revert to a previous state, you can easily import the exported file and restore your flow.

- *Streamlined collaboration*: Exporting flows enables sharing with other users and collaborators. This feature becomes valuable when you want to distribute your automation solutions among colleagues or external partners, who can then import the flow into their own Power Automate environments.

- *Efficient environment migration*: With Power Automate supporting multiple environments, such as development, testing, and production, exporting and importing flows allows smooth movement between these environments. This ensures consistency and continuity throughout different stages of the development life cycle.

- *Accelerated workflow creation*: Creating templates from exported flows accelerates the process of building new flows with similar designs and functionalities. This reusability of workflows and configurations saves valuable time and effort across various projects.

Error Handling

In Power Automate, you have several options for handling errors and exceptions that may occur during the execution of a flow. These options give you control over how your flow behaves in different error scenarios. Here are the main error handling features in Power Automate:

- *Run after configuration*: You can configure each action or step in your flow to determine its behavior based on the outcome of the previous action. You can specify whether the flow should continue, divert to error handling steps, or follow alternative paths based on success, failure, timeout, or skipped status of the preceding action.

- *Retry policy*: You can define a retry policy for failed actions, specifying how many times the action should be retried and the delay between retries. This is useful for handling transient errors or situations where a failed action might succeed if retried after a certain delay.

- *Scope and error handling actions*: The Scope action allows you to group a set of actions together and define the error handling behavior for that specific group. Within a scope, you can add actions like

"Terminate," "Run After," or "Configure run after" to handle specific error scenarios.

- *Condition-based error handling*: You can use conditional statements, such as If/Else or Switch, to evaluate specific conditions and define different actions or paths based on the evaluation result. This allows you to handle different error scenarios based on the conditions you specify.

- *Custom error messages and notifications*: You can utilize actions like "Send an email" or "Send a notification" to send customized error messages or notifications to specific individuals or groups when an error occurs. This helps in providing detailed information about the error and notifying the relevant stakeholders.

By leveraging these error handling options in Power Automate, you can effectively handle exceptions, retry failed actions, provide notifications, and ensure the smooth execution of your flows, even in the presence of errors or exceptions.

Let's look at a simple example based on the "Get changes for product status" action in our flow. Go to flow details page, edit and click "Add a parallel branch" next to this action. Refer to Figure 5-42.

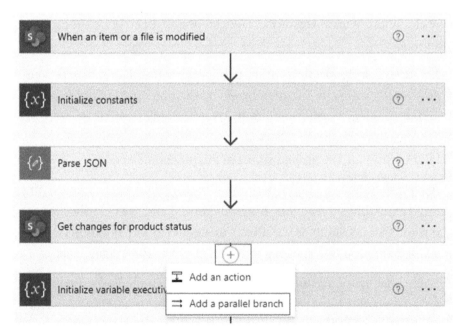

Figure 5-42. *Adding a parallel branch*

Next, let's add a "Send an Email(V2)" action to the flow. In the To field of the email action, enter your email address so that you receive the notification. To provide context, update the subject of the email to "The product data approval flow needs your attention" and the body to a similar content. Once you have added the email action, you can further configure its behavior by selecting the ... dots on the email action and clicking "Configure run after." Refer to Figure 5-43.

Figure 5-43. *Configuring run after*

From there, you can check the "has failed" option to ensure the email action runs only if it encounters a failure. Additionally, you can also check the "has timed out" option to enable the email action to run in case of a timeout during execution. Once you have selected the desired options, click the Done button to save the run after configuration. For a visual guide, you can refer to Figure 5-44.

Figure 5-44. *Configuring run after*

Figure 5-44 demonstrates the configured run after settings for the email action, where it will now run if the "Get changes for product status" action has failed or timed out. As a flow administrator, this setup ensures that you will receive a notification when such issues occur, prompting you to investigate and address the problem.

This example showcases how you can use the "Configure run after" feature. It can be used for more intricate scenarios, allowing you to define alternative steps to execute in case of failures. This feature allows you to handle errors, provide appropriate notifications or alerts, retry failed actions, or take alternative actions based on the specific error or condition encountered during the flow's execution. By leveraging this capability, you can design robust error handling and notification systems within your flows to address a wide range of error scenarios.

You can access an action settings by clicking the Settings option. This option can be found by clicking the ellipsis (…) next to the action. You can see this option just above the "Configure run after" option.

Clicking Settings allows you to access and modify various configuration options for the selected action. These settings can vary depending on the specific action and its capabilities. Here are a couple of common settings that are often available:

- *Timeout*: The Timeout setting allows you to specify the maximum duration the action should wait for a response or completion. If the action exceeds the specified timeout period, it will be considered as a timeout error. You can set a custom timeout value that suits your workflow requirements. The Timeout duration needs to be specified ISO 8601 format. For example, P1DT2H30M represents 1 days, 2 hours, 30 minutes.

- *Retry policy*: The Retry Policy setting enables you to define how the action should handle failures or errors. You can configure the number of retries and the delay between each retry attempt. This is useful for handling transient errors or situations where a failed action might succeed if retried after a certain delay. In the context of the retry policy in Power Automate, a fixed interval of Count 3 and Interval PT30S means that the specified action will be reattempted 3 times in total, with a fixed interval of 30 seconds between each retry if there is a failure.

Refer to Figure 5-45 for a visual guide where I specified a retry policy and timeout.

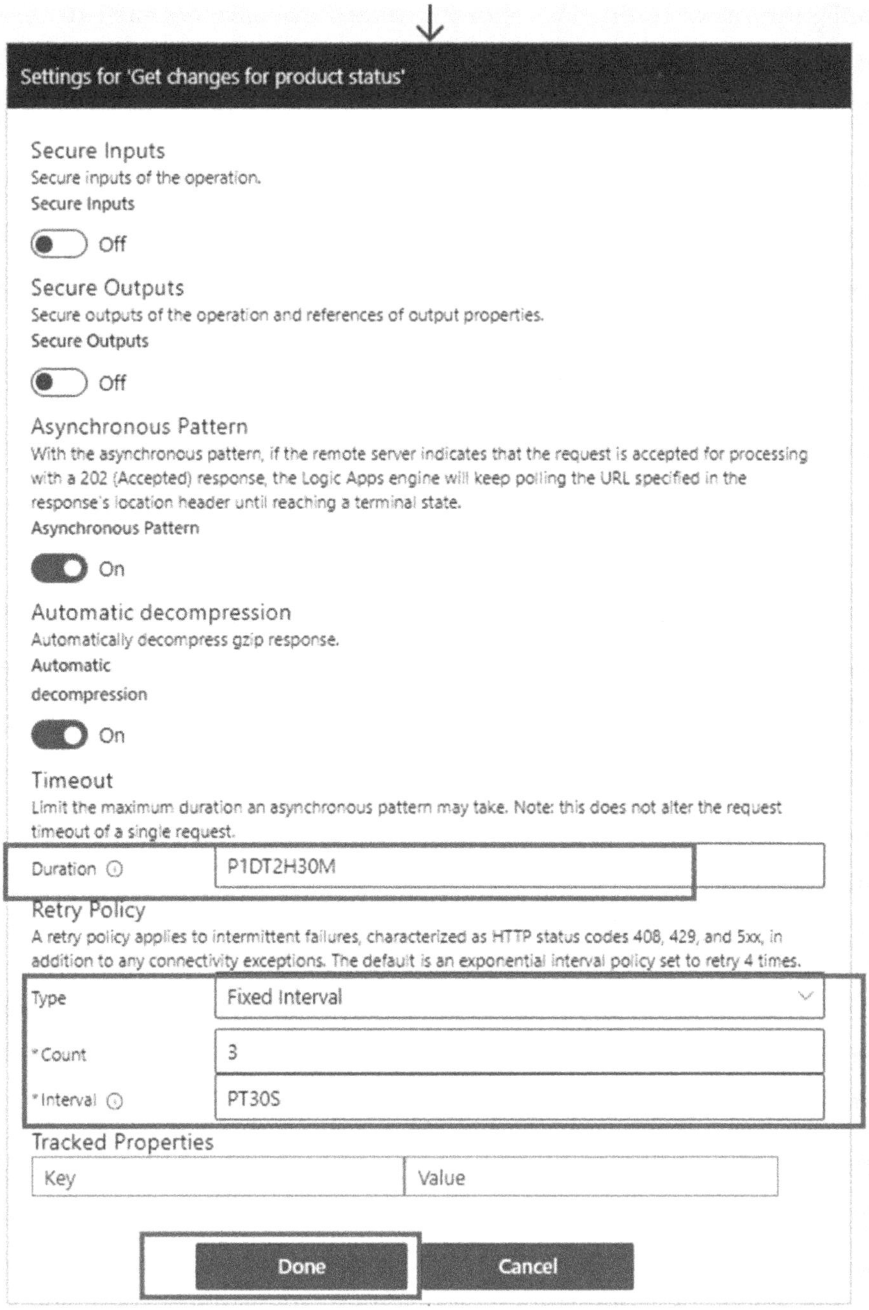

Figure 5-45. *Action settings*

By configuring these settings, you can fine-tune the behavior of each action to align with your workflow requirements. This includes handling potential errors, defining timeouts to prevent long-running actions, and optimizing the overall performance and reliability of your Power Automate flows.

Note   The error handling steps shown for the "Get changes for product status" action are purely for demonstration purposes and may not be directly applicable to your specific use case involving that particular action. It is important to customize the error handling approach based on your unique requirements and the characteristics of the action in question.

Solutions and Child Flows

In the Power Automate portal, you will find a feature called Solutions that provides an organized and centralized approach to managing your Power Apps and flows. Solutions in Power Automate are a way to group related components, such as flows, connectors, and Power Apps, into a single package. They facilitate the packaging and distribution of these assets across different environments, streamlining the deployment and management process.

Solutions enable you to group related flows together and organize them into logical units. They offer control over the deployment and visibility of flows, making it easier to handle them in different environments. Additionally, solutions allow you to package and export flows as solution packages, which can be shared or imported into other environments.

Child flows are a powerful feature in Power Automate. They enable the creation of reusable workflows that can be used as subroutines within other flows. Child flows encapsulate a set of actions or complex logic, which can be invoked from other flows.

Implementing child flows allows you to break down intricate workflows into smaller, more manageable units. This modular approach promotes reusability, as the same child flow can be used across multiple flows. By utilizing child flows, you simplify the design and maintenance of your workflows while improving their scalability and maintainability. These child flows can be easily created and managed within the Power

Automate interface, and they can be invoked from other flows using the Run a Child Flow action.

In addition, when creating a solution in Power Automate, you have the option to include both canvas Power Apps and flows within the same solution. This allows you to package them together as a cohesive solution that can be exported, imported, and managed as a single unit.

By adding both a Power App and an automated flow to a solution, you can create a complete end-to-end solution that combines the user interface and interaction capabilities of a Power App with the workflow automation capabilities of a flow. This is especially useful when you want to build integrated applications that involve user input, data processing, and system integration. Power Apps and Power Automate are tightly integrated within the Power Platform. You will be able to call a flow from Power App by adding Power Automate connectors.

Project Progress Review

In the previous chapter, we made progress in building a modern workplace for Cloudhadi. We created essential artifacts such as forms, dashboard views, and the Manage Products app. Our primary focus in this chapter was on developing the Product Data Approval flow, which allows product executives to submit documents for approval.

Using Power Automate and JSON formatting, we designed an end-to-end workflow for document approval, involving the product lead and inspection lead. We established permissions and notifications within the flow, ensuring a streamlined approval process.

It's important to note that there is always room for improvement when it comes to dashboard design and Power Automate flows. Our main objective was to provide a solid foundation and incorporate the latest and recommended practices to facilitate learning and understanding.

By completing the Product Data Approval flow, we have achieved a significant milestone in building a modern workplace for the organization users. We have now implemented solution for the requirements UC-D9, UC-D11, and UC-D14 requirements listed in the "Document Use Cases" section of Chapter 2.

Summary

This chapter introduced you to the powerful capabilities of Power Automate when it comes to automating business processes. However, it's important to note that the features we covered in this chapter only scratch the surface of what Power Automate has to offer. Power Automate provides a wide range of connectors, templates, actions, and data sources that can be leveraged for various automation scenarios. Additionally, it allows you to build AI models to further enhance your automation capabilities.

Throughout this chapter, we focused specifically on using Power Automate with SharePoint Online. You gained a solid understanding of how to utilize triggers, actions, and API calls within Power Automate to interact with SharePoint artifacts. We also explored the use of expressions and learned how to construct them effectively. We discussed important concepts such as solutions and child flows and delved into error handling techniques using the run after feature and retry policy.

By implementing the process automation for Product Data documents in the Cloudhadi Workplace project, you not only learned the fundamentals of Power Automate but also gained hands-on experience in applying these concepts. We adhered to a design-first approach and progressed through the development of the flow in various stages aligned with the initial design. Throughout each stage, testing and analysis were conducted.

While this chapter provided a strong foundation, there is much more to explore and discover within Power Automate. You are now in a great position to delve deeper into its features and unleash its full potential. In the next chapter, we will shift our focus from low-code solutions to a code-first approach as we explore the development of a web part using SharePoint Framework (SPFx).

CHAPTER 6

SharePoint Framework (SPFx)

In the previous chapters, we covered the fundamentals of SharePoint Online and analyzed business requirements for a project. We developed forms and formatted columns and views using JSON. We also explored Power Apps and Power Automate, creating canvas apps and automating business processes.

In this chapter, we will delve into a code-first approach for customizing SharePoint Online to meet complex business requirements. We will introduce the SharePoint Framework (SPFx), which is a modern development model that utilizes the user context and browser connection. With SPFx, we can customize SharePoint solutions using any JavaScript framework, and in this case, we will be using React. You'll become familiar with the basic concepts involved in React when we develop a web part.

Our approach will be centered around a design-first learning-by-doing methodology. We will walk through the step-by-step development of an SPFx web part, starting with the planning and design phase before moving on to implementation. Throughout this process, you will gain a solid understanding of custom development using SPFx and learn how to implement various business requirements.

Once the web part is developed, we will deploy it to a SharePoint App Catalog and host it on the workplace home page. Finally, we will provide an overview of SPFx extensions, allowing you to explore additional capabilities and concepts.

By the end of this chapter, you will have a good grasp of designing, developing, and deploying SPFx web parts. We will be completing some of the project requirements during the process. It's important to note that while we focus on the latest recommended concepts and provide a comprehensive example, covering every aspect of SPFx is beyond the scope of this chapter. The aim of the chapter is to equip you with the necessary knowledge to explore further and apply SPFx to your specific projects.

© Hari Narayn 2023
H. Narayn, *Building the Modern Workplace with SharePoint Online*,
https://doi.org/10.1007/978-1-4842-9726-1_6

App Catalog

To prepare for developing an SPFx web part, we need to create a dedicated location where we can upload and deploy it. This is done by creating an App Catalog site. There are two ways to create an App Catalog site: at the global level or at the site level.

To create a global App Catalog site, follow these steps:

1. Go to `https://admin.microsoft.com` and sign in with your admin account.

2. Click Show All and navigate to SharePoint in the left navigation bar.

3. Under More Features, go to the Apps section and click Open. Refer to Figure 6-1.

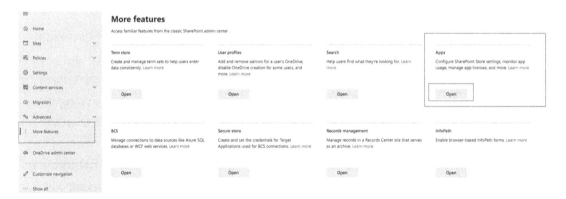

Figure 6-1. *Creating the App Catalog site*

4. On the page that appears, select App Catalog and click OK to create an App Catalog site.

5. In the Title field, enter **App Catalog** and set the URL as AppCatalog.

6. Add yourself as the administrator of the App Catalog site.

7. Click OK to create the App Catalog site.

Once the App Catalog site is created, you can access it and view the Apps for SharePoint section within the site's contents. This is where we will upload and deploy our SPFx web parts once they are developed. Refer to Figure 6-2.

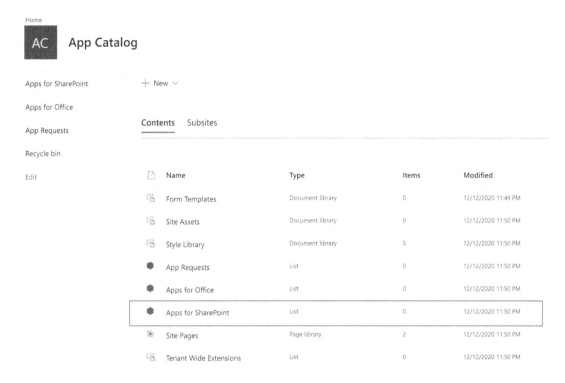

Figure 6-2. Apps for SharePoint

Alternatively, you can create an App Catalog site at the site level. This means that each SharePoint site collection can have its own App Catalog. For that, install the latest version of PowerShell on your machine. Then run the following cmdlets in order:

```
Install-Module PnP.PowerShell -Scope CurrentUser
Connect-PnPOnline -Url $TenantURL -Interactive
Add-PnPSiteCollectionAppCatalog -Site $SiteURL
```

In the second line, it will prompt you to enter credentials; use your tenant admin account credentials. Replace $TenantURL with your tenant URL, which is https:// cloudhadi-admin.sharepoint.com/ in my case, and replace $SiteURL with your site URL, which is https://cloudhadi.sharepoint.com/sites/Workplace in my case.

This will create a site-level catalog in your workplace site. This approach allows you to have an App Catalog specific to the site collection, enabling you to manage and deploy web parts within that site collection only. If you navigate to your SharePoint site and go to the Site Contents page, you will find the Apps for SharePoint section. This section allows you to manage and upload apps specifically for that site. You can click Apps for SharePoint and upload apps directly to the site-level catalog.

The main difference between a global App Catalog and a site-level App Catalog is the scope of deployment. A global App Catalog is shared across the entire SharePoint tenant and allows you to deploy web parts to multiple site collections. On the other hand, a site-level App Catalog is specific to a particular site collection and restricts deployment to that site collection only. The choice between using the global App Catalog or a site-level App Catalog depends on your specific requirements and governance policies. If you have a need to deploy web parts across multiple site collections, the global App Catalog provides a convenient and centralized approach. However, if you prefer more localized control and want each site collection to have its own App Catalog, you can opt for the site-level App Catalog instead.

Both types of App Catalogs serve the purpose of providing a centralized location for managing and deploying SPFx web parts within the SharePoint environment. In the chapter, we will be using the global App Catalog, which is shared across the entire SharePoint.

Development Environment

To set up your development environment for creating your first web part, you'll need to download and install the following open-source software on your machine:

1) *Node.js*: In the context of SPFx, Node.js is the runtime platform on which the SPFx web part will run. For the latest version of SPFx, you need Node.js v16.13+ for SharePoint Online. Follow these steps to install it:

   a. Go to the Node.js website at `https://nodejs.org/en/`.

   b. Visit the blog post for Node.js v16.13.0 release at `https://nodejs.org/en/blog/release/v16.13.0`.

   c. Download the appropriate package for your operating system. For example, if you have a 64-bit version of Windows, select `https://nodejs.org/dist/v16.13.0/node-v16.13.0-x64.msi` to download the MSI installer.

   d. Run the downloaded installer and follow the installation instructions.

   e. Once installed, open the command prompt, and run `node -v` to verify that Node.js is installed correctly. You should see a version starting with v16 or higher.

2) *Visual Studio Code*: Visual Studio Code is a recommended code editor for developing the web part. If you haven't already installed it, you can download it from the official website at `https://code.visualstudio.com`.

3) *Gulp, Yeoman, and SharePoint Generator*: Gulp is a build system that helps you build, bundle, and package the web part. Yeoman is a scaffolding tool that generates files based on your configuration. `@microsoft/generator-sharepoint` is a Yeoman generator that simplifies the creation of SharePoint client-side projects, including web parts, by providing project templates and automation for setup and configuration.

To install these tools, follow these steps:

a. Open the command prompt.

b. Navigate to the folder where you want to place the SPFx web part. For example, I created a folder called `Cloudhadi-ServicePortal` for the project. Use the command `cd C:\Projects\ Cloudhadi-ServicePortal` to navigate to `C:\Projects\Cloudhadi-ServicePortal`.

c. Run the following command to install Gulp, Yeoman, and the SharePoint Generator globally on your machine:

```
npm install gulp yo @microsoft/generator-sharepoint --global
```

Node Package Manager (NPM) is the package manager for JavaScript and is automatically installed with Node.js. Installing packages globally using the `--global` flag allows you to use the tools from any location on your machine. Wait for the installation to be completed. This may take a few minutes.

Once you have completed these installations, you'll have set up your development environment with Node.js, Visual Studio Code, Gulp, Yeoman, and the Yeoman SharePoint Generator. You are now ready to start developing your SPFx web part.

Service Portal Web Part

To begin fulfilling the requirements of the Cloudhadi modern workplace project, let's dive right into creating the Service Portal web part. The Service Portal web part is an essential component of the project and will play a crucial role in providing the desired functionalities.

To ensure that you have the same versions of the tools installed as mentioned, you can open the command prompt and run the following command:

```
node -v && npm -v && yo --version && gulp --version && npm show @microsoft/
sp-core-library version
```

The expected execution result should look like this:

> v16.13.0
>
> 9.7.1
>
> 4.3.1
>
> CLI version: 2.3.0
>
> Local version: 4.0.2
>
> 1.17.3

Here's the breakdown of the versions:

- Node.js: v16.13.0

- npm: v9.7.1

- Yeoman (yo): v4.3.1

- Gulp CLI version: 2.3.0

- Gulp Local version: 4.0.2

- SharePoint Framework (SPFx): v1.17.3

These versions should match the ones mentioned in your previous response.

If you find any discrepancies, you can try installing the specific versions using the `npm install` command. For example, if the Gulp version is different, you can install the specific version using `npm install gulp@4.0.2`.

By ensuring that you have the same versions of the tools installed, you can minimize any potential inconsistencies and ensure compatibility in your development environment.

To proceed with creating the SharePoint Framework (SPFx) project, make sure you are in your project directory (e.g., `C:\Projects\ Cloudhadi-ServicePortal`) and run the following command:

```
yo @microsoft/sharepoint
```

yo stands for Yeoman, a scaffolding tool that generates project structures and files based on predefined templates, known as *generators*. When you run this command, the generator prompts you with a series of questions to configure your SPFx project. You can provide your answers to these questions, as shown in Figure 6-3.

Based on your responses to these questions, the generator creates the necessary project structure, configuration files, and starter code files for your SPFx project. It sets up the foundation for developing web parts, extensions, or application customizers in SharePoint Online, depending on your chosen options.

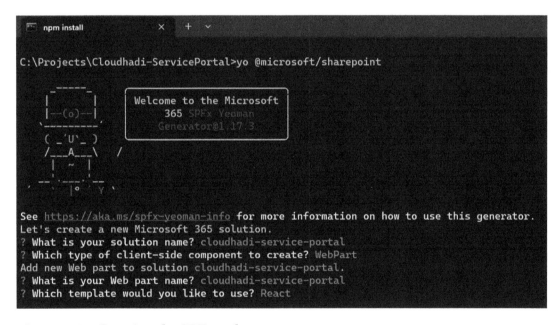

Figure 6-3. *Creating the SPFx web part*

After entering all the required information, the command will generate the web part based on the provided configuration. The process may take a few minutes to complete. Once the generation process is finished, you will see a message in the command prompt that says "Congratulations! Solution Cloudhadi-ServicePortal is created."

This message indicates that the web part project has been successfully created and is ready for further development. You can now start working on your SPFx web part using the generated project structure and files. To open the solution in Visual Studio Code (VS Code), enter Code. in the command prompt. This command will launch VS Code and open the solution directory as the current workspace. The dot (.) represents the current directory. In VS Code, you may encounter a pop-up notification asking if you trust the authors of this solution. When you see this pop-up, you can click Yes to proceed with opening the solution. Alternatively, you can navigate to the solution directory and open the solution file in VS Code.

Once the solution is opened in Visual Studio Code, you can start working on your SPFx web part and making modifications to the code, configuration files, and other project-related files.

SPFx Solution Files

Before previewing the web part, let's take a moment to understand some of the files that are generated by the Yeoman generator for SharePoint in your solution. Understanding the purpose and structure of these files will help you navigate and make modifications to your SPFx project effectively. These files are essential for developing and configuring the SPFx web part.

Here are some of the key files you'll find in the solution:

1) config: This folder contains the configuration files for your SPFx project, including the config.json file, which specifies various build and bundle settings. config.json defines the entry point for your web part. You can see that it is pointing to CloudhadiServicePortalWebPart.js by default. The .ts file gets compiled into .js; hence, the path points to .js. The package-solution.json contains the packaging information such as the name of the web part, the ID, and the version. serve.json contains server configurations. We can run and test the web part in a Workbench before deploying to the App Catalog. We specify the Workbench URL in the serve.json file.

2) src: This folder is where you'll primarily work on your web part code. It contains the following files:

a. `webparts:` This folder contains the web part(s) you'll be building. It includes a sample web part named after your solution (e.g., `CloudhadiServicePortalWebPart.ts`).

b. `loc:` This folder contains localization files for your web part, allowing you to provide translations for different languages.

c. `index.ts:` This file serves as the entry point for your web part's code. It initializes and renders the web part.

3) `Components:` The `Components` folder is where the React (`.tsx`) files are located. Since we chose React as the framework for our web part, these files contain the building blocks of your solution. Each file represents a separate component that contributes to the functionality of our web part.

4) `package.json:` This file is a standard npm package configuration file. It lists the dependencies and `devDependencies` required for your project and includes various scripts for building, testing, and deploying the web part.

5) `tsconfig.json:` This file specifies the TypeScript compiler settings for your project, including the target ECMAScript version and module resolution options.

6) `webpack.config.js:` This file is the webpack configuration file for your project. It defines how your web parts code is bundled and transformed during the build process.

7) `CloudhadiServicePortalWebPart.manifest.json:` The `manifest.json` file is like a document that describes the web part and how it should behave. It includes information such as its unique ID, name, and description. It also specifies where the web part can be used, like in SharePoint or Teams. The file also contains some settings for the web part, like whether it requires custom scripting or supports different themes.

These are just a few examples of the files that are generated by the Yeoman generator for SharePoint. Each file serves a specific purpose and plays a role in developing, building, and deploying your SPFx web part.

Next, let's look at the entry point web part file generated for our project in bit detail.

CloudhadiServicePortalWebPart.ts

The entry point of the web part is the CloudhadiServicePortalWebPart.ts file, located in the src/webparts/cloudhadiServicePortal directory of your solution. It is named with the convention of ending with WebPart.ts, indicating that it is a TypeScript file. TypeScript is the primary language used in SPFx web parts.

Take some time to explore and familiarize yourself with the contents of CloudhadiServicePortalWebPart.ts. Here's a brief overview of the code within this file. Don't worry if certain parts are unclear now; as you develop more SPFx web parts, you will become familiar with them.

1) The required imports are included for React, ReactDOM, and SharePoint Framework components and libraries. These libraries are imported because we are developing this web part using React. React provides the framework for building the user interface, while ReactDOM is responsible for rendering React components.

2) The necessary interfaces and types are defined. BaseClientSideWebPart represents the BaseClientSideWebPart class, which provides the basic functionality and structure for the web part. It is a key component for building SPFx web parts. IPropertyPaneConfiguration and PropertyPaneTextField are related to the property pane configuration of the web part. They help define the properties that can be configured by users in the SharePoint UI.

3) The CloudhadiServicePortalWebPart class is defined, extending the BaseClientSideWebPart class from SPFx. The web parts properties and their types are declared. The CloudhadiServicePortalWebPart class defines methods for rendering the web part, initializing it, handling environment messages, managing theme changes, disposing of the web part, and configuring the property pane. It also includes the definition of the web parts properties and uses React to render the component. The code sets up the basic structure and functionality of the web part.

4) The `render` method is implemented, which creates a React element and renders it to the DOM element of the web part. The `getPropertyPaneConfiguration` method is implemented to define the property pane configuration for the web part, including the fields to be displayed.

Overall, the code sets up the basic structure and functionality of the web part, including rendering the React component, handling theme changes, retrieving the environment message, and configuring the property pane.

This provides a general overview of some important files that are essential to getting started. While we continue with the development process, you will become more familiar with the remaining files and code. Before we begin development, let's run this solution in SharePoint Workbench to test it.

Running the Web Part

When you run the SPFx solution locally, it uses HTTPS for secure communication between the SharePoint Workbench and your local development environment. However, the development certificate used for HTTPS is self-signed and not trusted by default.

The command `gulp trust-dev-cert` is used in SPFx to trust the development certificate generated by the local development environment. By running this command, you explicitly trust the self-signed certificate, allowing the SharePoint Workbench to communicate securely with your local development environment without any browser warnings or errors. This step ensures a smooth and trusted connection during local development and testing of SPFx solutions.

Navigate to the command prompt and run the command `gulp trust-dev-cert` from your project folder. After executing the command, a pop-up will appear. Take a moment to read through it, and then click Yes to proceed. Following that, run the command `gulp build` to initiate the build process for your solution.

When you execute `gulp build`, it triggers the build pipeline of your SPFx project. This process compiles the TypeScript code, bundles the assets, and generates the necessary JavaScript files. Additionally, it performs various optimizations and checks for any errors or issues in the project.

During the build, the required dependencies and configurations are processed to create the final build output. The duration of the build process may vary depending on the complexity and size of the project. It is important to ensure that there are no errors reported in the command prompt during this step, as any errors need to be resolved before proceeding to the next stages of development and testing.

Note   To clear the console screen, you can use the `cls` command. This command will remove all the previous commands and output from the console, giving you a clean slate.If you want to stop the execution of a running command, you can press Ctrl+C on your keyboard. This will interrupt the command and bring up a confirmation message asking if you want to terminate the command. To confirm and stop the command, enter **Y** and press Enter.

To preview your web part, you need to make some changes to the `serve.json` file in your solution. Open the `serve.json` file and locate the {`tenantDomain`} placeholder. Replace {`tenantDomain`} with the URL of your SharePoint site. This configuration ensures that the development server serves your web part on the specified SharePoint site. Once you have made the necessary changes, save the `serve.json` file. This step is important as it allows you to view and test your web part in the SharePoint Workbench. Refer to Figure 6-4.

Figure 6-4. *Updating the Workbench URL*

To preview your web part in the SharePoint Workbench, return to the command prompt and execute the command `gulp serve`. This command not only initiates the build process but also opens the preview in the SharePoint Workbench. The SharePoint Workbench is a developer-focused design surface that allows you to test and preview web parts without the need for deploying them to a SharePoint environment. Within the SharePoint Workbench, you can interact with the client-side page and canvas, enabling you to add, remove, and test your web parts during the development phase. To add the `cloudhadi-service-portal` web part, click the + symbol. Refer to Figure 6-5.

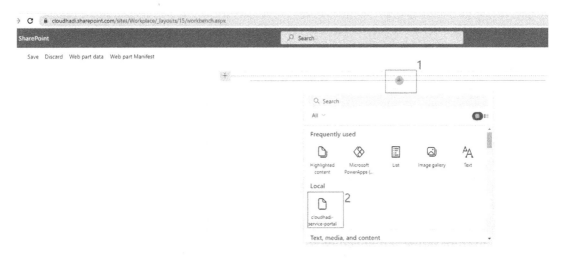

Figure 6-5. *Adding a web part in Workbench*

Once the web part is added, you will be able to see its content in the SharePoint Workbench. Also, by clicking the pencil icon, you can access its property pane. Refer to Figure 6-6.

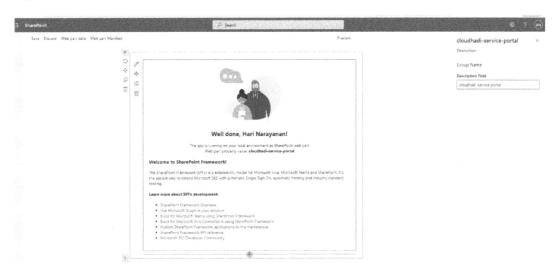

Figure 6-6. *Web part in Workbench*

If you navigate to your solution's source code, specifically the `src/components/CloudhadiServicePortal.tsx` file, you can observe that the displayed content originates from this React file. Therefore, we can commence our development from this `.tsx` file. The `CloudhadiServicePortalWebPart.ts` file serves as the entry point for the web part and is responsible for rendering the React file when the web part is loaded. If any property configurations are required for the web part, they can be implemented in the `CloudhadiServicePortalWebPart.ts` file. In the upcoming section, we will design our solution for the Service Portal, and subsequently, we can modify the code accordingly.

Requirements Recap

According to the Service Portal use cases, we have a requirement to include a feature in the workplace home page that allows users to submit requests and view existing requests. This requirement is specified in the UC-SD1 use case in Chapter 2. To fulfill this requirement, we need to establish a connection between the web part and the Service Portal list, which will be used to store and update request information.

The interface for the web part should consist of two tabs: Submit Request and View My Requests along with FAQs. The Submit Request tab will redirect the user to a form where they can input the necessary request details and submit it. On the other hand, the View My Requests tab will direct the user to a page where they can see their previous requests displayed as a list. By clicking each request, they will be able to access more detailed information about that specific request.

Before we delve into the solution design and development, let me provide you with an introduction to React. Once the solution design is finalized, we can proceed to the web part's code and commence the coding process.

Note   If you're new to JavaScript and React, I recommend reading my book on React called *Just React*. The book provides a comprehensive guide to learning React and covers various aspects of React development. It is available on Springer at `https://link.springer.com/book/10.1007/978-1-4842-8294-6` and can also be found on Amazon in different regions.

It's important to note that while this chapter focuses on SPFx concepts and developing web parts for SharePoint Online, it assumes you have a fundamental knowledge of JavaScript and React. While it provides guidance on using React within the context of SPFx development, it does not extensively cover the fundamentals of React or JavaScript. Therefore, if you are new to React, reading the *Just React* book will provide you with a solid foundation to understand and work effectively with React in the context of SPFx web part development.

Introduction to React

In simple terms, React is a JavaScript library that helps us create user interfaces (UIs). It allows us to build UIs by breaking them down into smaller, reusable pieces of code called components.

A component is like a building block of a UI. It is a JavaScript file that we develop using TypeScript, which later gets converted into JavaScript. There are parent components and child components. A child component is a component that is nested inside another component, which is the parent component. All components maintain a parent-child relationship. It's also possible to have a web part consisting of a single component.

To better understand this, you can navigate to the `CloudhadiServicePortal.tsx` file located in Solution ➤ src ➤ Webparts. In this file, replace the existing code with the code in Listing 6-1.

Listing 6-1. CloudhadiServicePortal.tsx

```
import * as React from 'react';
import styles from './CloudhadiServicePortal.module.scss';
import {ICloudhadiServicePortalProps} from './
ICloudhadiServicePortalProps';

const CloudhadiServicePortal = (props: ICloudhadiServicePortalProps) => {
  return (
    <div className={styles.welcome}>
      Service Portal - Welcome {props.userDisplayName}
    </div>
  );
};

export default CloudhadiServicePortal;
```

`CloudhadiServicePortal.tsx` is the TypeScript file for the `CloudhadiServicePortal` component. The file `extension .tsx` is used because we are using TypeScript. Let's go through the code line by line.

In React, the `import React from react` statement is used to import the necessary functions and types from the React library. When we write JavaScript XML (JSX) code, which is a syntax extension used in React to define components and their structure, it needs to be transformed into regular JavaScript code that the browser can understand.

The React library provides the necessary tools and functions to convert JSX into plain JavaScript. It includes the `React` object, which contains the core functionality of React, such as creating and rendering components, managing component state, and handling component life-cycle methods.

By importing `React`, we can use its features and utilities within our code, such as creating React elements, defining functional or class components, and leveraging React's component life-cycle methods. It allows us to build dynamic and interactive user interfaces using React's declarative approach.

In summary, importing `React` is essential to utilize the React library's functionality and write React components using JSX syntax.

Next, we import the `.scss` file for applying styles to the component. By importing the `.scss` file into our component, we can access predefined CSS classes and styles defined within that file. This allows us to apply specific styles to elements within our component, such as setting colors, font sizes, margins, and more.

The styles variable that we import represents an object containing the mapping of class names to their corresponding CSS styles defined in the `.scss` file. By accessing the properties of this styles object, we can apply those styles to the elements in our component. Using `.scss` and importing the associated styles allows us to easily manage and apply consistent styles to our components, making our UI more visually appealing and organized.

Importing and passing `ICloudhadiServicePortalProps` as a parameter to the component `CloudhadiServicePortal` allows us to access the SPFx property pane configurations or any other properties defined in the `ICloudhadiServicePortalProps` interface.

The `ICloudhadiServicePortalProps` interface defines the shape or structure of the properties that can be passed to the `CloudhadiServicePortal` component. By including `props: ICloudhadiServicePortalProps` as a parameter in the function, we are indicating that the component expects to receive an object of type `ICloudhadiServicePortalProps` as its input.

With this, we can access the properties defined in ICloudhadiServicePortalProps within the component body. These properties can include values or configurations from the SPFx property pane, such as user input, settings, or other data required for the component's functionality.

For example, if ICloudhadiServicePortalProps defines a property called userDisplayName. You can see this if you go to ICloudhadiServicePortalProps.ts inside the same folder. We can access the user display name within the component as props.userDisplayName. This allows us to use the passed property value and incorporate it into the component's rendering logic or perform other operations based on its value.

By passing ICloudhadiServicePortalProps to the component, we establish a way to pass data and configurations from the parent component or from outside sources, making our component more flexible and customizable based on the specific needs of our application or web part.

In the code snippet, the div element you see inside the return() method is written in JSX, a syntax extension of JavaScript used in React. JSX allows us to define the structure and content of our components in a more declarative way.

The <div> element has a CSS class assigned to it using the className attribute. In this case, the CSS class is specified as {styles.welcome}. The styles object is imported from the CloudhadiServicePortal.module.scss file, which contains custom styles defined for different classes.

By applying the CSS class styles.welcome to the <div>, we can utilize the predefined styles for the welcome class defined in the associated SCSS file.

Within the <div>, we have the text "Service Portal - Welcome" followed by the value of the userDisplayName property. The props object represents the properties passed to the component, and we can access the userDisplayName property using props.userDisplayName. This allows us to dynamically display the user's display name within the component.

So, the code snippet renders a <div> element with the custom styles defined in the SCSS file and displays the text "Service Portal - Welcome" followed by the value of the userDisplayName property passed through the props object. This enables the component to greet the user with their specific display name.

By using the export default statement, we make the class available for importing into other components.

To see the changes, we made in the code, let's stop the current running solution by using Ctrl+C in the command prompt. Then, we can run the `gulp serve` command again. Once the solution is running, go back to the SharePoint Workbench that we opened earlier. You will notice that now, instead of the default content, you will see the text "Service Portal" followed by your name displayed on the page. This indicates that our code modifications have been successfully applied and the web part is rendering the updated content as expected.

By following this process, we can quickly iterate and see the changes we make to our web part in real time, allowing us to develop and test our solution more efficiently.

Now that you have a basic understanding of SPFx files and how to work with them, let's move on to designing and building our solution. By designing and building the solution, you'll gain practical knowledge and experience in creating the desired functionality for the Service Portal.

We'll start by discussing the solution design and then proceed to implement it using SPFx. This approach allows us to learn and apply concepts in a hands-on manner. So, let's dive into solution design!

Service Portal Solution Design

To build our Service Portal solution, we need three main components: `CloudhadiServicePortal`, `RequestDetails`, and `RequestList`.

The `CloudhadiServicePortal` component serves as the main entry point and contains three tabs: Create a New Request, My Requests, and Pending Requests. This component acts as the home page for our portal.

The `RequestDetails` component is responsible for handling individual request creation. Users can enter details such as the request title and description using this component's user interface. They can then submit their request, initiating the request creation process.

The `RequestList` component plays a crucial role in managing the other two tabs. It needs to be rendered twice within the `CloudhadiServicePortal` component.

The first instance of the `RequestList` component is for the My Requests tab. In this tab, all users can view their requests, regardless of their status. It provides a comprehensive overview of each user's submitted requests.

The second instance of the `RequestList` component is specifically for the Pending Requests tab, which is accessible only to service executives. This tab allows service executives to view all pending requests and take necessary actions on them. For enhanced functionality, checkboxes are provided for selecting individual requests, and buttons corresponding to different status options (such as In Progress, Resolve, Reject, and Complete) enable executives to manage the pending requests efficiently.

By dividing the functionality between these components, we can create a user-friendly Service Portal where users can easily submit requests and track their status, while service executives can efficiently manage and take actions on pending requests.

Let's outline the development stages, each representing a distinct and testable part of our solution.

Stage 1: Setting Up the Web Part and Developing the Root Component

1. Install necessary dependencies like Fluent UI and PnP libraries for styling and SharePoint interaction.

2. Configure SPFx context and make any required changes in the `tsconfig` file.

3. Create additional interfaces and components for Request Details and Request List.

4. Develop the root component as the portal homepage.

5. Fetch the current logged-in user and determine if they belong to the Service Executives group.

6. Create three tabs: Request Details, My Requests, and Pending Requests. Pass the context and user information to the appropriate components.

7. Style the components using CSS classes.

8. Test the functionality in the Workbench.

Stage 2: Developing the Request Details Component

1. Develop a form with fields for the request details and apply validations.

2. Implement the submission of a new request by adding an item to the Service Portal list using the PnP library.

3. Provide functionality to reset the form, display error/success messages, and handle validation errors.

4. Style the component using CSS classes.

5. Test the functionality in the Workbench.

Stage 3: Developing the Request List Component

1. Create a grid or table to display the requests with important fields as columns.

2. Implement functionality to view more details of a request by clicking the ID column.

3. For nonservice users:

   a. Fetch and display all items from the Service Portal list associated with the logged-in user using the PnP library.

4. For service users:

   a. Fetch and display all pending items from the Service Portal list using the PnP library, excluding those with Completed or Rejected status.

   b. Add checkboxes to select requests and buttons for different status actions: In Progress, Resolve, Reject, and Complete.

5. Implement validations, success/error messages, and styling using CSS classes.

6. Test the functionality in the Workbench.

Stage 4: Deployment and Adding the Web Part to the Home Page

1. Package the solution using the `gulp` package command to generate the .sppkg file.

2. Upload the .sppkg file to the SharePoint tenant App Catalog.

3. Navigate to the workplace site and edit the home page.

4. Add the Service Portal web part to the page and save the changes.

5. Publish the page to make the web part visible.

6. Verify the functionality of the web part by submitting requests, viewing them, and performing actions.

Following this design-first approach and implementing these stages will help in planning and smoothly developing the Service Portal solution.

Development: Stage 1

This stage of development focuses on setting up the project by installing dependencies, configuring the necessary settings, creating the initial component files, and developing the root component. This stage is crucial for laying the foundation of the project before diving into the actual implementation. This involves six steps.

Step 1: Installing Dependencies

Before proceeding with component development, let's install the dependency packages.

To enhance the user interface of our solution, we will install the Fluent UI library, which is widely used in SharePoint Online for its styling. Let's proceed with the installation process:

1. Open your Visual Studio Code solution and navigate to the View menu.

2. Click Terminal. Alternatively, you can press Ctrl+ to open the Terminal at the bottom of the screen.

3. In the Terminal, run the command `npm install @fluentui/react`. This command will install the necessary packages from the Fluent UI library into your solution.

   Refer to Figure 6-7 for a visual guidance.

Figure 6-7. *VS Code Terminal*

By installing Fluent UI, we can leverage its components and styling to create a visually appealing and consistent user interface for our Service Portal solution.

Next, install the required PnP modules. Run the following command:

```
npm install @pnp/sp
```

The command installs the `@pnp/sp` package from the npm registry as a dependency in your project.

`@pnp/sp` is a JavaScript library that provides a Fluent API (PnP stands for Patterns and Practices) for working with SharePoint in a client-side context. It simplifies the process of interacting with SharePoint sites, lists, libraries, and other SharePoint artifacts. By installing `@pnp/sp`, you gain access to a wide range of functionalities and methods that allow you to perform operations such as creating, reading, updating, and deleting items in SharePoint lists, querying data, uploading files, managing permissions, and much more.

Next run `npm install @pnp/sp`.

The command installs the @pnp/core package from the npm registry as a dependency in your project. PnP Core offers a set of utility methods and classes that encapsulate complex REST API calls and operations, making it easier for developers to interact with SharePoint data and services

Next, run the following command:

```
npm install @pnp/spfx-controls-react
```

The command npm install @pnp/spfx-controls-react is used to install the @pnp/spfx-controls-react package as a dependency in your project. This package is a set of reusable React controls and components designed specifically for SPFx solutions.

Step 2: Setting Up the Context

Setting up the context in the root TypeScript file of the SPFx web part allows us to pass the necessary context information to the child components. The context object provides access to important information and functionalities related to the SharePoint environment and the current user.

By passing the context object to the child components, we enable them to access this information and utilize the available functionalities. This allows for seamless integration with SharePoint and the ability to perform SharePoint-related operations, such as fetching data, interacting with lists and libraries, and more.

To set up the context in the CloudhadiServicePortalWebPart.ts file, there are three changes that need to be made.

1. Update the import statement to include WebPartContext:
   Find the import code that includes BaseClientSideWebPart:

   ```
   import { BaseClientSideWebPart } from '@microsoft/sp-
   webpart-base';
   ```

   Then add WebPartContext to the import statement:

   ```
   import { BaseClientSideWebPart, WebPartContext } from '@microsoft/
   sp-webpart-base';
   ```

   The WebPartContext class is part of the SharePoint Framework (SPFx) and is used to provide contextual information and resources to SharePoint web parts. It represents the context in which the web part is executed and provides access to various properties, methods, and services.

2. Update the ICloudhadiServicePortalWebPartProps interface to include the context property:
Locate the interface declaration:

```
export interface ICloudhadiServicePortalWebPartProps {
    description: string;
}
```

Add the context property to the interface:

```
export interface ICloudhadiServicePortalWebPartProps {
    description: string;
    context: WebPartContext;
}
```

The ICloudhadiServicePortalWebPartProps interface defines the properties that can be passed to the CloudhadiServicePortal web part. In this case, it includes two properties.

3. Update the render method to include the context parameter:
Find the render method, and inside the render method, use the context.

```
public render(context: WebPartContext): void {
  const element: React.ReactElement<ICloudhadiServicePortalProps>
  = React.createElement(
    CloudhadiServicePortal,
    {
      description: this.properties.description,
      isDarkTheme: this._isDarkTheme,
      environmentMessage: this._environmentMessage,
      hasTeamsContext: !!context.sdks.microsoftTeams,
      userDisplayName: context.pageContext.user.displayName,
      context: context
```

```
        }
      );
      ReactDom.render(element, this.domElement);
    }
```

The context is a special object that contains important information about the SharePoint environment in which the web part is running. By passing this context to the `CloudhadiServicePortal` component during rendering, you're giving the component access to SharePoint-specific resources and functionalities.

In the provided code snippet, the context object is passed as a prop to the `CloudhadiServicePortal` root component, which can then pass it down to its child components as needed. This ensures that the necessary context information is available throughout the component hierarchy for any SharePoint-related operations or data retrieval.

Step 3: Updating tsconfig

To update the `tsconfig.json` file in your project, locate the `tsconfig.json` file in the root directory of your project. Find the `compilerOptions` section within the file. Inside the `compilerOptions` section, locate the `target` property and set its value to `es2017`. It should look like this:

```
"compilerOptions": {
  "target": "es2017",
  // other options...
}
```

Next, find the `lib` property within the `compilerOptions` section. Add `es2017` to the array of values for the `lib` property. It should look like this:

```
"compilerOptions": {
  // other options...
  "lib": [
    "es5",
    "dom",
    "es2015.collection",
    "es2015.promise",
```

```
    "es2017"
  ]
}
```

Save the `tsconfig.json` file.

By updating the `target` and `lib` options in the `tsconfig.json` file, you have configured the TypeScript compiler to target ES2017 and include the necessary polyfills and typings for ES2017 features. In simple words, without these steps, we might not be able to use some of the latest JavaScript features in our code.

Now that we have finished our preconfiguration steps, it's time to create the initial component structure. But before we dive into that, let's take a moment to understand how we can use the VS Code Terminal to serve our solution.

Moving forward, you can conveniently use the built-in Terminal within Visual Studio Code to serve your solution, eliminating the need to switch back to the command prompt. This streamlines your development process. It is important to note that you should close the command prompt before running the solution from the VS Code Terminal.

Once you have started the solution using the Terminal, you can either refresh the existing Workbench in your browser, instead of adding the web part again to a newly launched Workbench. This allows you to test and evaluate the functionality and appearance of your web part within the SharePoint environment.

Also note that during development, you can keep `gulp serve` running in the command prompt or Terminal to automatically update your solution as you make changes. This way, you don't need to stop and restart `gulp serve` every time you modify your code.

After making changes to your components or any other files, you can easily see the updated version of your solution by simply refreshing the Workbench page in your browser. This streamlines the development process and enables faster iteration. Remember to save your changes and wait a few seconds for the build to complete. Then, refresh the Workbench page to ensure that the browser reflects the latest code modifications.

Step 4: Updating the Root Interface and Creating New Interfaces

An interface is a way to define the structure or shape of an object. It specifies the names and types of properties that an object should have. By using an interface, you can ensure that the components or parts of your application communicate with each other in a predictable and consistent manner. It helps with type checking, code organization, and maintaining code quality by providing clear definitions and contracts for the expected properties and their types.

In the `components` folder, you will find a default interface called `ICloudhadi ServicePortalProps.ts` for the root component `CloudhadiServicePortal.tsx`. This interface defines properties such as `description`, `userDisplayName`, and `context`.

As a first step, locate `ICloudhadiServicePortalProps.ts` and add the `context` property there. The `ICloudhadiServicePortalProps.ts` file will look like this now:

```
import { WebPartContext } from '@microsoft/sp-webpart-base';
export interface ICloudhadiServicePortalProps {
  description: string;
  isDarkTheme: boolean;
  environmentMessage: string;
  hasTeamsContext: boolean;
  userDisplayName: string;
  context: WebPartContext;
}
```

Next, to create interfaces for the new components, follow these steps:

1. In the components folder, locate the `ICloudhadiServicePortalProps.ts` file and make a copy of it.

2. Rename the copied file to `IRequestDetailsProps.ts`.

3. Open the `IRequestDetailsProps.ts` file and replace the existing code with the following:

   ```
   import { WebPartContext } from '@microsoft/sp-webpart-base';
   export interface IRequestDetailsProps {
      context: WebPartContext;
   }
   ```

4. Create another interface file and name it `IRequestListProps.ts`.

5. Open the `IRequestListProps.ts` file and add the following code:

```
import { WebPartContext } from '@microsoft/sp-webpart-base';

export interface IRequestListProps {
    context: WebPartContext;
    isServiceUser: boolean;
}
```

By creating these interfaces, we define the expected properties for the corresponding components. In the `IRequestDetailsProps` interface, we include the `context` property of type `WebPartContext.` We can add any additional properties specific to the Request Details component here if needed.

Similarly, in the `IRequestListProps` interface, we included the context property and added an additional property `isServiceUser` of type Boolean. We can add any other properties specific to the Request List component here if needed.

These interfaces serve as contracts that specify the structure and types of the properties that the components should receive. They help ensure consistency and provide a clear definition of the expected properties, making it easier to work with the components and maintain code quality.

Step 5: Creating Components

To create a new component called `RequestDetails`, you can follow these steps:

1. Navigate to the `Components` folder in your project.

2. Locate the file named `CloudhadiServicePortal.tsx` and make a copy of it.

3. Paste the copied file into the same `Components` folder.

4. Rename the copied file to `RequestDetails.tsx`.

By copying and renaming the file, you now have a new component file called `RequestDetails.tsx` that you can modify and customize for our specific requirements.

Copy the provided code in Listing 6-2 to the `RequestDetails` component for now. We will further develop this component in the upcoming sections. This code serves as a temporary placeholder for displaying the request details.

Listing 6-2. RequestDetails.tsx: Initial Code

```
import * as React from 'react';
import { IRequestDetailsProps } from "./IRequestDetailsProps";
const RequestDetails = (props: IRequestDetailsProps) => {

  const {context} = props;
  return (
    <div>
      <h2>Request Details {context.pageContext.user.displayName}</h2>
    </div>
  );
};

export default RequestDetails;
```

This temporary placeholder code defines a functional component called RequestDetails that takes in props of type IRequestDetailsProps. It extracts the properties context from the props object. It then renders a simple HTML structure with a heading displaying the user's display name.

Next, follow the same steps to create a new component called RequestList.tsx. Copy the provided placeholder code in Listing 6-3 to the component for now.

Listing 6-3. RequestList.tsx: Initial Code

```
import * as React from 'react';
import { IRequestListProps } from "./IRequestListProps";
const RequestList = (props: IRequestListProps) => {
  const {context, isServiceUser } = props;
  return (
    <div>
      <h2>Request List - {context.pageContext.user.displayName},
      {isServiceUser}</h2>
    </div>
  );
};

export default RequestList;
```

Step 6: Develop the Root Component

So now we have the interfaces and components basic set up. Now, let's focus on implementing the portal home page, which involves setting up the root component. The root component will consist of three tabs as per the design requirements.

- The first tab is a form that allows users to submit a new request.

- The second tab is a table that displays all the submitted requests of the logged-in user.

- The third tab is a table that displays all pending requests from all users. However, this tab will be visible only if the logged-in user is a member of the Service Executives group.

Replace the existing code in `CloudhadiServicePortal.tsx` with the code in Listing 6-4. I will provide an explanation of the code using comments to mark different sections for easy identification during the explanation.

Note   It's important to note that after pasting the code, you might encounter compiler errors in the `styles` section. This is expected since the SCSS module code has not been added yet. However, in the next step, when the SCSS module code is incorporated, these compiler errors will be automatically resolved.

Listing 6-4. ClouhadiServicePortal.tsx: Final Code

```
/* Section - Dependency imports - packages */
import * as React from 'react';
import { useEffect, useState } from 'react';
import { Icon } from '@fluentui/react';
import { spfi, SPFx } from "@pnp/sp";
import "@pnp/sp/webs";
import "@pnp/sp/lists";
import "@pnp/sp/items";
import "@pnp/sp/site-users/web";

/* Section  - Dependency imports - internal */
import styles from './CloudhadiServicePortal.module.scss';
```

```
import { ICloudhadiServicePortalProps } from './
ICloudhadiServicePortalProps';
import RequestDetails from './RequestDetails';
import RequestList from './RequestList';

const CloudhadiServicePortal = (props: ICloudhadiServicePortalProps): JSX.
Element => {

/* Section  - Component body */

  // Get the context from props.
  const { context } = props;

  //State variables.
  const [activeTab, setActiveTab] = React.useState('createRequest');
  const [isServiceUser, setIsServiceUser] = useState(false);

  // handle tab click.
  const handleTabChange = (tab: string): void => {
    setActiveTab(tab);
  };

  //Get the groups of logged in users
  const checkServiceUser = async (): Promise<void> => {
    try {
      const sp = spfi().using(SPFx(props.context));
      const groups = await sp.web.currentUser.groups();
      const userGroups = groups.map((g) => g.Title);

      if (userGroups.includes("Service Executives")) {
      setIsServiceUser(true); }
      else { setIsServiceUser(false); }

    } catch (error) {
      console.log("Error fetching user groups:", error);
    }
  };

  // During component load for the first time.
  useEffect(() => {
```

```
    checkServiceUser().catch((error) => {
      console.log("Unhandled error in fetching groups:", error);
    });
  }, []);

  // Defining the tabs
  const tabData = [
    {
      tabId: 'createRequest',
      iconName: 'Glimmer',
      label: 'Create a New Request',
      visible: true
    },
    {
      tabId: 'myRequests',
      iconName: 'ContactList',
      label: 'My Requests',
      visible: true,
    },
    {
      tabId: 'pendingRequests',
      iconName: 'GroupedList',
      label: 'Pending Requests',
      visible: isServiceUser
    }
  ];
/*Section return function */
  return (
    <div className={styles.cloudhadiServicePortal}>
      <div className={styles.tabContainer}>
        {tabData.filter((tab) => tab.visible).map((tab) => (
          <div
            key={tab.tabId}
            className={`${styles.tab} ${activeTab === tab.tabId ? styles.
            activeTab : ''}`}
            onClick={() => handleTabChange(tab.tabId)}
```

```
      >
        <Icon iconName={tab.iconName} className={styles.tabIcon} />
        {tab.label}
      </div>
    ))}

  </div>
  <div className={styles.tabContent}>
    {activeTab === 'createRequest' && (
      <RequestDetails context={context} />
    )}
    {activeTab === 'myRequests' && (
      <RequestList context={context} isServiceUser={false} />
    )}
    {isServiceUser && activeTab === 'pendingRequests' && (
      <RequestList context={context} isServiceUser={true} />
    )}
  </div>

  </div>
  );
};
/*Section Export */
export default CloudhadiServicePortal;
```

Let's break down the code.

1. Dependency Imports: packages:

   - React: The React library is used for creating React components.

   - useEffect and useState: These hooks from the React library are used for handling side effects and managing state in functional components.

   - Icon from Fluent UI React: This component provides a set of customizable icons that can be used in the UI.

   - spfi and SPFx from @pnp/sp: These functions from the Patterns and Practices (PnP) library are used for interacting with SharePoint.

- Modules from @pnp/sp: These modules (webs, lists, items, siteusers/web) from the @pnp/sp library provide functionalities for working with SharePoint webs, lists, items, and site users.

2. Dependency Imports: internal:

- styles from CloudhadiServicePortal.module.scss: The styles object contains CSS classes specific to the CloudhadiServicePortal component.

- ICloudhadiServicePortalProps from ICloudhadiServicePortalProps: The ICloudhadiServicePortalProps interface defines the expected props for the CloudhadiServicePortal component.

- RequestDetails from RequestDetails: The RequestDetails component is responsible for displaying request details.

- RequestList from RequestList: The RequestList component is responsible for displaying a list of requests.

  These import statements ensure that the required packages, libraries, styles, and components are available for use within the CloudhadiServicePortal component.

3. Component body:

- const { context } = props;: Destructures the context property from the props object and assigns it to a constant variable context. This allows accessing the context property directly within the component.

- const [activeTab, setActiveTab] =useState(createRequest);: Declares a state variable activeTab and a corresponding setter function setActiveTab using the useState hook. The initial value of activeTab is set to createRequest. The useState hook is a built-in hook in React that allows functional components to have state variables. It returns an array with the current state value and a setter function, enabling state management within functional components.

- `const [isServiceUser, setIsServiceUser] = useState(false);`: Declares a state variable `isServiceUser` and a corresponding setter function `setIsServiceUser` using the `useState` hook. The initial value of `isServiceUser` is set to `false`.

- `handleTabChange`: Defines a function `handleTabChange` that takes a `tab` parameter of type string. This function updates the value of `activeTab` using the `setActiveTab` setter function.

- `checkServiceUser`: Defines an asynchronous function `checkServiceUser` that fetches the groups of the logged-in user. It uses the `spfi` and `SPFx` methods from the `@pnp/sp` library to create a SharePoint client object and retrieve the current users groups. The retrieved groups are stored in the `groups` variable.

- The line `const sp = spfi().using(SPFx(context));` is initializing the SPFx context using the PnP library. Here's a breakdown of what each part does:

1. `spfi()`: This function is provided by the PnP library and is used to create a new instance of the SharePoint Framework context. It returns an object that provides various methods and properties to interact with SharePoint.

2. `.using(SPFx(context))`: This method is used to configure the SharePoint Framework context with the provided `context` object. The `context` object typically contains information about the current SharePoint site, user context, and other relevant data. It allows the PnP library to interact with SharePoint using the provided context.

   By initializing the SharePoint Framework context using `spfi().using(SPFx(context))`, you are setting up the PnP library to work with the specific SharePoint environment and leverage its features and capabilities. This allows you to perform operations such as querying lists, retrieving items, updating data, and more using the PnP library within your React component.

- `const userGroups = groups.map((g) => g.Title);`: Extracts the titles of the user groups from the `groups` array using the `map` function. The resulting array is assigned to the `userGroups` constant.

- `if (userGroups.includes("Service Executives")) { setIsServiceUser(true); } else { setIsServiceUser(false); }`: Checks if the `userGroups` array includes the string `"Service Executives"`. If it does, the `isServiceUser` state variable is set to true using the `setIsServiceUser` setter function; otherwise, it is set to `false`. This checks if the currently logged-in user is a service executive or not, by checking if the user belongs to the Service Executives group.

- `catch`: The `catch` block catches any errors that occur during the asynchronous operations and logs an error message along with the specific error to the console.

- `useEffect`: The useEffect hook is used to perform side effects in functional components. In this case, it calls the `checkServiceUser` methods to fetch user groups and check if the user is service user, during the initial component load. The empty dependency array [ ] as the second argument ensures that the effect runs only once.

- The `tabData` variable is an array of objects defining the tabs. Each object represents a tab and contains properties like `tabId`, `iconName`, `label`, and `visible`. The `visible` property of the last tab is dependent on the value of the `isServiceUser` state variable, allowing dynamic visibility based on the logged in user.

4. `Return function:`

   This section represents the JSX code for rendering the components UI. Let's break it down:

   - The outermost `<div>` has the class name `styles.cloudhadiServicePortal`, which is a CSS module class name imported from the associated SCSS file. Inside the outer `<div>`, there is another `<div>` with the class name `styles.tabContainer`. This `<div>` contains the tabs. We will add all these class names to the style file in the next section. Ignore the errors for now.

- The tabs are dynamically rendered based on the `tabData` array. The `filter()` method is used to filter out tabs with `visible` set to `true`, and the `map()` method is used to generate a `<div>` element for each visible tab.

- Each tab `<div>` has the class name `styles.tab`, and if the `activeTab` matches the tabs `tabId`, it also gets the class name `styles.activeTab`.

- Clicking a tab triggers the `onClick` event, which calls the `handleTabChange()` function and passes the tabs `tabId` as an argument.

- Inside the outer `<div>`, there is another `<div>` with the class name `styles.tabContent`. This `<div>` represents the content area below the tabs.

- The content that is rendered depends on the `activeTab` value. If `activeTab` is `createRequest`, the `<RequestDetails>` component is rendered with the specified props. If `activeTab` is `myRequests`, the `<RequestList>` component is rendered with `isServiceUser` set to `false`. If activeTab is `pendingRequests` and the user is a service user (`isServiceUser` is `true`), the `<RequestList>` component is rendered with `isServiceUser` set to `true`.

Overall, this JSX code creates a tab-based UI where the content dynamically changes based on the selected tab and user permissions.

The `RequestDetails` component is always displayed to show the request form, regardless of the user's role. It provides a way for users to create new requests.

The `RequestList` component is displayed in two instances for service executives. The first instance shows "My Requests," which displays the requests specific to the logged-in user. This tab is visible to all users, allowing them to view their own requests.

The second instance of the `RequestList` component, visible only to service executives (`isServiceUser === true`), displays "Pending Requests." This tab shows all the pending requests, providing an overview of the requests that require attention from service executives.

In summary, the `RequestDetails` component is always visible for request creation, while the `RequestList` component is displayed twice: once to show "My Requests" for all users, and again to show "Pending Requests" specifically for service executives.

Next, let's add the necessary classes to the CloudhadiServicePortal.module.scss file to make the app functional. Replace the current code inside the file with the code provided in Listing 6-5.

Listing 6-5. CloudhadiServicePortal.module.scss: Classes for Root Component

```scss
.cloudhadiServicePortal {
  .tabContainer {
    display: flex;
    justify-content: space-between;
    background-color: #2596be;
    padding: 10px;
  }

  .tab {
    cursor: pointer;
    padding: 10px;
    color: white;
    font-size: 16px;
  }

  .tabIcon {
    margin-right: 8px;
    font-size: 18px;
    vertical-align: middle;
  }

  .activeTab {
    background-color: white;
    color: chocolate;
    border: 2px solid green;
  }

  .activeTab::after {
    content: "";
    position: absolute;
    bottom: -2px;
    left: 0;
```

```
  width: 100%;
  height: 2px;
  background-color: green;
  transform: scaleX(0);
  transition: transform 0.3s ease-in-out;
}

.activeTab:hover::after,
.activeTab:focus::after {
  transform: scaleX(1);
}

.tabContent {
  padding: 10px;
}
}
```

Now that the root component is set up, we can proceed with testing stage 1 of the web part development.

Note   You can find all the final code files for this project in the Chapter 6 folder of the book's GitHub repository. Refer to the repository for the code files. You can access the repo at https://github.com/apress/building-modern-workplace-SharePoint-online-2e.

Testing: Stage 1

Follow these steps to test the functionality of the web part:

1. Open the Terminal in Visual Studio Code and run the command gulp serve. If you already have gulp serve running and the Workbench launched in the browser, simply refresh the page. If you encounter any issues, stop the current run using Ctrl+C and then rerun gulp serve. If Workbench is newly launched, add the cloudhadi-service-portal web part.

2. Once added, you will see two tabs: "Create a New Request" and
   "My Requests." Clicking each tab will highlight it, and you will
   notice the corresponding placeholder content for RequestDetails
   and RequestList displayed on their respective tabs. Refer to
   Figure 6-8 for reference.

Figure 6-8. *Stage 1, portal tabs, organization user*

3. Now, open a new browser profile and log in with your service
   executive account. Make sure that the account has been added to
   the Service Executives group. You can check this by navigating to
   your site, going to Site Contents, going to Site Permissions, and
   going to Service Executives Group.

4. Once logged in with the service executive account, copy the
   Workbench URL from your serve.json file or from the opened
   browser window, and paste it into the service user browser. Add
   the web part and you can now see three tabs: "Create a New
   Request," "My Requests," and "Pending Requests." Click each
   tab to verify if they are working correctly. Refer to Figure 6-9 for
   reference.

5. Once logged in with the service executive account, copy the
   Workbench URL from your serve.json file or from the opened
   browser window, and paste it into the service user browser. Add the
   web part and you can now see three tabs: "Create a New Request,"
   "My Requests," and "Pending Requests." Click each tab to verify if
   they are working correctly. Refer to Figure 6-9 for reference.

Figure 6-9. *Stage 1, portal tabs, service user*

With the completion of web part development, stage 1, we have successfully finished testing. Now, let's proceed to the next stage of the development process.

Development: Stage 2

During this stage of development, our focus will be on creating the Request Details component. By the end of this stage, all users, including service users and other organizational users, will be able to enter the necessary details and submit their requests. These requests will be saved in the Service Portal list within our SharePoint site.

To start with, replace the existing code in `RequestDetails.tsx` with the code in Listing 6-6. I will provide an explanation of the code using comments to mark different sections for easy identification during the explanation.

Note   As before, note that after pasting the code, you might encounter compiler errors in the styles section. This is expected since the SCSS module code has not been added yet. However, in the next step, when the SCSS module code is incorporated, these compiler errors will be automatically resolved.

Listing 6-6. RequestDetails.tsx: Final Code

```
/*Section - imports */

import * as React from 'react';
import { useState } from 'react';
```

```
import { Stack, TextField, Dropdown, PrimaryButton, DefaultButton,
IDropdownOption } from '@fluentui/react';
import styles from './CloudhadiServicePortal.module.scss';
import { spfi, SPFx } from "@pnp/sp";
import "@pnp/sp/webs";
import "@pnp/sp/lists";
import "@pnp/sp/items";
import "@pnp/sp/site-users/web";
import { AssignFrom } from "@pnp/core";
import { IRequestDetailsProps } from "./IRequestDetailsProps";

const RequestDetails = (props: IRequestDetailsProps): JSX.Element => {

  /*Section - component body */

  const [requestTitle, setRequestTitle] = useState('');
  const [requestDescription, setRequestDescription] = useState('');
  const [relatedTo, setRelatedTo] = useState('');

  const [message, setMessage] = useState('');
  const [IsSuccess, setIsSuccess] = useState(false);
  const { context } = props;
  const sp = spfi().using(SPFx(context));
  const spSite = spfi(`${context.pageContext.web.absoluteUrl.split('/
sites')[0]}/sites/workplace/`).using(AssignFrom(sp.web));
  const getRandomInt = (min: number, max: number): number => {
    min = Math.ceil(min);
    max = Math.floor(max);
    return Math.floor(Math.random() * (max - min + 1)) + min;
  };

  const handleReset = (): void => {
    setRequestTitle('');
    setRequestDescription('');
    setRelatedTo('');
  };

  const handleSubmit = async (): Promise<void> => {
```

```
  if (!requestTitle || !requestDescription || !relatedTo) {
    setMessage('Please fill in all the required fields.');
    return;
  }
  try {

    const reqID = `CSR${getRandomInt(10000, 99999)}`;
    await  spSite.web.lists.getByTitle(`Service Portal`)
      .items.add({
        Title: reqID,
        RequestTitle: requestTitle,
        RequestDescription: requestDescription,
        Relatedto: relatedTo,
        RequestStatus: "New"
      });
    handleReset();
    setIsSuccess(true);
    setMessage(`Service request Created! ${reqID}`);
  }
  catch (Ex) {
    setMessage('Service request creation failed. Please contact
    IT team');
  }

};


const handleRelatedToChange = (event: React.FormEvent<HTMLDivElement>,
option?: IDropdownOption): void => {
  if (option) {
    setRelatedTo(option.key.toString());
  }
};

/*Section - return function */
return (
  <div className={styles.container}>
    <h2 className={styles.title}>New Service Request</h2>
```

```
<div className={styles.formGrid}>
  <Stack tokens={{ childrenGap: 15 }}>
    <TextField label="Request Title"
      value={requestTitle}
      onChange={(event, newValue) => setRequestTitle(newValue || '')}
      required className={styles.fluentControl} />
    <TextField label="Request Description"
      value={requestDescription}
      onChange={(event, newValue) => setRequestDescription
      (newValue || '')}
      multiline rows={4} required className={styles.fluentControl} />
    <Dropdown
      label="Related to"
      defaultSelectedKey={relatedTo}
      onChange={handleRelatedToChange}
      options={[
        { key: 'Access', text: 'Access' },
        { key: 'Materials', text: 'Materials' },
        { key: 'Equipment', text: 'Equipment' },
        { key: 'General', text: 'General' }
      ]}
      required
      className={styles.fluentControl}
    />
    <Stack className={styles.buttonContainer} horizontal tokens={{
    childrenGap: 20 }}>
      <PrimaryButton text="Submit" onClick={handleSubmit}
      className={styles.fluentControl} />
      <DefaultButton text="Reset" onClick={handleReset}
      className={styles.fluentControl} />
    </Stack>
  </Stack>
  {message && (
    <div className={IsSuccess ? styles.successLabel : styles.
    errorLabel}>
```

```
        <span>{message}</span>
      </div>
    )}
  </div>
</div>
);
};

export default RequestDetails;
```

Let's break down the code.

1. Imports:

    - React: The React library is used for creating React components.

    - useState: This hook from the React library is used for managing state in functional components.

    - Stack, TextField, Dropdown, PrimaryButton, DefaultButton, IDropdownOption: These are components imported from the @ fluentui/react library. They are used to build the user interface of the RequestDetails component.

    - styles: This imports the CSS module styles from the CloudhadiServicePortal.module.scss file. It allows styling the RequestDetails component using the defined styles.

    - spfi, SPFx: These are imported from the @pnp/sp library. They are used for accessing SharePoint functionality, such as interacting with lists, items, and site users.

    - @pnp/sp/webs, @pnp/sp/lists, @pnp/sp/items, @pnp/sp/site-users/web: These imports specify additional functionalities provided by the @pnp/sp library, such as working with SharePoint webs, lists, items, and site users.

    - IRequestDetailsProps: This import specifies the type definition for the IRequestDetailsProps interface, which defines the props expected by the RequestDetails component.

2. Component body:

Here's an explanation of each part:

a) State Variables:

- requestTitle and setRequestTitle: These variables are created using the useState hook and represent the value and setter function for the request title.

- requestDescription and setRequestDescription: These variables represent the value and setter function for the request description.

- relatedTo and setRelatedTo: These variables represent the value and setter function for the "Related to" dropdown field.

- status and setStatus: These variables represent the value and setter function for the "Status" dropdown field.

- message and setMessage: These variables represent the message to be displayed after submitting the form.

- IsSuccess and setIsSuccess: These variables represent the success status of the form submission.

- SPSite: The AssignFrom method is used to access the context of the service portal list, ensuring the proper functioning of the web part when accessed from different contexts, such as Microsoft Teams. The reason for using AssignFrom is to handle scenarios where the web part is accessed from outside the site context, like in Microsoft Teams. In typical cases, we can directly access the site context using sp.web. However, when the web part is used in Teams, the Teams environment does not have direct access to the context of the workplace site. The line of code context. pageContext.web.absoluteUrl.split(/sites)[0]}/sites/ workplace/ constructs a URL for the workplace site by combining the root URL of the current site with /sites/workplace/.

b) Props:

In React, components can receive input through properties, commonly referred to as *props*. Props are a way to pass data from a parent component to its child components. In the provided code, the component expects to receive props through the `props` parameter. The prop `context` represents the context of the component. It could contain information related to the current execution environment.

Props allow for dynamic and flexible component behavior by allowing external data to be passed into the component. The parent component that renders this component would provide these props when using it in JSX syntax. In the context of the provided code, the CloudhadiServicePortal component serves as the parent component, while the `RequestDetails` component is the child component.

When the `RequestDetails` component is rendered within the `CloudhadiServicePortal` component, it receives props from its parent component. These props are provided in the JSX syntax when rendering the child component, as shown in stage 1 of the code. For `RequestDetails`, only one prop is passed, which is context.

c) `Helper functions:`

- `getRandomInt`: This function generates a random integer between the given `min` and `max` values. This is for setting the request ID, which gets stored in the `Title` field of the service portal item. This function will be called during the click of the Submit button.

d) `Event handlers:`

- `handleSubmit`: This asynchronous function is called when the form is submitted. It validates the form fields and then uses the PnP library to add a new item to the Service Portal list with the provided values. The status is set to the default value New. After successful submission, it resets the form and sets the success message with the request ID.

- `handleReset`: This function resets the form fields to their initial values.

- handleRelatedToChange: This function is triggered when the "Related to" drop-down value changes. It updates the relatedTo state variable based on the selected option.

  Overall, this code manages the state of form fields, handles form submission, and updates the state variables accordingly. It interacts with the Service Portal list using the PnP library to add new items to the list.

3. Return function:

   Let's look at the JSX code that defines the structure and layout of the RequestDetails component. It renders a form for creating a new service request. Let's break it down:

   - <div className={styles.container}>: This <div> element represents the outer container of the component. It applies the CSS class container from the CloudhadiServicePortal.module. scss stylesheet.

   - <h2 className={styles.title}>New Service Request</ h2>: This <h2> element displays the title "New Service Request" We will add the styles for the component to this scss file in the next stage.

   - <div className={styles.formGrid}>: This <div> element represents a grid layout for the form elements.

   - <Stack tokens={{ childrenGap: 15 }}>: This <Stack> component from the @fluentui/react library sets up a vertical stack layout for its child components. The tokens prop specifies the spacing between the child components as 15 pixels.

   - <TextField label="Request Title" ... />: This <TextField> component is used for inputting the request title. It displays a label "Request Title" and binds its value to the requestTitle state variable. The onChange event handler updates the requestTitle state when the value changes.

   - <TextField label="Request Description" ... />: This <TextField> component is like the previous one but is used for inputting the request description. It displays a label "Request Description" and binds its value to the `requestDescription` state variable.

- `<Dropdown label="Related to" ... />`: This `<Dropdown>` component is used for selecting the "Related to" category of the service request. It displays a label "Related to" and binds its value to the `relatedTo` state variable. The available options are specified using the `options` prop.

- `<Stack className={styles.buttonContainer} ... />`: This `<Stack>` component is used to display the Submit and Reset buttons horizontally. The buttons are defined using `<PrimaryButton>` and `<DefaultButton>` components. The onClick event handlers are set to call the `handleSubmit` and `handleReset` functions, respectively.

- `{message && (...)}`: This is a conditional rendering statement. If the message variable is truthy, it renders a `<div>` element with either the CSS class `successLabel` or `errorLabel` based on the value of the `IsSuccess` variable. The message content is displayed inside a `<span>` element. Finally, the closing `</div>` tags complete the structure of the component.

  This code defines the UI and behavior of the `RequestDetails` component. It utilizes various components from the `@fluentui/react` library and from our custom SCSS for styling and functionality.

4. `Export:`

   The export default `RequestDetails` statement is used to export the `RequestDetails` component as the default export from the module where it is defined. By exporting it as the default export, other modules can import the `RequestDetails` component without specifying its exact name, using the `import` statement. For example, we import it using the following in the root component:

   ```
   import RequestDetails from './RequestDetails';
   ```

Next, let's add the necessary classes to the `CloudhadiServicePortal.module.scss` file to make the Request Details Form functional. Append the classes provided in Listing 6-7 to the existing code within the file, while ensuring that the previously added classes for the root component remain intact.

Listing 6-7. CloudhadiServicePortal.module.scss: Classes for the Request Details Component

```scss
// Classes for Request Details

.container {
    max-width: 700px;
  margin: 0 auto;
  box-shadow: 0 2px 4px 0 rgba(0, 0, 0, 0.2), 0 25px 50px 0 rgba(0, 0,
  0, 0.1);
  padding: 20px;
  border: 2px solid #ccc;
  border-radius: 10px;
}

.title {
  font-size: 24px;
    font-weight: 600;
    padding-bottom: 10px;
    padding-left: 30%;
    color: #0078d4;
}

.formGrid {
  display: grid;
  grid-template-columns: 1fr;
  gap: 15px;
}

.fluentControl .ms-TextField {
  width: 100%;
}
```

```css
.fluentControl .ms-Dropdown {
  width: 100%;
}

.buttonContainer {
  display: flex;
  justify-content: center;
  padding:20px;
}

.successLabel {
  background-color: #70c985;
  color: white;
  padding: 10px;
  margin-top: 10px;
  padding-top: 10px;
  border-radius: 5px;
}

.errorLabel {
  background-color: lightcoral;
  color: white;
  padding: 10px;
  margin-top: 10px;
  border-radius: 5px;
}
```

Now that the request details form component is set up, we can proceed with testing stage 2 of the web part development.

Testing: Stage 2

Follow these steps to test the functionality of the web part in stage 2:

1. Open the Terminal in Visual Studio Code and run the command `gulp serve`. If you already have `gulp serve` running and the Workbench launched in the browser, simply refresh the page.

If you encounter any issues, stop the current run using Ctrl+C and then rerun `gulp serve`. If Workbench is newly launched, add the `cloudhadi-service-portal` web part.

2. Once added, you will see two tabs: "Create a New Request" and "My Requests." Clicking the "Create a New Request" tab will highlight it, and you will notice the form displayed on the tab. Enter the details shown in Figure 6-10.

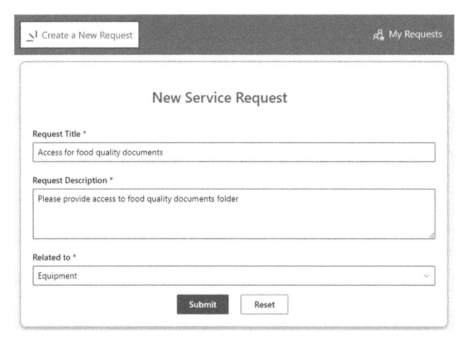

Figure 6-10. *Stage 2, creating a new service request*

3. To submit the form, click the Submit button. After clicking the button, a new item will be created in the Service Portal list. The item will have the following field values:

    – *Title*: A randomly generated number prefixed with CSR (e.g., CSR12345)

    – *RequestTitle*: The value entered in the Request Title text field

    – *RequestDescription*: The value entered in the Request Description text field

- *Relatedto*: The selected value from the "Related to" drop-
down list

- *RequestStatus*: The default status New

After successfully creating the item, the form fields (`requestTitle`,
`requestDescription`, `relatedTo`) will be cleared. A success
message will be displayed. If the item creation is successful, the
message will indicate that the service request was created. If
there's an error during the item creation process, the message will
indicate that the creation failed.

Following these steps, navigate to the Service Portal list and verify
that a new item has been created with the entered details. You can
refer to Figure 6-11 for an example of how the list should look like
with the newly created item.

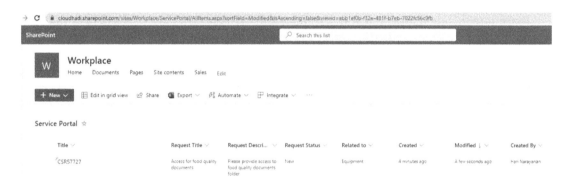

Figure 6-11. *Stage 2, created service request*

4. Now, try to submit the form without entering any or all the field
    values. The form will be validated to ensure that the required fields
    (`requestTitle`, `requestDescription`, and `relatedTo`) are filled in.
    If any of the fields are empty, an error message will be displayed.

5. Enter some details in the form fields. After entering the details, if
    you click the Cancel button, all the field values (`requestTitle`,
    `requestDescription`, `relatedTo`, `status`) will be reset to empty
    values. The form will be cleared, allowing you to start fresh and
    enter new details.

This completes the testing of stage 2, where you have tested the creation of a new service request, performed form validation, and verified the resetting of the form by clicking the Cancel button. Try to create 5 to 10 items so that you have enough items while testing the next stage. Log in with different user accounts such as the service user and create few additional items.

Development: Stage 3

During this stage of development, our primary objective is to create the Request List component. By the end of this stage, all users, including service users and other organizational users, will have the ability to view their request details and current status by navigating to the My Requests tab. Service users will have an additional tab specifically for viewing pending requests, and they will be able to take action on those requests directly from that tab. Any status updates made by the service users will be reflected in the Service Portal list within our SharePoint site.

To initiate this development stage, replace the existing code in `RequestList.tsx` with the code provided in Listing 6-8. An explanation will follow.

Note   As before, note that after pasting the code, you might encounter compiler errors in the `styles` section. This is expected since the SCSS module code has not been added yet. However, in the next step, when the SCSS module code is incorporated, these compiler errors will be automatically resolved.

Listing 6-8. RequestList.tsx: Final Code

```
/*Section - Imports */
import * as React from 'react';
import styles from './CloudhadiServicePortal.module.scss';
import { useEffect, useState } from 'react';
import { spfi, SPFx } from "@pnp/sp";
import "@pnp/sp/webs";
import "@pnp/sp/lists";
import "@pnp/sp/items";
import { AssignFrom } from "@pnp/core";
```

```
import { IRequestListProps } from "./IRequestListProps";
import { Stack, Checkbox, Link, PrimaryButton, DefaultButton, Dialog,
DialogType, DialogFooter } from '@fluentui/react';

const RequestList = (props: IRequestListProps): JSX.Element => {
  /*Section - component body */
  const [listData, setListData] = useState([]);
  const [isDialogOpen, setIsDialogOpen] = useState(false);
  const [selectedItem, setSelectedItem] = useState(null);
  const [message, setMessage] = useState('');
  const [isSuccess, setIsSuccess] = useState(false);
  const { context, isServiceUser } = props;
  const sp = spfi().using(SPFx(context));
  const spSite = spfi(`${context.pageContext.web.absoluteUrl.split('/
  sites')[0]}/sites/workplace/`).using(AssignFrom(sp.web));
  const getMyItems = async (): Promise<any[]> => {

    const myItems = await spSite.web.lists.getByTitle(`Service
    Portal`).items
      .select("Author/EMail", "ID", "Title", "RequestTitle", "Relatedto",
      "RequestStatus", "RequestDescription")
      .expand("Author")
      .filter(`Author/EMail eq '${context.pageContext.user.email}'`)();
    return myItems;
  }

  const getPendingItems = async (): Promise<any[]> => {
    const newItems = await spSite.web.lists.getByTitle(`Service
    Portal`).items
      .select("Author/Title", "ID", "Title", "RequestTitle", "Relatedto",
      "RequestStatus", "RequestDescription")
      .expand("Author")
      .filter(`RequestStatus ne 'Completed' || RequestStatus ne
      'Rejected'`)()

    return newItems;
  }
```

```
useEffect(() => {

  const getItems = async (): Promise<void> => {
    try {

      let items: any[];

      if (isServiceUser) {
        items = await getPendingItems();
      }
      else {
        items = await getMyItems();
      }
      const updatedItems = items.map(item => ({
        ...item,
        checked: false
      }));

      setListData(updatedItems);

    } catch (error) {
      console.log("Error fetching pending items:", error);
    }
  };

  getItems().catch((error) => {
    console.log("Unhandled error in fetching items:", error);
  });
}, [isSuccess]);

const showDetailsDialog = (item: unknown): void => {
  setSelectedItem(item);
  setIsDialogOpen(true);
};

const hideDetailsDialog = (): void => {
  setIsDialogOpen(false);
};
```

```
const updateStatus = async (updatedStatus: string): Promise<void> => {
  const selectedItems = listData.filter(item => item.checked);
  if (selectedItems.length === 0) {
    setMessage('Please select a request to set status.');
    return;
  }

  try {
    await Promise.all(
      selectedItems.map(async (item) => {
        await sp.web.lists.getByTitle("Service Portal").items.
        getById(item.ID).update({
          RequestStatus: updatedStatus,
        });
      })
    );

    setMessage('Status updated for selected request/s!');
    setIsSuccess(true);
  } catch (error) {
    setMessage('Status update failed. Please contact IT team');
  }
};

const handleCheckboxChange = React.useCallback(
  (ev?: React.FormEvent<HTMLElement | HTMLInputElement>, checked?:
  boolean, itemId?: number) => {
    setListData(prevListData =>
      prevListData.map(item => {
        if (item.ID === itemId) {
          return {
            ...item,
            checked: checked
          };
        }
        return item;
      })
```

```
    );
  },
  []
);
/*Section - return function */
return (
  <div className={styles.requestList}>
    <h2 className={styles.title}>{isServiceUser ? `Pending Requests` :
    'My Requests'}</h2>
    {isServiceUser && <Stack className={styles.buttonList} horizontal
    tokens={{ childrenGap: 20 }}>
      <PrimaryButton text="In Progress" onClick={() => updateStatus("In
      Progress")} className={styles.btnInProgress} />
      <PrimaryButton text="Resolve" onClick={() =>
      updateStatus("Resolved")} className={styles.fluentControl} />
      <PrimaryButton text="Complete" onClick={() =>
      updateStatus("Completed")} className={styles.btnCompleted} />
      <DefaultButton text="Reject" onClick={() =>
      updateStatus("Rejected")} className={styles.fluentControl} />
    </Stack>}
    {message && (
      <div className={isSuccess ? styles.successLabel : styles.
      errorLabel}>
        <span>{message}</span>
      </div>
    )}
    <table className={styles.table}>
      <thead>
        <tr>
          <th>ID</th>
          <th>Title</th>
          <th>Related To</th>
          {!isServiceUser && <th>Status</th>}
          {isServiceUser && <th>Requested By</th>
            <th>Action</th>}
```

```
      </tr>
    </thead>
    <tbody>
      {listData.map((item, index) => (
        <tr key={index}>
          <td> <Link onClick={() => showDetailsDialog(item)}>{item.
          Title}</Link></td>
          <td>{item.RequestTitle}</td>
          <td>{item.Relatedto}</td>
          {!isServiceUser && <td>{item.RequestStatus}</td>}
          {isServiceUser && <td>{item.Author.Title}</td>
            <td> <Checkbox checked={item.checked} onChange={(ev,
            checked) => handleCheckboxChange(ev, checked, item.
            ID)} /></td>
          </>}

        </tr>
      ))}
    </tbody>
</table>
{/* Details Dialog */}
<Dialog
  hidden={!isDialogOpen}
  onDismiss={hideDetailsDialog}
  dialogContentProps={{
    type: DialogType.normal,
    title: selectedItem?.Title || '',
  }}
  modalProps={{
    isBlocking: false,
    styles: { main: { maxWidth: 450 } },
  }}
>
  {selectedItem && (
    <div>
```

```
      <p><strong><em>Request Title:</em></strong> {selectedItem.
      RequestTitle}</p>
      <p><strong><em>Description:</em></strong> {selectedItem.
      RequestDescription}</p>
      <p><strong><em>Related To:</em></strong> {selectedItem.
      Relatedto}</p>
      <p><strong><em>Current Status:</em></strong> {selectedItem.
      RequestStatus}</p>
    </div>

  )}
  <DialogFooter>
    <PrimaryButton onClick={hideDetailsDialog} text="Close" />
  </DialogFooter>
</Dialog>
</div>
);
};

export default RequestList;
```

Let's delve into the code.

1. Imports:

   The import section includes the necessary imports to use
   React, SharePoint APIs, and Fluent UI React components in
   this component. Most of the imports we explained during
   `RequestDetails` section. Let's go through the additional ones.

   - IRequestListProps: This interface defines the props expected
     by the `RequestList` component. It is imported from the
     `IRequestListProps.ts` file.

   - Components from @fluentui/react: These components
     (Stack, Checkbox, Link, PrimaryButton, DefaultButton, Dialog,
     DialogType, DialogFooter) are part of the Fluent UI React library.
     They can be used to build the user interface of the application.

2. Component body:

    Here's an explanation of each part:

    a) State Variables:

    - listData and setListData: These are state variables initialized using the useState hook. listData stores an array of items, and setListData is a function to update the listData state.

    - isDialogOpen and setIsDialogOpen: These state variables are used to control the visibility of a dialog component.

    - selectedItem and setSelectedItem: These state variables are used to store the currently selected item in the dialog.

    - message and setMessage: These state variables are used to display a message in the UI.

    - isSuccess and setIsSuccess: These state variables are used to indicate the success status of status update operation from service user.

    And as before in Request Details, the SPSite variable is assigned with the current site using AssignFrom.

    b) Props:

    In the provided code, the component expects to receive props through the props parameter. Here's a breakdown of the props used in the code snippet:

    context: This prop represents the context of the component. It could contain information related to the current execution environment.

    isServiceUser: This prop is a Boolean value indicating whether the current user is a service user or not. It is likely used to conditionally render certain parts of the component or to control the behavior based on the user type.

    When the RequestList component is rendered within the CloudhadiServicePortal component, it receives props from its parent component. These props are provided in the JSX syntax when rendering the child component, as shown in stage 1 of the code. For `RequestList`, two props is passed, which were discussed earlier.

c) Event Handlers:

1. `getMyItems` and `getPendingItems`: These are asynchronous functions that retrieve items from the Service Portal list . They use the PnP library to construct a query to fetch specific properties (`select`) and expand the related `Author` field to include additional information. The `filter` method is used to filter the items based on the author's email or the request status. The retrieved items are returned as a promise.

2. `getItems` (used in the `useEffect` hook): This asynchronous function is responsible for fetching the items based on the condition of `isServiceUser`. If `isServiceUser` is true, it calls getPendingItems to retrieve the pending items. Otherwise, it makes a call to `getMyItems` to retrieve items specific to the current user. The retrieved items are then mapped to include a new property `checked` with an initial value of `false`. The updated items are set as the new state using `setListData`.

3. `showDetailsDialog`: This function is called when a user wants to show the details of a particular item. It takes an `item` object as a parameter and sets it as the `selectedItem` state. It also sets the `isDialogOpen` state to true to open the dialog component.

4. `hideDetailsDialog`: This function is called when a user wants to hide/ close the dialog. It sets the `isDialogOpen` state to `false,` effectively closing the dialog.

5. `updateStatus`: This function is called when the user wants to update the status of selected items. It first checks if any items are selected by filtering the `listData` array based on the `checked` property. If no items are selected, it sets the `message` state to display an error message and returns early. If there are selected items, it uses `Promise.all` to update the status of each selected item in parallel. It iterates over the selected items, retrieves the corresponding item in the list using its ID, and updates its `RequestStatus` property with the `updatedStatus` value. If all the updates are successful, it sets the message state to indicate the

success and sets the isSuccess state to true. If any errors occur during the update process, it sets the message state to display an error message.

6. handleCheckboxChange: This callback function is used to handle the checkbox change event. It is wrapped in the React.useCallback hook to optimize performance by memoizing the function instance. When a checkbox is checked or unchecked, this function is called with the event object (ev), the checked state, and the itemId of the corresponding item. Inside the function, the listData state is updated by mapping over the previous state (prevListData). For the item with a matching itemId, its checked property is updated based on the checked value passed to the function. The updated listData is set as the new state using setListData.

These event handlers are responsible for fetching data from SharePoint, updating the UI state, and performing actions based on user interactions. They provide the necessary functionality to handle the logic and behavior of the component.

3. Return function:

This part represents the rendering of the Request List component. Here's an explanation of how the code works:

1. The component is wrapped in a <div> with the class name requestList. The component renders a heading (<h2>) that displays either "Pending Requests" or "My Requests" based on the logged in user.

2. If isServiceUser is true, a <Stack> component is rendered. Inside the stack, there are several <PrimaryButton> and <DefaultButton> components with different text and click handlers. These buttons are used for updating the status of selected requests. Each button represents a status

3. If there is a message value (truthy), a <div> with either the class name successLabel or errorLabel is rendered. The successLabel class is applied when isSuccess is true.

4. A <table> is rendered with the class name table. It contains a <thead> and a <tbody>. The <thead> contains table headers, and the <tbody> contains rows of request items. Some of the headings are rendered based on logged

in user. For example, Requested by and action are available only for service users, whereas status is available for only other users.

5. Inside the <tbody>, each request item in the listData array is mapped and rendered as a table row (<tr>). The item's properties are displayed in different table cells (<td>). The display of certain cells is conditional based on the value of isServiceUser. This is same as earlier.

6. If isServiceUser is true, an additional column Action, with a checkbox is rendered for each request item. The checkbox's checked prop is set to the item's checked property, and the onChange event is handled by the handleCheckboxChange function.

7. At the end of the component, there is a <Dialog> component that represents a details dialog. It is conditionally rendered based on the value of isDialogOpen. The dialog displays detailed information about the selected request item. The dialog content includes the item's title and additional details such as the request title, description, related information, and status.

8. The dialog has a footer that contains a <PrimaryButton> component with the text "Close." Clicking this button triggers the hideDetailsDialog function to close the dialog.

Overall, this component renders a table-based request list with options for updating the status of selected requests and a details dialog for viewing additional information about a request item.

Next, let's add the necessary classes to the CloudhadiServicePortal.module.scss file to make the Request List functional. Append the classes provided in Listing 6-9 to the existing code within the file, while ensuring that the previously added classes for the root and Request Detail components remain intact.

Listing 6-9. CloudhadiServicePortal.module.scss: Classes for Request List Component

```
//Request list component

  .requestList {
    margin-top: 20px;
  }
```

```css
.table {
  width: 100%;
  border-collapse: collapse;
  overflow-y: auto;
  height: 300px;
  margin-top:10px;
}

.table th,
.table td {
  border: 1px solid #ccc;
  padding: 8px;
  text-align: left;
}

.table th {
  background-color: #f0f0f0;
  font-weight: bold;
}
.buttonList {
  display: flex;
  justify-content: center;
  padding-top: 2px;
  padding-bottom: 25px;
}
  .btnInProgress {

  background-color: lightcoral;
  min-width: 120px !important;
}
.btnCompleted {
  background-color: #2596be;
}
```

Now that the request list component is set up, we can proceed with testing stage 3 of the web part development.

Testing: Stage 3

Follow these steps to test the functionality of the web part in stage 3:

1. Open the Terminal in Visual Studio Code and run the command `gulp serve`. If you already have `gulp serve` running and the Workbench launched in the browser, simply refresh the page. If you encounter any issues, stop the current run using Ctrl+C and then rerun `gulp serve`. If Workbench is newly launched, add the `cloudhadi-service-portal` web part.

2. The user interface consists of two tabs: Create a New Request and My Requests. When you click the My Requests tab, it becomes highlighted, indicating that it is currently selected. As a result, all the requests associated with your account are displayed in the tabs content area. This ensures that only items created by your account are shown on the My Requests tab. You can verify this by comparing the displayed items with the entries in the service portal list on the site. If you go to the service portal list on the site, and compare these items, you can notice that only items created by your account are displayed on the My Requests tab.

    Refer to Figure 6-12 for the My Requests tab.

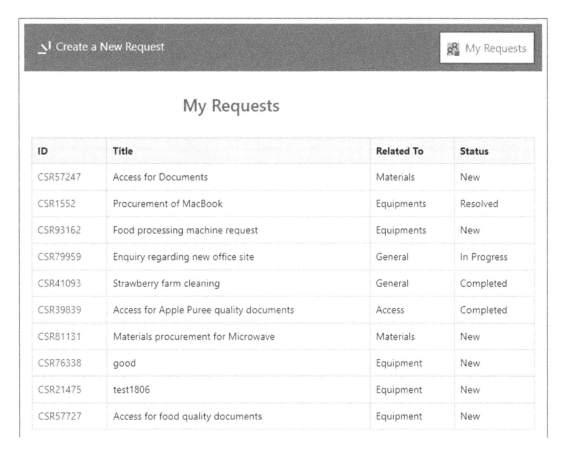

ID	Title	Related To	Status
CSR57247	Access for Documents	Materials	New
CSR1552	Procurement of MacBook	Equipments	Resolved
CSR93162	Food processing machine request	Equipments	New
CSR79959	Enquiry regarding new office site	General	In Progress
CSR41093	Strawberry farm cleaning	General	Completed
CSR39839	Access for Apple Puree quality documents	Access	Completed
CSR81131	Materials procurement for Microwave	Materials	New
CSR76338	good	Equipment	New
CSR21475	test1806	Equipment	New
CSR57727	Access for food quality documents	Equipment	New

Figure 6-12. *Stage 3, My Requests*

3. If you click the ID of a request, a small popup dialog will appear, displaying all the relevant information related to that request. You can view details such as the request title, description, related information, and current status. This allows you to quickly access and review the details of a specific request. You can refer to Figure 6-13 for a visual reference.

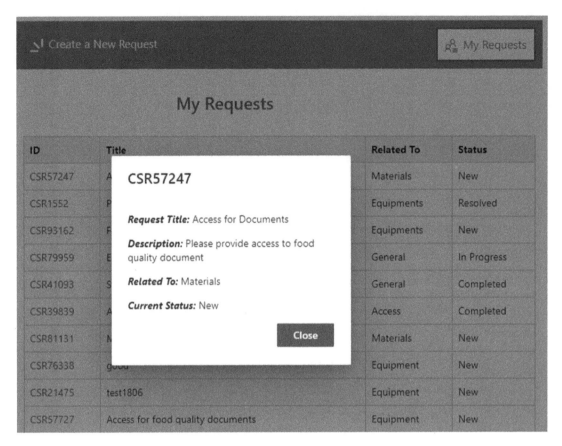

Figure 6-13. *Stage 3, individual request dialog*

(If you already have the web part open with the service account, you can skip the next step, step 5. This means you don't need to repeat the process of opening the web part with the service account, as you have already done it in stage 1.)

4. Now, open a new browser profile and log in with your service executive account. Make sure that the account has been added to the Service Executives group. You can check this by navigating to your site ➤ site contents ➤ site permissions ➤ Service Executives. Once logged in with the service executive account, copy the Workbench URL from your serve.json file or from the opened browser window, and paste it into the service user browser. Add the web part and you can now see three tabs: Create a New Request, My Requests, and Pending Requests.

5. When you click the My Requests tab, you will see the items that were created using the service account. If there are any requests associated with that account, they will be displayed on this tab. Refer to Figure 6-14 for my example.

My Requests

ID	Title	Related To	Status
CSR9305	Material access for service users	Access	New
CSR444444	Suser	Materials	Resolved

Figure 6-14. *Stage 3, My Requests (from another user)*

6. Next, let's test an important part of stage 3. By clicking Pending Requests, you will be able to view all the pending requests from all users, meaning all the requests except the ones with a status of Completed/Rejected. Similar to My Requests, you can click the ID value in the ID column to view more details in a small dialog.

In the Pending Requests tab, you will notice a checkbox next to each request. You can select one or multiple requests by clicking the checkboxes. At the top of the page, there are four buttons, each representing a different status. When you select one or more requests and click a status button, the status of the selected requests will be updated accordingly.

You can refer to Figure 6-15 for a visual representation of this functionality.

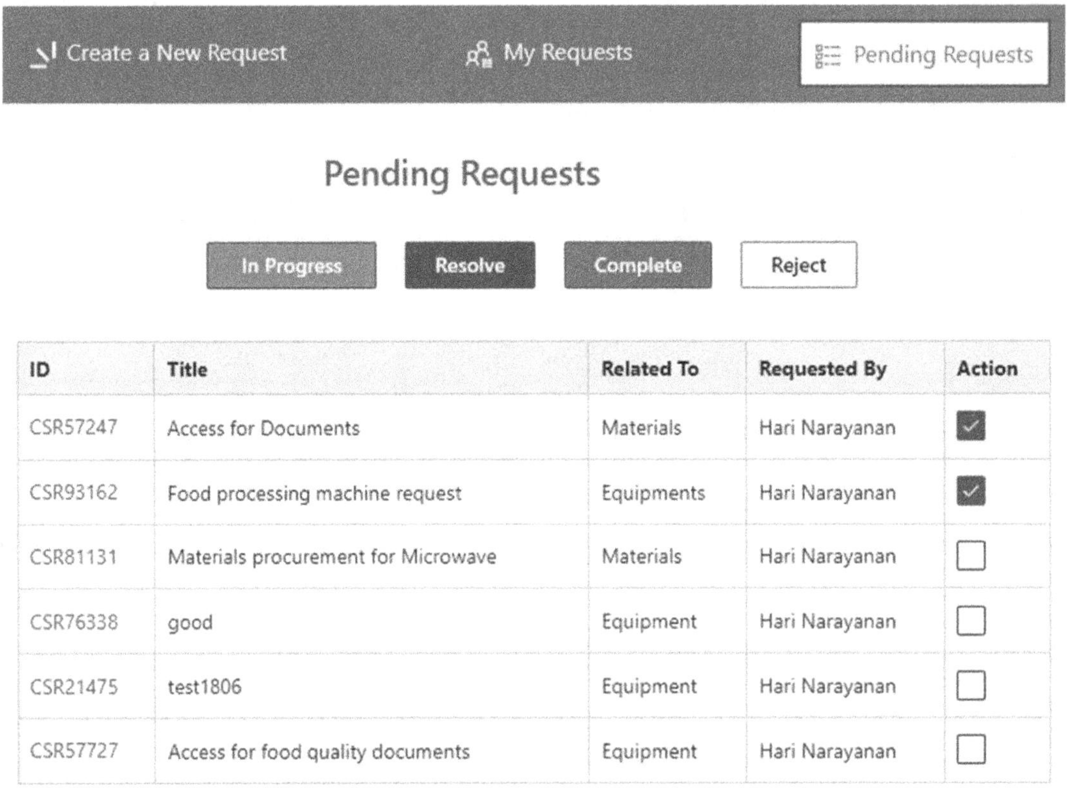

Figure 6-15. *Stage 3, actioning a service request*

After successfully updating the status, a confirmation message will be displayed below the buttons, indicating that the status has been updated. If any of the selected requests have their status set to Completed, those items will no longer appear in the table, as they are no longer pending.

To verify the status update, you can navigate to the Service Portal list and observe that the corresponding item's status has been modified according to the status button you clicked. You can test this by selecting different items with different statuses and observing the changes reflected in the list.

You have successfully completed the testing for stage 3 of the web part development. Throughout this stage, you thoroughly tested various functionalities, including user-specific requests, the details dialog for individual requests, and the ability to take actions on service requests from a service account.

By accomplishing these tasks, you have successfully developed a web portal that allows users within the organization to submit requests and view their own requests.

Most importantly, service executives have the capability to view all pending requests and take necessary actions on them.

With the completion of this stage, you have reached the final stage of the web part development, where you will perform additional testing and prepare for deployment.

Note   It's important to note that the primary focus of this design and development activity was to establish a strong foundation and learn the fundamentals of designing and developing an SPFx web part. The emphasis was on adopting the latest and recommended techniques and cultivating logical thinking when designing a component-based solution.

While the current web part may have scope for improvement in terms of styling and additional functionalities, it's important to recognize that this project served as a starting point to build upon. There are numerous possibilities to enhance the web part, such as refining the visual design, incorporating more advanced features, and integrating with other tools such as Power Automate or Microsoft Teams.

I encourage you to continue exploring and expanding the capabilities of this web part. By leveraging your knowledge gained from this experience, you can further enhance the web part's functionality, user experience, and integration possibilities to meet specific requirements or organizational needs.

Deployment

Now we have reached a stage where we can build and deploy this web part to our workplace site. Let's look at the steps to achieve this.

Here are the steps to deploy an SPFx web part to our tenant App Catalog and add it to a home page of the workplace site:

1. Build and package the web part.

   - From the VS Code Terminal, run the command `gulp bundle --ship` to create the production-ready bundle of your web part. Ensure to stop `gulp serve` if it is running.

   - Run the command `gulp package-solution --ship` to package the solution into an `.sppkg` file.

- After running this command, the generated `.sppkg` file can be found in the `sharepoint` folder within your SPFx project directory. By default, the filename will be in the format `solution-name.sppkg` where `solution-name` corresponds to the name specified in your project's `package-solution.json` file. In this case, it should be `cloudhadi-service-portal.sppkg`.

  For example, here's my file path where I can find the `.sppkg` file: `C:\Projects\Cloudhadi-ServicePortal\sharepoint\solution`.

  The `.sppkg` (SharePoint Package) file is a package file that contains all the necessary files and metadata required for deploying and installing an SPFx solution in a SharePoint environment. The `.sppkg` file includes the following components:

  - *Bundled JavaScript and CSS files*: These are the compiled and bundled JavaScript and CSS files that make up your SPFx solution. These files contain the logic and styling for your web part or extension.

  - *Manifest file*: The manifest file (`manifest.json`) describes your solution and provides SharePoint with information about the components, assets, and capabilities of your SPFx solution.

  - *Assets and localization files*: Any additional assets such as images or icons used by your solution may be included in the `.sppkg` file. If your SPFx solution supports multiple languages, the `.sppkg` file may include localized resource files.

  - *Permissions and capabilities*: The manifest file specifies the required permissions and capabilities needed by your solution to access SharePoint resources or perform specific actions.

2. Upload and deploy the package to the tenant App Catalog:

   - Go to your tenant App Catalog we created earlier. Refer to the section "App Catalog" earlier in this chapter.

   - Once in the App Catalog site, go to site contents and click Apps for SharePoint.

- Upload the `.sppkg` file generated in the previous step using the Upload button.

- Select "Make solution available to all sites" and then click Deploy to deploy the package. The app will be deployed and will be available to all sites in the tenant. Refer to Figure 6-16.

Figure 6-16. *Uploading and deploying an SPFx web part*

When you upload and deploy the `.sppkg` file to the SharePoint tenant App Catalog, SharePoint extracts the contents of the package and installs the solution, making it available for use within SharePoint sites.

To upload the SPFx web part to the site-level App Catalog, the steps are similar to those mentioned earlier, with the only difference being the URL where you upload the package.

3. Add a web part to the SharePoint Site home page:

- Navigate to the workplace site home page. Click the Edit or Edit page option to enter edit mode.

- In the page edit mode, click the + button in the top-left section.

- Search for *clouhadi* and find our web part. Click it to add it to the page. Refer to Figure 6-17.

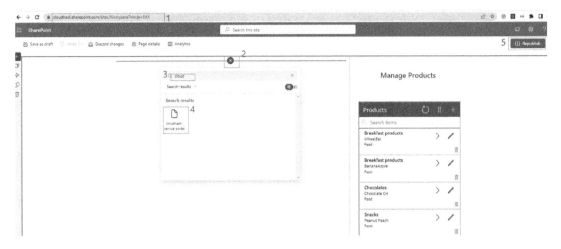

Figure 6-17. *Uploading and deploying an SPFx web part*

- Republish the page to see the web part in action. You can now observe the added web part on the page, as shown in Figure 6-18. Additionally, I have included a text web part for a heading and rearranged the products web parts by moving them to a vertical section. This arrangement provides some spacing between the web parts.

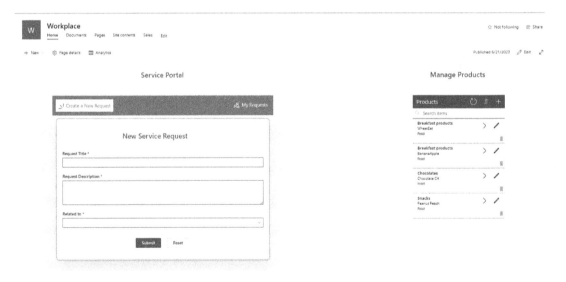

Figure 6-18. *SPFx web part added to SharePoint site*

Your SPFx web part has been successfully deployed to the SharePoint tenant App Catalog and added to a SharePoint site page. It's now ready for users to interact with on the Service Portal list. Try creating requests. Also, log in as a service user, access the "Pending requests" tab, and try to action the requests.

Project Progress Review

In the previous chapter, we successfully developed the Product Data approval flow, which streamlined the process of document submission and approval for product executives.

In this chapter, we focused on enhancing the user experience by designing and developing the Service Portal web part. This web part empowers Cloudhadi users by providing them with a convenient way to submit requests directly from their home page. By clicking the My Requests tab, users can now easily access and track their submitted requests.

Additionally, Service Executives now can view all pending requests and take necessary actions directly from their home page. This efficient workflow ensures timely processing and resolution of pending requests.

With the completion of the Service Portal web part, we have achieved a significant milestone in creating a modern workplace for our organization's users. The implementation of the UC-SD1 and UC-SD4 requirements, as outlined in the "Service Portal Use Cases" section of Chapter 2, showcases our commitment to providing effective solutions that meet the needs of our users.

Note   You can find all the final code files for this project in the Chapter 6 folder of the book's GitHub repository. The web part final code can also be found under the same folder. Once you clone the web part, before you run the project, make sure you run `npm install` so that all dependencies get installed. Refer to the repository at `https://github.com/apress/building-modern-workplace-SharePoint-online-2e`.

Overview of SPFx Extensions

Let's discuss an overview of SPFx extensions here to understand their purpose and potential applications.

SharePoint Framework extensions are powerful tools that allow developers to extend and customize the SharePoint user interface. They provide the ability to add custom functionalities and components to various aspects of SharePoint, including site pages, lists, libraries, and forms. Here's an overview of the main types of SPFx extensions:

1. Application Customizer:

    - Application Customizers enable developers to inject custom scripts or components into SharePoints header or footer sections.

    - They allow for modifications to the overall look and feel of SharePoint sites, including custom branding elements.

    - Application Customizers are typically used to create global customizations that are applied across multiple pages or sites.

2. Field Customizer:

    - Field Customizers allow developers to customize how fields in SharePoint lists and libraries are displayed.

    - Custom rendering logic can be added to fields, such as rendering them as clickable links, progress bars, or interactive components.

    - Field Customizers enhance the user experience and provide additional functionality for specific fields.

3. Command Set:

    - Command Sets enable developers to add custom actions, buttons, and menu items to SharePoints command bar (toolbar).

    - Custom actions can be created to trigger specific functionalities, such as executing custom code, performing operations on selected items, or integrating with external systems.

    - Command Sets are particularly useful for creating custom actions for list items, documents, or other SharePoint entities.

4. Form Customizer:

- Form Customizers are a newer addition to the SPFx ecosystem and focus on customizing the forms used for creating and editing list items or document properties in SharePoint lists and libraries.

- They allow for modifications to the layout, behavior, and appearance of the forms to better align with organizational needs.

- Form Customizers are built using web technologies like JavaScript, TypeScript, HTML, and CSS.

SPFx extensions provide a flexible way to tailor the SharePoint user interface to meet specific business requirements, enhance user productivity, and integrate with external systems or services. They can be deployed to the SharePoint App Catalog or site collection's App Catalog, making them available for use across multiple sites. With SPFx extensions, developers can extend and customize SharePoint in a way that suits their organization's unique needs.

Summary

The main objective of this chapter was to provide you with a starting point for SPFx development, focusing on design, development, and deployment aspects. You gained knowledge on designing and developing SPFx solutions, including creating an App Catalog, packaging the app, and deploying it to the catalog.

We also explored the basic concepts of React, covering topics such as hooks for state management, component interactions using props, conditional rendering, and performing operations with SharePoint. Throughout this process, we built a Cloudhadi service portal where users can submit and view requests, while Service Executives can act on those requests.

By developing the Service Portal web part, we have made significant progress in creating a robust and user-friendly digital workplace for Cloudhadi. However, there is still plenty of room for further enhancements. You can refine the design, add more functionalities, and integrate with other tools like Power Automate and Teams. These improvements can greatly enhance the overall functionality and productivity of the Service Portal.

Modern Search

In this chapter, we will explore a topic that is essential for efficient information retrieval within our Cloudhadi portal: search functionality. SharePoint Search provides a robust solution for locating the necessary information quickly and easily. While SharePoint offers both classic and modern search experiences, our focus will primarily be on SharePoint's modern search capabilities.

At the top of every page on our Workplace site, we have a search box. Utilizing this feature, we can search for specific content within the site, and the results will be displayed on a default page called `search.aspx`. However, to enhance the search experience and provide more flexibility, we will delve into the capabilities of the PnP Modern Search web parts, introduced in 2017 under the SharePoint Framework (SPFx) model of modern development. These web parts, available in the PnP Modern Search solution, offer powerful tools that allow SharePoint superusers, webmasters, and developers to create highly customizable and personalized search-driven experiences.

Our focus in this chapter will be on configuring and customizing search using the PnP Modern Search web parts. The latest version, PnP v4, utilizes Microsoft Graph APIs to enhance search capabilities. By the end of this chapter, you will gain familiarity with Modern Search concepts and learn how to apply customizations to tailor the search experience to our specific needs.

It's important to note that this chapter primarily focuses on building fundamental search configurations and serves as an introduction to PnP Modern Search. There is much more to discover and explore beyond the fundamentals covered here, providing ample opportunity for further customization and refinement of the search functionalities.

© Hari Narayn 2023
H. Narayn, *Building the Modern Workplace with SharePoint Online*,
https://doi.org/10.1007/978-1-4842-9726-1_7

Out-of-the-Box Search

SharePoint offers an out-of-the-box search feature that allows users to perform searches within the platform. To access this functionality, simply navigate to the home page of your Workplace site. From there, you can utilize the provided search box to initiate a search query. For example, you can enter the term **food** into the search box to begin searching for relevant content, as depicted in Figure 7-1.

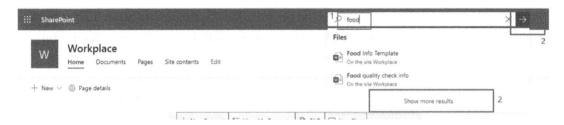

Figure 7-1. *SharePoint search box*

After entering a search query in the SharePoint search box, the results will be displayed. If you quickly find the desired information, you can directly click the relevant result. However, if you want to explore more search results, you can click the right arrow or select Show More Results. This action will take you to the search page, as illustrated in Figure 7-2.

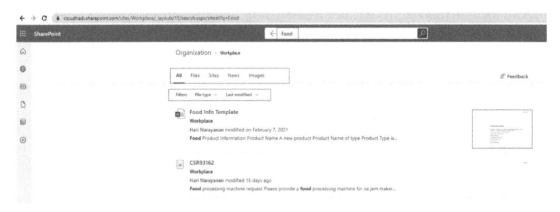

Figure 7-2. *Default search page*

In the default search page, when searching for the *food* keyword, all the matching results will be displayed, accompanied by a filter option at the top. By clicking the filter drop-down, you can refine the results based on the last modified date. Some of the results may also offer a preview of the corresponding file. Additionally, there are five tabs above the results that categorize different types of search results.

If you navigate to the Service Portal list, Products list, or Product Data library and perform a search in the top search box, the results will be limited to the respective list or library you have selected. The watermark on the search box indicates the scope within which the search will be executed.

However, the out-of-the-box (OOB) search box in SharePoint has its limitations in terms of providing an enhanced search experience. This is where the PnP Modern Search solution comes into play, as it enables the creation of enhanced search-based solutions within the SharePoint Modern experience. We will delve into the details of this solution shortly.

Requirements Recap

According to the requirements provided by Cloudhadi, our objective is to conduct a search for all Product Data documents. Furthermore, we need to implement filters based on Product Type, Document Type, and Modified fields.

PnP Modern Search

To obtain the PnP Modern Search solution, you can visit the GitHub repository specifically designed for Modern Search. From there, you can download the SPFx package called `pnp-modern-search-parts-v4.sppkg` by accessing the following link: `https://github.com/microsoft-search/pnp-modern-search/releases/download/4.9.0/pnp-modern-search-parts-v4.sppkg`.

Once the package is downloaded, you can proceed to integrate it into your Workplace site and explore the various features offered by the web parts involved.

To start the integration process, navigate to the tenant App Catalog site. Upload the downloaded `.sppkg` file in the Apps for SharePoint section and deploy it. While deploying, ensure to click Make This Solution Available to All Sites in the Organization, as illustrated in Figure 7-3.

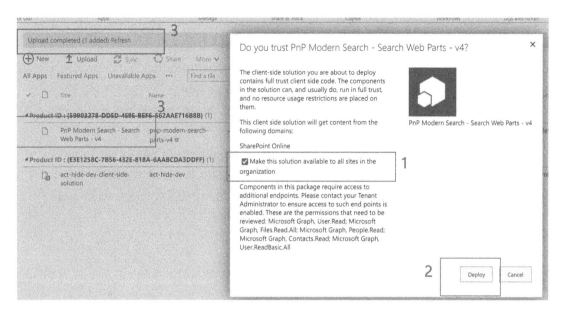

Figure 7-3. *Deploying PnP Modern Search to App Catalog*

To create a custom search page for your Workplace site, follow these steps:

1. Return to the Workplace site.

2. Click the Settings option.

3. From the settings menu, select Add a Page.

4. This action will open the page creation interface, as depicted in Figure 7-4.

By following these steps, you can initiate the process of adding a custom search page to your Workplace site.

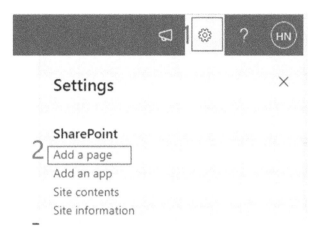

Figure 7-4. *Adding a page in Settings*

To proceed, select the Blank template after clicking Add a Page in the Workplace site settings. Then, click Create Page, following the steps illustrated in Figure 7-5. This will enable you to create a new page using the Blank template.

Figure 7-5. *Choosing a template and creating a page*

After successfully creating the page, you will be redirected to the page editing screen. On this screen, you can make changes to the page layout and content. Begin by typing in **ModernSearch** as the desired title for the page.

Next, add the One-Third Left Column section to the page, as demonstrated in Figure 7-6. This section layout option allows you to display content in a left-aligned column, occupying one-third of the page width. By selecting this layout, you can customize and configure the search-related components in this section of the page.

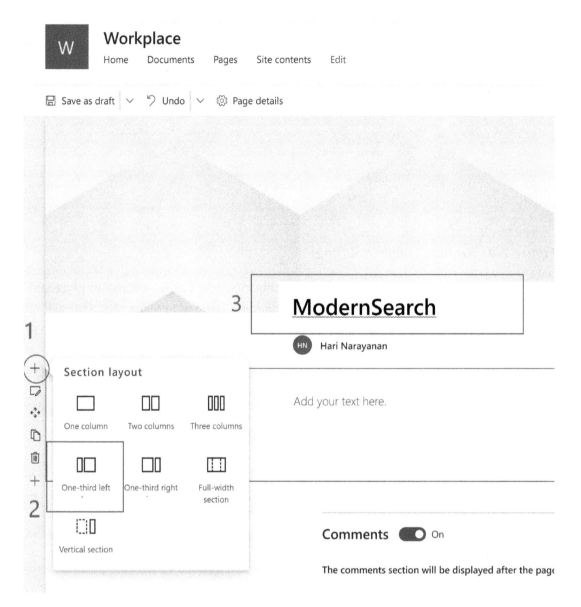

Figure 7-6. *Adding a section*

After adding the One-Third Left Column section, proceed to include the PnP—Search Results web part on the right side of the screen, as illustrated in Figure 7-7.

This web part will be placed within the newly added section, allowing you to configure and customize the search results display on your custom search page.

Figure 7-7. *Adding the PnP—Search Results web part*

Follow the same steps as before to add a section on the left side of the screen, but this time select the PnP-Search-Filters web part. Once both web parts are added, you can proceed with their configuration.

To begin configuring the Search Results web part, click the Configure button. Figure 7-8 illustrates the initial configuration of the Search Results web part, which you can refer to while making the necessary adjustments and customizations.

Figure 7-8. *PnP—Search results: query and result source*

To achieve the desired search results, follow these steps:

1. Select SharePoint Search as the data source for the Search Results web part.

2. Update the query text to {searchTerms}*. This modification ensures that the search results encompass all local SharePoint sites.

3. Set the Result Source ID to Documents to narrow down the scope of the search to all documents within the site.

4. Refine the search further by configuring the refinement filters to include the path filter. Use the filter Path: [yourSiteURL]/ProductData* to restrict the search to the Product Data documents specifically.

5. Also, click "web part title" on the web part and change it to **Product Data documents**.

6. By implementing these settings, you will be able to view all approved Product Data documents in your search results. Note that for the documents to appear in the search, they must be approved, as content approval is enabled in the library.

7. If you need additional documents to work with in the search, you can upload more files into the Product Data library and ensure they go through the approval process.

Following these steps will enable you to set up the search configuration as required, providing accurate and filtered search results for the approved Product Data documents.

If you click Next from the bottom of the web part properties panel, you can change the layout, show results count, and more.

Continuing with the configuration, add the PnP-Search Filters web part to the left section, similar to how you added the search results web part. The PnP-Search Filters web part allows users to apply filters to refine their search results.

Click the Configure button for the Filter web part and choose the data source from the Search Results web part. This connection ensures that the filter conditions are based on the search results obtained from the Search Results web part. Additionally, set the operator to AND to ensure that all filter conditions must match for effective filtering. Refer to Figure 7-9 for a visual representation of this configuration.

The PnP-Search Filters web part provides a user-friendly interface to apply various filter conditions on search results. By connecting it to the Search Results web part and setting the operator to AND, you ensure that only the results matching all the selected filter conditions will be displayed. This allows for a more refined and precise search experience.

Figure 7-9. *Connecting the Filter web part to the search results*

Before proceeding with setting up the filters, let's temporarily save and publish the page. This will allow us to explore the result sources, search schema, and managed properties in the upcoming section. By understanding the search schema, we will gain insights into how to configure the filter options accurately based on fields such as Product Type, Document Type, and Modified date.

Once we have a clear understanding of the managed properties associated with these fields, we can return to the page and effectively add the desired filters using the PnP-Search-Filters web part, and further configure the search Results web part.

Result Sources

You have selected Document result source while configuring the web part in the previous section. Result sources as predefined locations where SharePoint looks for information when you perform a search. These result sources act as filters or boundaries that determine which content is included in the search results.

Imagine you have a vast collection of movies available on Netflix. Each genre on Netflix represents a result source. If you're in the mood for a specific type of movie, such as a comedy or a thriller, you would go to the result source or genre category labeled Comedy or Thriller to find movies in that genre. Similarly, result sources in SharePoint work like genre categories on Netflix and help narrow down the search to specific areas or types of content.

In a SharePoint site, you can find result sources by going to the Site Settings. Result sources are listed in the Search category (you can see it highlighted in the Figure 7-10 in the next section). They can be configured to include specific sites, libraries, lists, or even external content sources. By defining and customizing result sources, you can control which content is included in the search results and provide more targeted and relevant information to users.

Result sources play a crucial role in improving the search experience by enabling users to find the most relevant information quickly and efficiently. By utilizing result sources effectively, you can streamline search results and ensure that users are presented with content that is most likely to meet their needs.

Search Schema

In SharePoint, the search function relies on a search index to provide users with relevant information. The search index is like a giant database that stores and organizes content from various sources within SharePoint. It enables users to find information quickly and efficiently.

The search index is created and maintained based on a search schema. Think of the search schema as a blueprint that defines how the search index is structured and what information can be searched. It consists of crawled properties, crawled property categories, crawled-to-managed property mappings, and managed property settings. By understanding the crawled and managed properties within the search schema, you can effectively configure filters and search queries to retrieve precise search results in SharePoint.

Crawled properties represent the content and metadata extracted during the crawling process. When SharePoint crawls content, it collects information from documents, such as their title, author, modified date, and more. These properties are stored as crawled properties in the search index.

Managed properties, on the other hand, are created based on crawled properties and are used for searching and filtering. They define what can be searched for and how it can be searched. Managed properties can be customized and mapped to specific crawled properties to enhance search functionality.

To view the crawled properties associated with specific fields like Product Type, Document Type, and Modified, you can navigate to the Site Settings of your Workplace site, access Site Collection Administration, and then go to Search schema. This allows you to examine and manage the properties that contribute to the search experience. Refer to Figure 7-10.

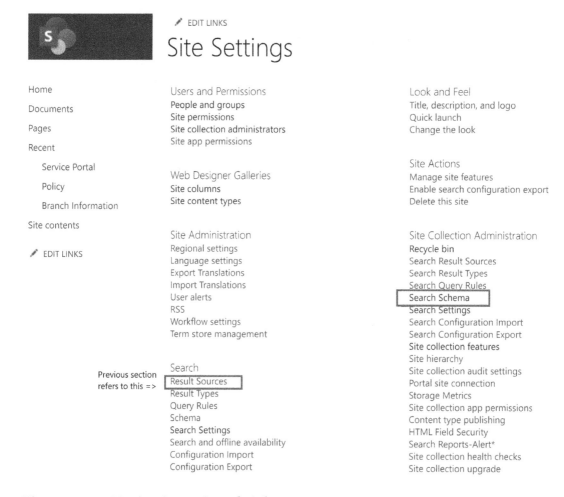

Figure 7-10. Navigating to Search Schema

On the page that appears, locate and click Crawled Properties. Then, perform a search for *producttype* in the search bar, as demonstrated in Figure 7-11. This action will help you find the specific crawled property associated with the Product Type field.

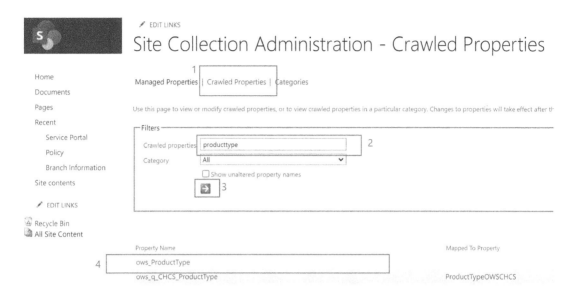

Figure 7-11. *Crawled Properties page*

On the displayed page, search for *producttype* in the Property Name section to find the corresponding crawled property. In this case, you will likely come across a crawled property named ows_ProductType, which represents the metadata for the product type. Similarly, you can search for *modified* and *documenttype* to find the crawled properties ows_Modified and ows_DocumentType for the Modified date and Document Type fields, respectively.

It's important to note that although crawled properties contain the content and metadata of items, they need to be mapped to managed properties to be included in the search index. Managed properties are the properties that are written to the search index and used for search queries.

To recap, content and metadata must be crawled to create/update crawled properties, which represent the information of crawled items. However, the search index relies on managed properties. Therefore, it's necessary to map crawled properties to managed properties. The search index then utilizes these managed properties to provide search results based on user queries.

Managed properties are defined with various settings that determine how the content is displayed in search results and how users can search for it. For instance, if you want users to filter results by Product Type, the managed property for Product Type must be set as "refinable." In our case, we need three refinable properties: Product Type, Document Type, and Modified date.

In the search schema, you can either create new managed properties or leverage existing managed properties provided out of the box (OOB). By searching for *refinable* in the search schema, you will find numerous managed properties that are available for refinement. Let's proceed by mapping three of these properties to the corresponding crawled properties for Product Type, Document Type, and Modified date. You can start by searching for *refinablestring*, as depicted in Figure 7-12.

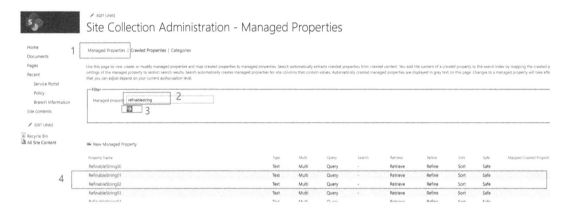

Figure 7-12. *Refinable managed properties*

Next, locate and click RefinableString01 in the search schema. Note that you may not be able to edit most of the properties in the search schema. For RefinableString01, observe that the property type is Text, and the Refinable option is set to Yes – Active.

Scroll down to the bottom of the page and click Add a Mapping next to Mappings to Crawled Properties. Then, perform a search for *producttype* and select the crawled property ows_ProductType from the search results. Finally, click OK to confirm the mapping, as depicted in Figure 7-13. This mapping ensures that the crawled property ows_ProductType is now mapped to the managed property RefinableString01.

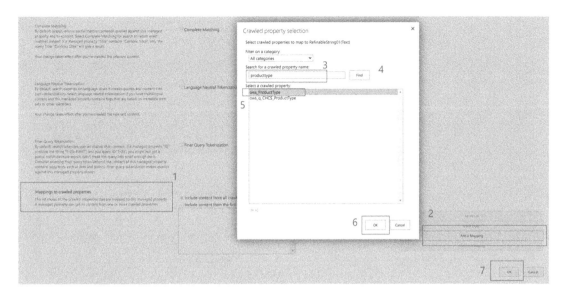

Figure 7-13. *Mapping to crawled properties*

Following the previous steps, repeat the process to map the crawled properties to managed properties for Document Type and Modified date. Search for *refinablestring02* in the search schema and add a mapping to the appropriate crawled property, ows_DocumentType. Similarly, search for *refinabledate01* and map it to the crawled property ows_Modified for the Modified date.

Once you have completed these changes, it is important to reindex the Product Data library. This ensures that the mapping to the search index is updated during the next scheduled crawl. To reindex the library, navigate to the Product Data library, access the library settings, and click "Advanced settings." Within the advanced settings, locate the Reindex Document library option, as shown in Figure 7-14. Select this option to initiate the reindexing process for the library.

Performing the reindexing will synchronize the changes made to the mapping of crawled properties and managed properties with the search index. As a result, the search functionality will accurately retrieve and display the desired results based on the refined managed properties for Product Type, Document Type, and Modified date.

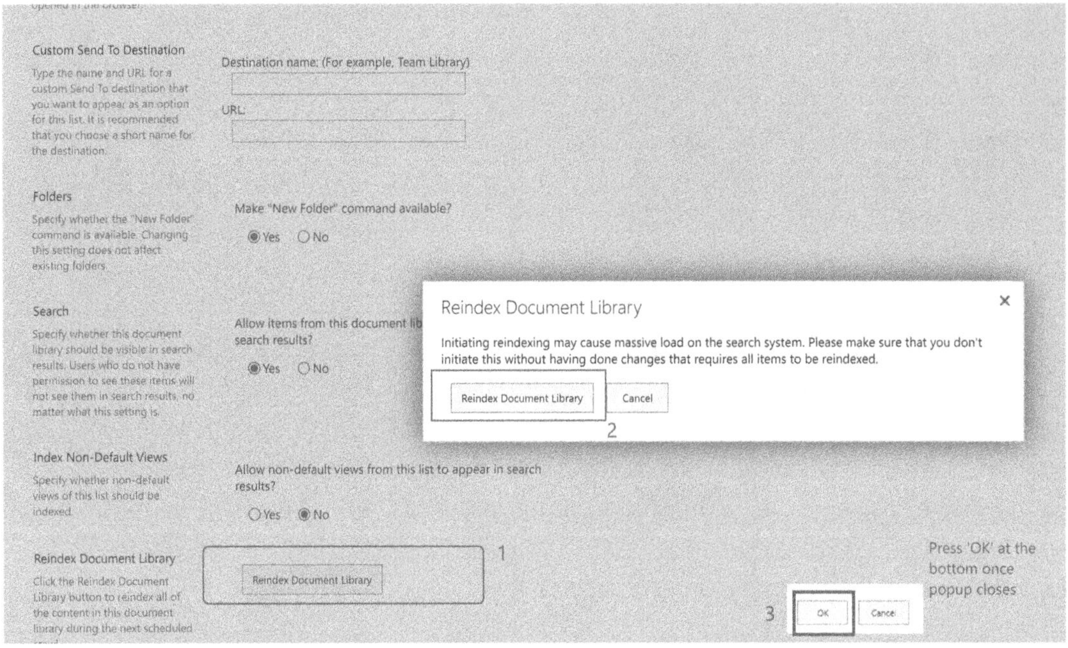

Figure 7-14. *Reindexing the document library*

As depicted in Figure 7-14, click Reindex Document Library and confirm the action in the subsequent pop-up. Once you have completed this step, remember to scroll down and click OK at the bottom of the screen to save your changes.

Note that the time it takes for the search index to update in SharePoint Online may vary. While it typically does not take longer than 15 minutes, the duration can depend on various factors, such as the size of the library and the current workload on the SharePoint Online service. It is recommended to allow some time for the reindexing process to complete and the search index to reflect the updated mapping changes.

Filters

To enable the filter functionality, we have successfully connected the Filter web part to the Search Results web part through the Filter web part properties (as shown in the previous Figure 7-9). However, for the filters to function properly, we need to update the managed metadata properties in both web parts. Additionally, it is essential to establish a two-way connection by connecting the Search Results web part to the Filter web part through the Search Result web part properties. This will ensure that the filter selections made by users dynamically update the search results. Once the reindexing process is completed, allow some time for the changes to take effect. Afterward, you can return to the search page and proceed with editing the page to implement the desired filter functionality.

To enable the filter functionality, follow these steps:

1) Edit the properties of the Search Results web part and add the three managed properties to the Selected Properties field. Check the boxes for RefinableDate01, RefinableString01, and RefinableString02 in the Selected Properties drop-down (refer to Figure 7-15). This ensures that the search results will include Product Type, Document Type, and Modified.

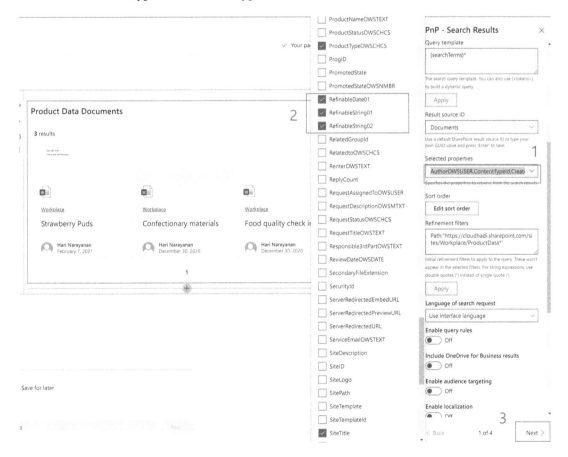

Figure 7-15. *Selected properties, Search Results web part*

2) Close the drop-down and proceed to the next page. Choose the Details List layout instead of Cards. Scroll down and click

"Manage columns" on the right side of the screen. This allows you to define which columns appear in the results. Refer to Figure 7-16.

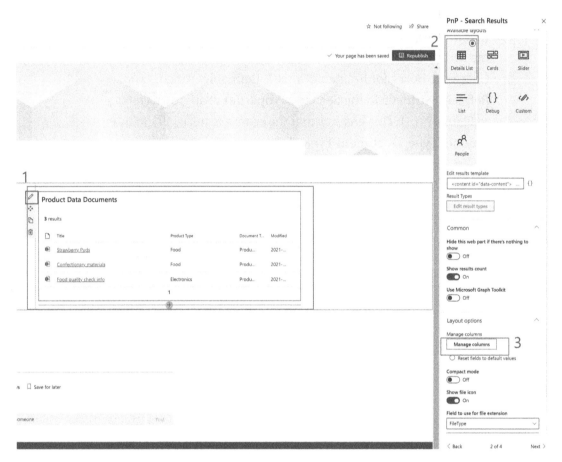

Figure 7-16. *Layout, Search Results web part*

3) In the "Manage columns" pop-up, add the columns as shown in Figure 7-17. Set the minimum and maximum width accordingly and check the boxes for the Sortable and Resizable columns. This will ensure that you can resize the columns by dragging and dropping from the results.

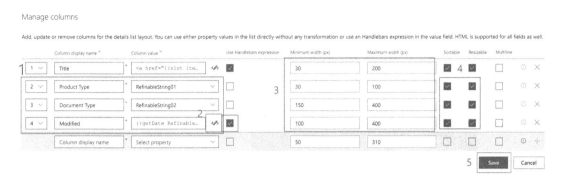

Figure 7-17. *"Manage columns" page*

4) To format the Modified property as a date field, enable the "Use Handlebars expression" option for the property. By doing so, you can utilize the handlebars templating language to customize the column formatting in the Search web parts. Once you check the Use Handlebars checkbox, a pencil icon will appear next to the property. Click the pencil icon to access the handlebars expression editor. In the handlebars expression editor, update the expression to `{{getDate RefinableDate01 "MMM DD, YYYY"}}` to format the Modified property as desired. This expression instructs the web part to display the date in the format of Month Day, Year (e.g., Jan 01, 2023). After making the necessary changes, click Save to apply the handlebars expression. You can refer to Figure 7-18 for visual guidance. Once you have completed these steps, remember to save the managed columns to ensure that all the configurations are preserved.

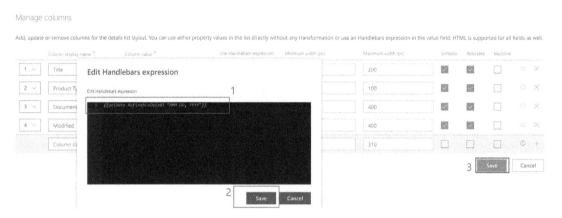

Figure 7-18. *"Edit Handlebars expression" box*

5) With the configurations in place, the Results web part displaying the Product Type, Document Type, and Modified date is now ready. The Modified date will be presented in the desired [MMM, DD, YYYY] format. The next step is to establish a two-way connection with the Filters web part. To establish the connection, click the Next button in the web part properties window. In page 3, enable the toggle for Connect to a Filters Web Part to establish the connection. From the "Use Filters from this component" drop-down menu, select the Filters web part. Refer to Figure 7-19.

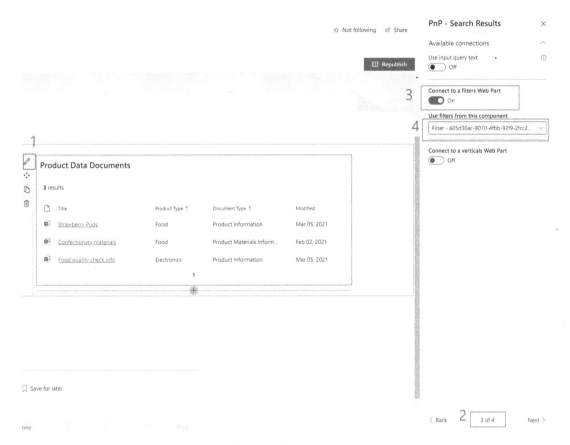

Figure 7-19. *Connecting to a Filters web part*

By completing these steps, the two-way connection between the Results web part and the Filters web part will be established. This connection enables the filtering functionality, allowing users to refine their search results based on the selected filter criteria.

Proceed to the next step to configure the Filters web part by editing it and customizing the filter options for Product Type, Document Type, and Modified date.

To customize the Filters web part, follow these steps:

1. Use the pencil icon on the Filters web part and click Edit in the Customize Filters section, as demonstrated earlier in Figure 7-9.

2. In the Edit Filters pop-up window, add the columns for Product Type, Document Type, and Modified, as depicted in Figure 7-20.

3. Choose the appropriate filter fields for each column based on your requirements.

4. For Product Type and Document Type, select the Check Box template and enable the Show Count option.

5. For Modified, choose the Date Range template.

6. Check the Expand by Default option for all the columns to display the filter options expanded by default.

7. Leave the Sort settings unchanged.

8. Feel free to experiment with different configurations for these settings, if desired.

9. Once you have finished configuring the filter options, click Save to save your changes.

By following these steps, you can customize the Filters web part by adding the desired columns and defining the filter options for Product Type, Document Type, and Modified.

Figure 7-20. *Edit Filters screen*

After completing all the necessary settings, close the properties window and proceed to publish the page. Once published, the search page will resemble the one shown in Figure 7-21, with the configured search results and filters.

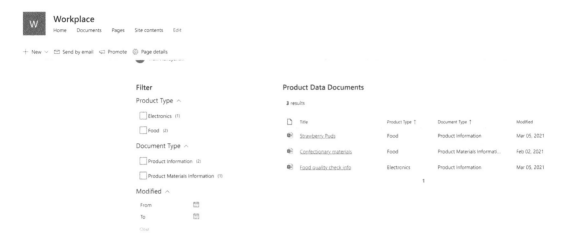

Figure 7-21.   Search results and filter

Before finalizing the setup, take the opportunity to test the filter functionality by filtering the results based on Product Type, Document Type, and different date ranges. It is recommended to add enough content from the Product Data library for testing purposes. Please ensure that all the documents in the library are approved, as the search results will display only approved documents.

By testing the filters and ensuring the inclusion of approved content, you can confirm that the search page is functioning correctly and that users can effectively filter and retrieve the desired results based on their search criteria.

By completing the configuration process, you have successfully set up a search page that fulfills all the requirements for the Cloudhadi Workplace search. Users now can search for product data documents, apply filters based on Product Type or Document Type, and sort the search results as desired.

In addition to the Search Results and Filter web parts, the Modern Search package also includes the Search Verticals and Search Box web parts. The Search Verticals web part enables users to browse data from multiple data sources, providing a more comprehensive search experience. You can configure the verticals to suit your specific needs and data sources.

In the next section, we will explore how queries can be sent from the home page of the Workplace site to the search results page. This functionality allows users to enter search queries directly from the home page and be directed to the search results page for the relevant search results.

Search Box

To incorporate a search box into your Workplace site, follow these steps:

1. Navigate to the home page of your Workplace site and enter the edit mode for the page.

2. Add a new section above the service portal section.

3. Search for the *PnP-Search Box* web part.

4. Add the PnP-Search Box web part to the newly created section, as illustrated in Figure 7-22.

By following these steps, you will successfully add the PnP-Search Box web part to your Workplace site's home page. This search box will function similarly to the out-of-the-box search box, allowing users to enter free text queries that will be sent to the Search Results web parts. Additionally, you can configure the search box to specify a page URL where the queries will be sent as query string parameters or URL fragments.

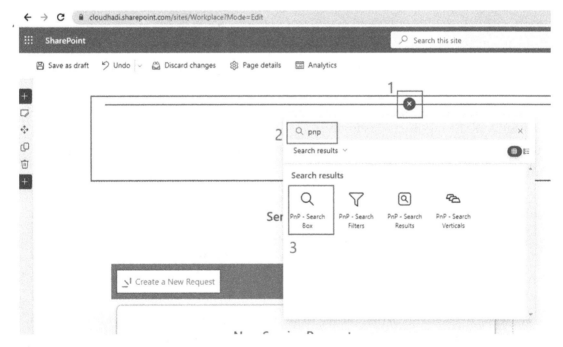

Figure 7-22. PnP, Search Box web part

Once you have added the PnP-Search Box web part, proceed with the configuration steps shown in Figure 7-23. Enable the toggle for Send the Query to a New Page and provide the URL for the `modernsearch.aspx` page. Select Query String Parameter as the method for sending the query and assign a parameter name. Additionally, include placeholder text in the search box to provide guidance for users when entering their search queries.

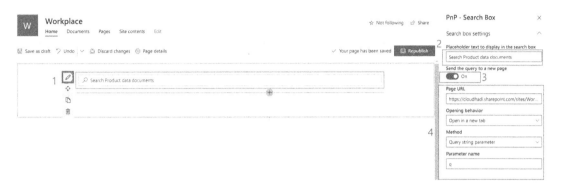

Figure 7-23. *Configuring the search box*

By following these steps, you can ensure that when users enter a keyword in the search box on the home page and initiate a search, they will be redirected to the search results page with the keyword passed as a query string parameter in the URL. For instance, if someone searches for *food*, they would be directed to `{SiteURL}/ ModernSearch.aspx?q=Food.` By configuring the PnP-Search Box web part in this manner, it will send the entered queries to the specified page as a query string parameter.

To ensure that the Search Results web part can receive and process this query string parameter, you need to navigate to the `modernsearch.aspx` page and make the necessary adjustments. Edit the page and access the properties of the Search Results web part. Within the properties pane, depicted in Figure 7-24, activate the Use Input Query Text toggle and configure the settings.

Specify the Input Query Text as a dynamic value and establish a connection with the Page Environment under the Connect to Source section. Select Query Parameters for the Query String option and choose q as the parameter's property. This parameter corresponds to the keyword passed from the search box on the home page. All these modifications can be made within section 3 of the properties pane under Available Connections.

Following these steps will ensure that the Search Results web part can receive and process the query string parameter, allowing it to display the relevant search results based on the user's entered keyword.

Figure 7-24. *Using input query text*

The final step is to modify the query template in the properties pane of the Search Results web part to enable filtering based on the query string. Update the value to the following: `and(Path:"[yourSiteURL]/ProductData*", RefinableString01:{QueryString.q})`.

Once you have made this update, the search results will be dynamically updated based on the entered search query. For instance, if you search for *food* using the search box on the home page, you will be directed to the results page specifically for the search term *food*. The search results will be displayed as depicted in Figure 7-25. Additionally,

I made some adjustments to enhance the appearance of the Title web part and the Search Results web part, resulting in an improved overall visual presentation.

The Search Results web part will now filter the results based on the entered search query, focusing on the ProductData path, and refining the results using the RefinableString01 property. This ensures that the displayed search results are tailored to the specific search query, creating a more relevant and user-friendly search experience.

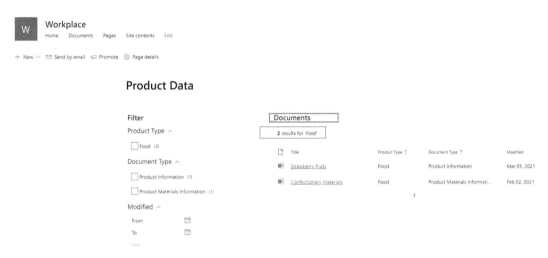

Figure 7-25. *Search results for the food keyword*

Note   To facilitate testing and debugging of search queries, the SharePoint Search Query Tool developed by the PnP team is highly recommended. This open-source tool offers valuable assistance in constructing and refining search solutions. For detailed information about the tool and to download it, visit `https://github.com/pnp/PnP-Tools/tree/master/Solutions/SharePoint.Search.QueryTool`.

Project Progress Review

In the previous chapter, we successfully developed a service portal web part that allows Cloudhadi users to submit requests and enables service executives to act on those requests.

In this chapter, our focus was on search functionality, where we configured search web parts using the PnP modern search approach. During the process, we effectively addressed several of our search use cases, specifically UC-S1, UC-S2, and UC-S4, as outlined in Chapter 2's "Search Use Cases" section.

I will leave it for you to explore UC-S3, which involves building a custom search results page that is configured to filter results for each product category, such as Food or Electronics. To achieve this, you will need to create a dedicated search page and add a search results web part to it. Update the refinement filters to ensure that only documents from the specific product category folder, such as Food, are returned in the search results. Additionally, you can add a search box to the desired location on the page, which will point to the newly created search results page.

By implementing these steps, you will be able to fulfill UC-S3 by creating a customized search experience tailored to specific product categories. This will enable users to easily search for and retrieve relevant documents within their desired product category.

Summary

In our discussion, we delved into the world of PnP Modern Search to enhance the search experience for our Cloudhadi Workplace site. We focused on leveraging SharePoint's modern search capabilities and customizing it using PnP Modern Search web parts.

We explored the PnP Modern Search web parts. These web parts offer a range of customizable and personalized search-driven experiences. We started with adding the Search Results and Filter web parts to a page and made necessary configurations. This involved mapping crawled properties to managed properties and setting up filter functionality. By mapping crawled properties to managed properties, we controlled how content is displayed in search results and enabled specific filtering options. These managed properties determined the scope and relevance of search results.

We explored customizations to enhance the visual presentation and usability of the search results. This included adjusting layouts, adding columns, and formatting data using handlebars expressions.

Another important aspect we discussed was the use of query parameters and result sources. We configured the Search Box web part to pass search queries to the search results page using query string parameters. By implementing these steps, we successfully enhanced the search experience within our Cloudhadi Workplace site. Users can now search for content, apply filters, and obtain more relevant results.

It's important to note that while we covered fundamental configurations, there are still endless possibilities for further exploration and customization of the PnP Modern Search solution to fine-tune the search functionality based on specific needs.

In conclusion, SharePoint and PnP Modern Search provide a powerful combination to create a personalized and efficient search experience. Users can quickly find the information they need within a SharePoint site, improving productivity and collaboration.

Teams and Power Virtual Agents

In this chapter, we will dive into the powerful world of Microsoft Teams. Teams is a versatile collaboration platform that offers a wide range of features such as online meetings, document sharing, live chat, and more. It has gained immense popularity, particularly during the COVID-19 pandemic, as it enables seamless virtual communication and facilitates effective teamwork. With deep integration into Microsoft 365 (M365), Teams provides a comprehensive solution for collaboration, including file storage, chat capabilities, and more.

Our primary focus in this chapter is to introduce you to Teams, Power Virtual Agents (PVAs), and Microsoft Graph. We will explore how to leverage SharePoint Online in conjunction with these platforms. To kickstart this process, we will reuse an existing SharePoint Framework (SPFx) web part and integrate it into Teams. This integration will lay the foundation for further enhancements. Subsequently, we will delve into the creation of a chatbot using Power Virtual Agents within Teams.

Additionally, we will provide a brief overview of Microsoft Graph, a unified API endpoint that offers extensive access to data and resources across the Microsoft 365 ecosystem.

By the end of this chapter, you will gain familiarity with the fundamentals of Teams, learn how to develop a chatbot using PVAs, and fulfill some of the requirements for Clouhadi. It's important to note that this chapter serves as an introduction to Teams and PVAs, leaving ample room for exploration and discovery of their full potential.

© Hari Narayn 2023
H. Narayn, *Building the Modern Workplace with SharePoint Online*,
https://doi.org/10.1007/978-1-4842-9726-1_8

SPFx in Teams

SharePoint Framework is a development framework offered by Microsoft for creating customizations and solutions for SharePoint. With the emergence of Microsoft Teams, SPFx can also be utilized to develop applications and integrations specifically tailored for Teams.

Let's explore an overview of SPFx in Teams:

- SPFx within Teams empowers developers to construct customized tabs, personal apps, and messaging extensions that seamlessly integrate with Microsoft Teams.

- SPFx web parts can be incorporated as tabs within Teams channels, enabling the presentation of SharePoint-based content and functionality directly within the Teams interface.

- Personal apps, developed through SPFx, can be installed and accessed by individual users within the Teams app, offering personalized experiences and access to SharePoint content.

- Messaging extensions built with SPFx allow users to interact with external systems, including SharePoint, facilitating content search, and sharing within Teams chats.

SPFx apps initially developed for SharePoint can be reused in Teams without any modifications. Furthermore, the functionality of SharePoint-based SPFx apps can be enhanced by leveraging Teams-specific capabilities, such as integration with Teams APIs, utilizing Teams authentication mechanisms, and incorporating Teams-specific UI components and extensions.

To begin, let's integrate our Service Portal web part, which we developed during Chapter 6, into Teams. Start by opening the SharePoint App Catalog. Select our Service portal app and click Sync to Teams. Refer to Figure 8-1.

Figure 8-1. *Syncing an app to Teams*

Wait for a few minutes. You will get a notification that the app is synced. Now the app is available to add in Teams.

Next access Teams through your web browser using the link `https://teams.microsoft.com` and logging in with your SharePoint credentials. Alternatively, you can also install the Teams app and log in there.

Click Apps at the bottom. Search for *cloudhadi*. You will be able to see the Service Portal available to add. Click the Add button. Refer to Figure 8-2.

Figure 8-2. *Finding the SPFx app*

Click the Add button in the pop-up window that appears. Refer to Figure 8-3 for visual guidance. By doing so, the Service Portal web part will be successfully added to your Teams environment.

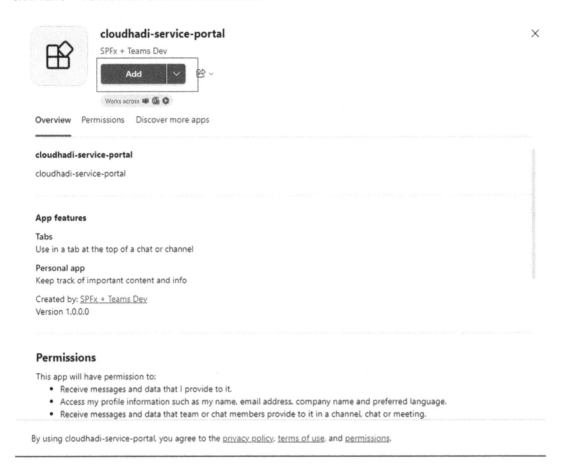

Figure 8-3. *Adding the SPFx app to Teams*

As you can see, the web part is automatically launched with the default tab titled Create a New Request. This tab serves as a convenient way to submit service requests directly within Teams, eliminating the need to navigate to the SharePoint site. For a visual reference, refer to Figure 8-4.

Figure 8-4. *New service request from Teams*

With this functionality, you can easily submit and view service requests, all within the Teams environment. Feel free to submit requests directly from Teams by utilizing the provided functionality within the web part. By clicking the My Requests option, you can conveniently view the requests that you have created within the Teams environment. Refer to Figure 8-5.

ID	Title	Related To	Status
CSR57247	Access for Documents	Materials	New
CSR1552	Procurement of MacBook	Equipments	Resolved
CSR93162	Food processing machine request	Equipments	New
CSR75959	Enquiry regarding new office site	General	In Progress
CSR41093	Strawberry farm cleaning	General	Completed
CSR39839	Access for Apple Puree quality documents	Access	Completed
CSR81131	Materials procurement for Microwave	Materials	New
CSR76338	good	Equipment	New
CSR21475	test1806	Equipment	New
CSR57727	Access for food quality documents	Equipment	New
CSR45484	New requestTeamsTest	Access	New

Figure 8-5. *My Requests from Teams*

Note   As you may recall from our development of the Service Portal web part in Chapter 6, we utilized the `AssignFrom` method to access the context of the service portal list. This was done to ensure that the web part functions properly in Teams. Since Teams does not have the context of the workplace site, accessing the service portal list using `sp.web` would not work when the web part is deployed in Teams. The approach we employed to obtain the web context allows for seamless functionality in both scenarios.

If you happen to navigate away from the app, don't worry! You can easily access the app again by following these steps: click the ... (ellipsis) icon located on the left side of Teams and then select cloudhadi-serviceportal from the available options. This will allow you to return quickly and conveniently to the app whenever needed.

What we have covered so far is merely the tip of the iceberg. There is a vast array of possibilities and features to explore within team development and utilizing SPFx within Teams. In the final section of the chapter, we will delve into adding an extension that facilitates seamless interaction between Teams and SharePoint.

However, before we proceed with that, let's shift our focus to building a bot using Power Virtual Agents. We will explore how to create and integrate the bot into Teams, further expanding the capabilities and functionality available to users.

Power Virtual Agents

Power Virtual Agents is a robust tool designed for creating intelligent chatbots. These chatbots can be configured to provide answers and assistance in response to user inquiries. PVAs offer the flexibility to be utilized as stand-alone web applications or integrated as discrete apps within Teams. In this chapter, we will explore the integration of PVAs specifically within Teams, leveraging their capabilities to enhance communication and support within the platform.

Now, let's dive deeper into PVAs and learn how they can empower you to create interactive and helpful chatbots within Teams.

Creating a Chatbot

To enable users to interact with the bot and create service requests directly within Teams, let's create a chatbot specifically for the service portal using Power Virtual Agents within Teams. The chatbot for the service portal allows users to seamlessly communicate and create service requests directly within Teams, eliminating the need to navigate to the portal. Follow these steps to proceed with the chatbot creation process:

1. *Open PVA*: Begin by navigating to Teams and locating the Apps
    icon in the left navigation bar. From there, search for Power Virtual
    Agents and click Open, as depicted in Figure 8-6.

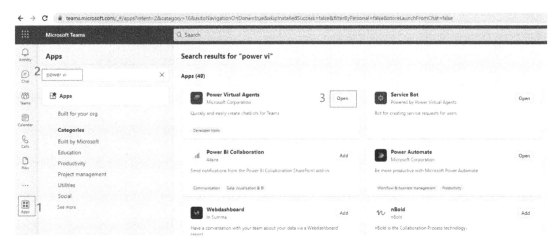

Figure 8-6. *Navigating to Power Virtual Agents*

2. *Welcome screen*: On the Power Virtual Agents welcome screen,
    you'll encounter various options, including a Copilot authoring
    preview and links to learning documentation. One noteworthy
    feature is the ability to create a chatbot within just 5 minutes,
    without requiring any coding. To begin, click Start Now and let's
    create the chatbot. Refer to Figure 8-7 for visual guidance on the
    welcome screen.

Figure 8-7. *PVA Welcome screen*

3. *Select a team*: A pop-up window will appear prompting you to select a team. From the available options, choose the desired team and then click Continue, as shown in Figure 8-8. It is possible to opt for the default team selection. Assigning a team serves a vital purpose when creating a chatbot using Power Virtual Agents within Teams. By selecting a team, you establish the ownership and management responsibilities for the chatbot. The chosen team will have control over the chatbot's configuration, deployment, and access permissions. Furthermore, this selection facilitates collaboration and enables seamless sharing of the chatbot with other team members, allowing them to interact with and utilize the chatbot within the specific team context.

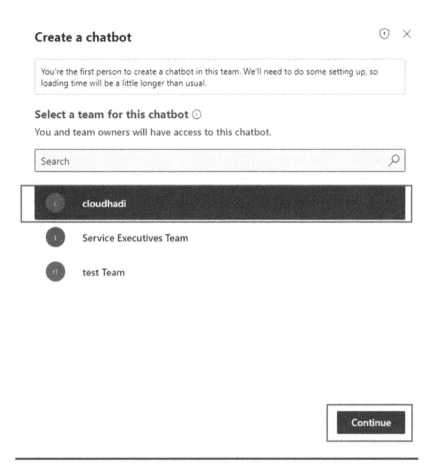

Figure 8-8. *Selecting a team*

4. *Create a bot*: After selecting a team and clicking Continue, it may
   take a few moments for the screen to load, where you can enter
   the details for your bot. Once the screen is visible, provide a name
   for your bot, such as Service Bot, and then click Create, as shown
   in Figure 8-9. This step initiates the creation of your chatbot within
   Power Virtual Agents.

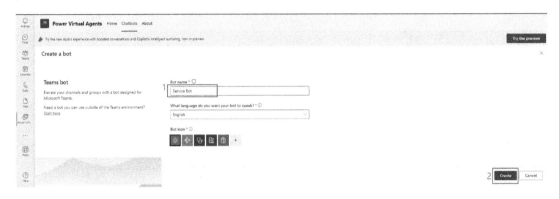

Figure 8-9. *Creating a chatbot*

Once your bot is successfully created, you will have access to
various options for authoring or automating topics, editing, and
testing the bot, and publishing it. These options are conveniently
displayed and can be explored within the Power Virtual Agents
interface, as illustrated in Figure 8-10. This allows you to
customize and fine-tune your bot's behavior, test its functionality,
and ultimately publish it for users to interact with.

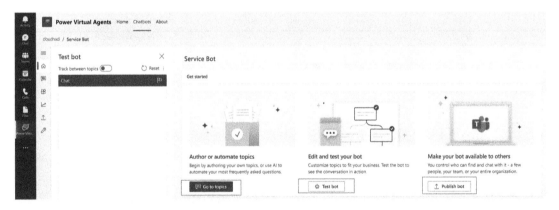

Figure 8-10. *Bot Welcome page*

5. *Create a topic*: Topics in the context of chatbots refer to specific
areas or subjects that the bot is trained to understand and respond
to. They represent the different conversation scenarios or user
intents that the bot is designed to handle. Each topic typically
focuses on a particular task, question, or type of interaction.

When authoring a chatbot using Power Virtual Agents, you can create and define multiple topics to cover a range of user inquiries or actions. For example, you might have topics like Book a Service Request, Check Order Status, or FAQs. Each topic contains a set of predefined triggers, user prompts, and bot responses that help guide the conversation flow.

By organizing your bot's capabilities into topics, you can effectively manage and control the bot's behavior in various conversation scenarios. It allows you to provide targeted responses and actions based on the user's input or intent, ensuring a more personalized and relevant interaction experience.

To define responses and interactions, the first step is to create a topic. Let's use two phrases, Service Request and Create Service Request, as triggers for this topic. Whenever a user types in either of these phrases, the bot will initiate a series of questions related to creating a service request.

To proceed, click Go to Topics. This will direct you to the Service Bot page, where you can create topics, test your bot, publish it, and more. Next, click New Topic and select From blank, as depicted in Figure 8-11.

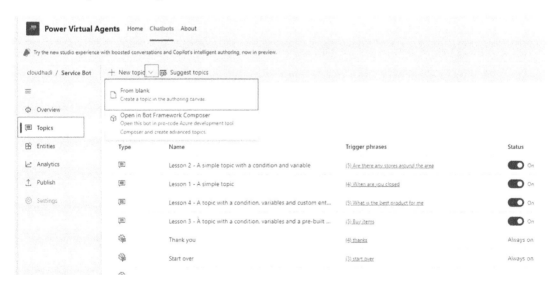

Figure 8-11. *Topics screen*

6. *Add trigger phrases*: To add trigger phrases to a topic in Power Virtual Agents, locate the Trigger phrases section and click it. Enter the trigger phrase in the input field that appears. Press Enter or click the + icon to save the trigger phrase. Refer to Figure 8-12 where I already added a trigger phrase Service request and in the process of adding the second phrase Create a service request.

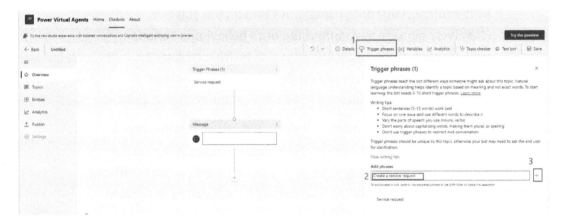

Figure 8-12. *Adding trigger phrases*

You can add multiple trigger phrases to a topic, enabling the bot to respond to various user inputs that match these phrases. By defining relevant trigger phrases, you ensure that the bot is activated and starts asking questions or providing responses when users enter those specific phrases during the conversation. Once a user types either of these two phrases, the bot will be triggered, and the next step is to configure the bot's response using the authoring canvas.

7. *Configure responses, Title*: Let's proceed with configuring the bot's response. Start by adding a message in the Message box. Then, click the + symbol to add a node and select the Add question option. This will add a node of type "Ask question" to the conversation flow.

In the Ask a Question box, type in the following question: **Can you please provide a title for your request?**

In the Identify section, click the icon, and select User's Entire Response to capture the user's complete response. For the Save response As field, click the pencil icon and enter **varTitle** as the variable name.

Refer to Figure 8-13.

Figure 8-13. *Configuring responses, Title*

By following these steps, we have messaged the user when they enter any of the defined triggers. We then proceed to ask the user a question and save their response in the varTitle variable.

8. *Configure responses, Description*: Let's proceed by adding a question for the request description. To do this, add a node and select "Add a condition." In the condition block, enter **varTitle** and choose a value. This step ensures that the question for the description will be asked only once the user provides the title.

Next, add another "Ask a question" node and prompt the user to provide the request description. Save the response in a separate variable named varDescription. By doing this, we now have the user's response for the description saved in the varDescription variable.

Refer to Figure 8-14.

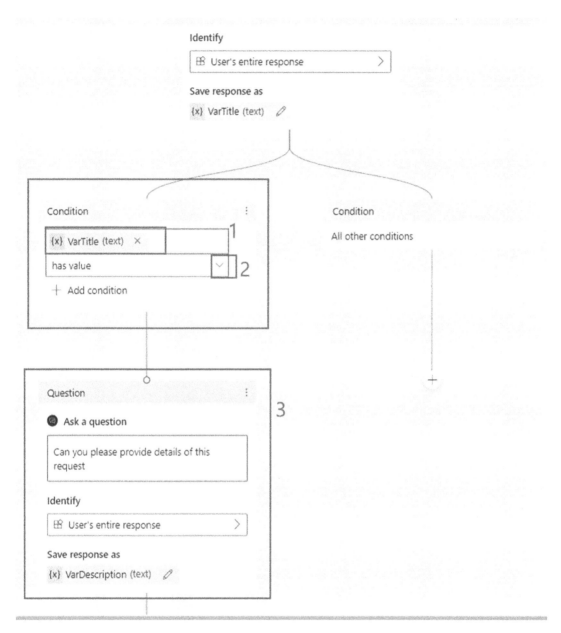

Figure 8-14. *Configuring responses, description*

This configuration ensures that the chatbot asks for the request description only after the user has provided the title, creating a structured conversation flow and capturing the necessary information.

9. *Configure responses, Related To*: Let's proceed by adding a
question for the related to field. To do this, add a node and select
"Add a condition." In the condition block, enter **varDescription**
and choose has value. This step ensures that the question for
the related to will be asked only once the user provides the
description.

Next, add another "Ask a question" node and prompt the user
to provide the related to. This time use the "Multiple choice
questions" option and add four options for the user. Save the
response in a variable named varRelatedTo.

Refer to Figure 8-15.

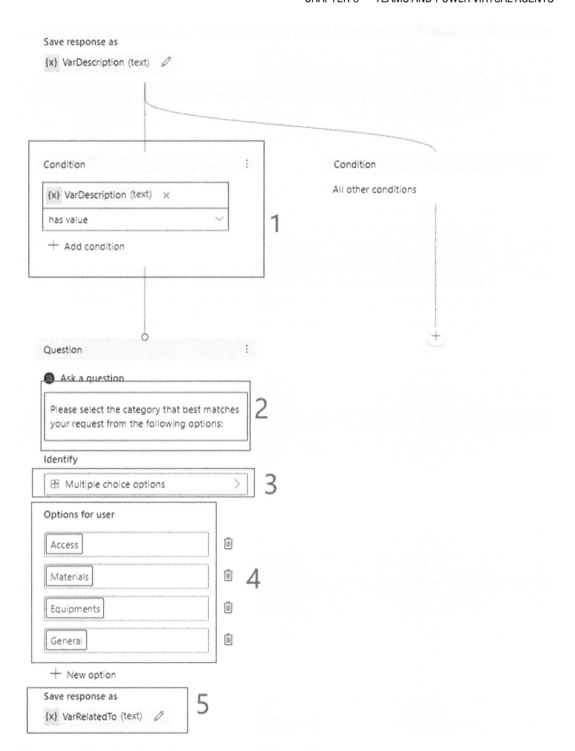

Figure 8-15. *Configuring responses, Related To*

By doing this, we now have the user's selection for the "related to" saved in the `varRelatedTo` variable. Note that when adding each option, a conditional block is automatically generated at the bottom. However, you can remove these conditional blocks by clicking the dots located next to them.

To avoid any loss of progress while adding a flow in the next step, ensure that you click the Save button located at the top-right corner. This will effectively save all the changes made to the topic thus far, guaranteeing that your modifications are securely stored and ready for the upcoming flow integration.

10. *Invoke a flow*: Now, let's incorporate a flow into this topic to save the service request to SharePoint. Begin by adding a condition that checks if `varRelatedTo` has a value. Following this, add a node titled "Call an action" and select the option "Create a flow." For visual guidance, please refer to Figure 8-16.

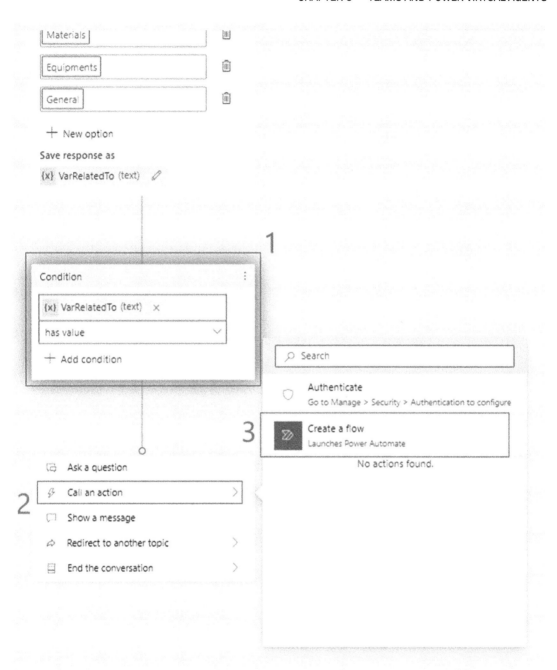

Figure 8-16. *Call an action, create a flow*

Power Automate will now launch within Teams. Select Power
Virtual Agents Flow Template to create the flow, as shown in
Figure 8-17.

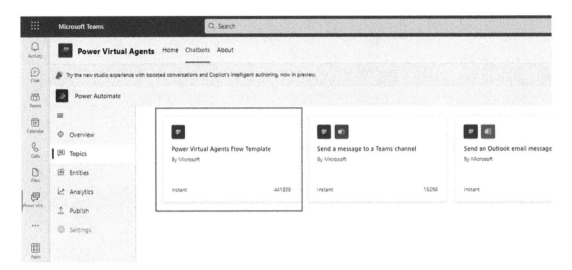

Figure 8-17. *Choosing a flow template*

11. *Configure the flow, stage 1*: The flow designer will open, and you
will see the Power Virtual Agents trigger. Proceed by adding three
text inputs: title, description, and relatedTo. Make sure to enter the
respective variable names you provided in the topic, as shown in
Figure 8-18.

Below the Power Virtual Agents trigger, add an Initialize Variable
action. Initialize a variable named `serviceNumber` and set its value
to CSR concatenated with the expression `rand(10000, 99999`.
This will generate a random number to be used for the title.

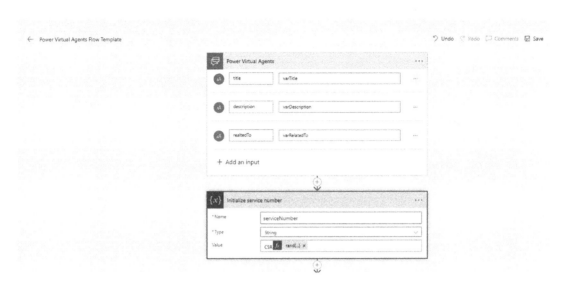

Figure 8-18. *Configuring the flow, stage 1*

12. *Configure the flow, stage 2*: Proceed by adding a "Create item"
     action from SharePoint. Within the Create Item screen, enter
     the necessary field values, as depicted in Figure 8-19. Assign
     the variable serviceNumber to the Title field. Utilize the
     respective dynamic content inputs for Request Title and Request
     Description, and select Custom value for the "Related to" drop-
     down, choosing the appropriate input from the dynamic content
     options. Set the Request Status Value to the default New.

     In the final block of the flow, titled Return Value(s) to Power
     Virtual Agents, include serviceNumber as the output variable. This
     ensures that the service number will be returned to Power Virtual
     Agents. When the flow execution is successful, indicating the
     creation of the service request in SharePoint, the output will be
     sent back to Power Virtual Agents.

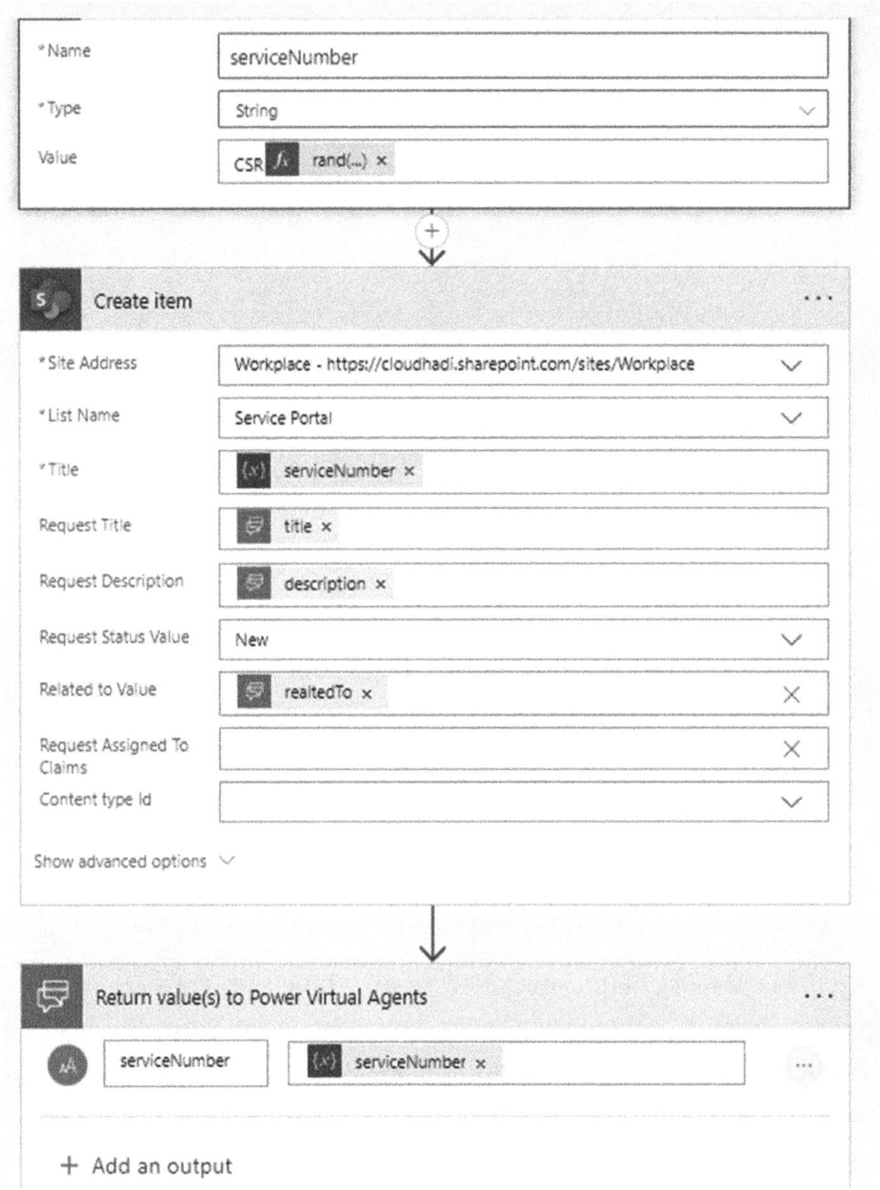

Figure 8-19. *Configuring the flow, stage 2*

By completing these configurations, the flow will seamlessly create a service request in SharePoint, while also providing the necessary output to Power Virtual Agents for further processing.

To save the configured flow, click the Save button located at the top-right corner. This ensures that your flow changes are securely saved. Afterward, click the Close button positioned above the flow to return to the topic authoring canvas.

13. *Send inputs to flow*: Now, click the "add node" option again, select "call an action," and now choose the flow that we created. Since we didn't provide a custom name for the flow, it will be displayed as the default Power Virtual Agents Flow Template.

In the action settings, you will find options to provide input values. Using the drop-down menus, select varTitle for the title input, varDescription for the description input, and varRelatedTo for the related to input. This ensures that the flow will receive and process the corresponding values from Power Virtual Agents.

As the final step, let's add a message block to provide feedback to the user that the service request has been created. In the message, you can include the service number as a reference. Use the Insert variable option and insert the service number variable to dynamically display the specific service number in the message. This personalized message will inform the user about the successful creation of the service request, providing them with the relevant reference information.

Refer to Figure 8-20.

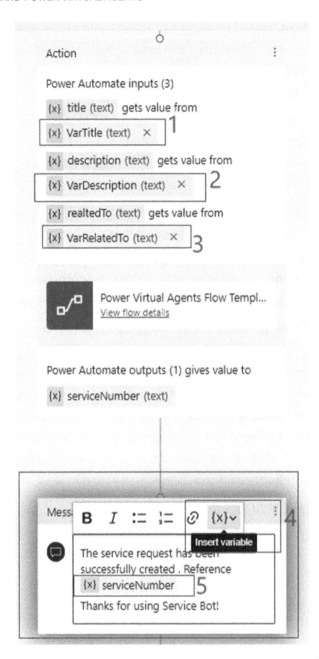

Figure 8-20. *Adding inputs to the flow action and adding a final message*

Save the topic using the Save button in the upper-right corner.

14. *Test the bot*: It's time to put our bot to the test! Click the Test Bot button located at the top-right corner of the screen. Test the bot by entering phrases like **service request** or **create service request** to trigger the relevant conversation flow. Refer to Figure 8-21 for an example of a test run, showcasing the bot's responses and interactions. This testing phase allows you to verify the behavior and functionality of the bot, ensuring that it performs as expected and delivers the intended user experience.

Figure 8-21. *Testing the bot*

As depicted in the figure, the bot is actively responding to your chat and engaging in a conversation by asking relevant questions. Furthermore, the bot successfully created a service request and furnished you with a reference number for further reference. To validate the creation of the service request, you can navigate to the service portal list in your SharePoint site, where you will find that your request has indeed been successfully created and recorded. This seamless integration between the bot and the SharePoint site ensures that your requests are efficiently managed and tracked within the workplace environment.

By following this approach, you can create multiple topics within the same bot to handle different conversation scenarios. However, for our service portal requirements, we won't be requiring additional topics. I will leave it for you to explore further. You can create more topics and do different configurations to enhance the bot's capabilities.

Now, let's move on to the next step: publishing and sharing the bot. This process involves making the bot available for users to interact with.

Publishing and Sharing the Bot

To publish the bot, navigate to the left-side navigation and select the Publish option. Click Publish and confirm by selecting Publish again in the pop-up window. For visual reference, please consult Figure 8-22. Publishing the bot makes it accessible and available for users to engage with, ensuring a seamless and interactive experience.

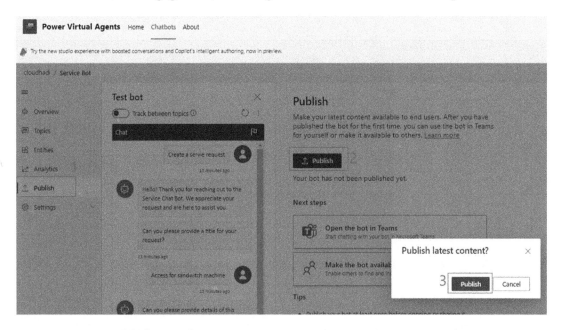

Figure 8-22. *Publishing a bot*

Once you click the Publish button, it will take a few seconds for the bot to be published. After that, it's time to share the bot with your organization so that everyone can access it. To do this, click the "Make the bot available to others" option, located below the Publish button as next steps. In the sliding window that appears, click "Availability options" at the bottom. In the resulting window, click "Show to everyone in my org" to share with everyone. Refer to Figure 8-23.

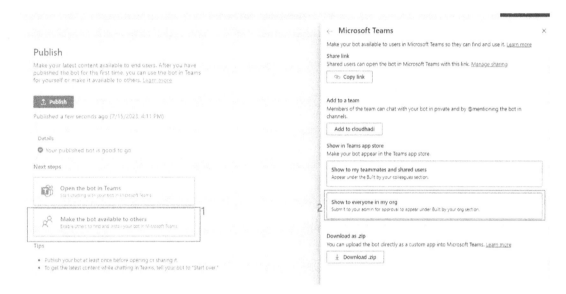

Figure 8-23. *Sharing the bot to everyone*

Click "submit for admin approval" from the screen that appears. Then click Yes from the pop-up.

Now, to approve the app, access the Teams admin center by visiting `https://admin.teams.microsoft.com/`. From there, navigate to Manage Apps under Teams Apps in the left navigation pane, as depicted in Figure 8-24. In this section, you will notice that one app is pending approval. Search for *Service Bot*, where you will find the app submitted with the status marked as Blocked. Select the app, and click Allow. Click Allow from the resulting pop-up as well. Refer to Figure 8-24.

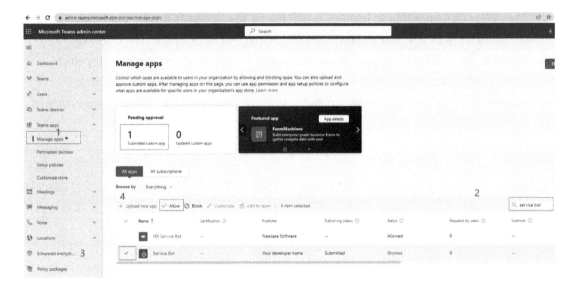

Figure 8-24. *Managing apps in the Teams admin center*

In case the allow didn't work, click the row corresponding to the Service Bot app; you will be directed to the Details page for the app. From there, click Publish. This action will publish the app, causing the status to change from Blocked to Allowed.

Upon returning to the Publish page in your teams, simply click the Refresh option in the "Make bot available to others" window. Upon doing so, you will observe that the Service Bot has been successfully published by your organization, as indicated in Figure 8-25. This confirmation signifies that the bot is now available and accessible to others within your organization, allowing for widespread usage and engagement.

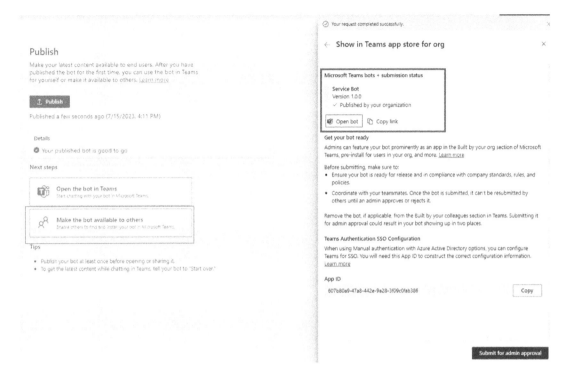

Figure 8-25. *Opening the published bot*

Click the Open Bot button, and a pop-up will appear, providing you with the option to add the Service Bot to your Teams. By clicking Add, you will successfully incorporate the app into your Teams environment, granting you access to the functionalities and features offered by the Service Bot. Alternatively, you can go to teams, search for the Service Bot, and click it. For visual reference, refer to Figure 8-26.

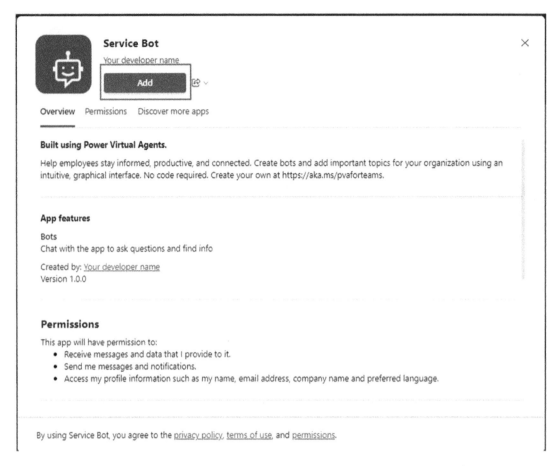

Figure 8-26. *Adding the app to Teams*

Upon accessing Teams, you will notice the presence of the Service Bot in the top-left corner of the navigation pane. By clicking it, you can initiate a chat with the bot and create a service request directly within the chat interface. For a visual example, refer to Figure 8-27.

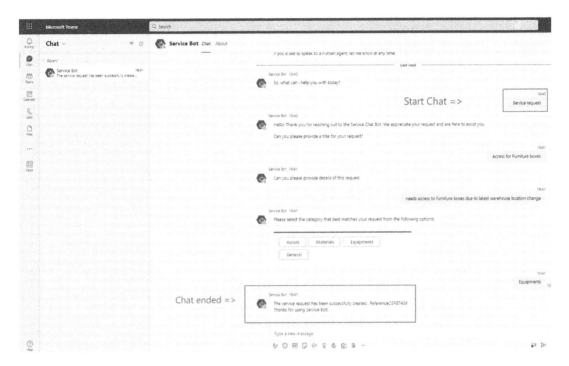

Figure 8-27. *Service Bot in operation*

Note   Every user within your organization will need to individually add the Service Bot app to their Teams to utilize its functionalities. This can be done by clicking the ... icon in the left navigation bar or by accessing the Apps section. If you want to ensure that the app is readily available to all users in your organization, you can set up global policies within the Teams admin center and add Service Bot to the list of pinned apps. By doing so, the app will be easily accessible and visible to all users, providing a consistent experience across the organization.

Now you have successfully created your first bot! This bot is capable of interaction with Teams, SharePoint, and Power Automate, opening numerous possibilities for streamlining processes and enhancing collaboration. You can further explore the potential of topics and create more intelligent chatbots. This allows you to delve deeper into advanced bot development, leveraging additional features and capabilities to create even more sophisticated conversational experiences.

Overview on Microsoft Graph

Microsoft Graph is a powerful API that allows developers to access and interact with various Microsoft 365 services, such as SharePoint and Microsoft Teams. It provides a unified endpoint for accessing resources and relationships across multiple Microsoft products, simplifying application development. Here's an overview of the key capabilities of Microsoft Graph when used with SharePoint and Teams:

1. Microsoft Graph and SharePoint:

    - *Retrieve SharePoint site data*: We can use Microsoft Graph to fetch information about SharePoint sites, including lists, libraries, and their contents. For instance, you can obtain a list of all lists within a SharePoint site or retrieve metadata for a specific document library.

    - *Manage SharePoint files and folders*: Microsoft Graph enables CRUD operations on files and folders in SharePoint document libraries. This means you can programmatically create, read, update, and delete files and folders, as well as perform various file operations.

    - *Access SharePoint lists and items*: Microsoft Graph provides the ability to work with SharePoint lists and items. You can retrieve list data, create new items, update existing ones, and delete items. This allows for automation and custom solutions built on top of SharePoint. Like we use PnP for accessing SharePoint data, you can use Graph.

    - *Perform search operations*: With Microsoft Graph, you can leverage powerful search capabilities for SharePoint content. You can execute queries to search for documents, lists, sites, and other SharePoint entities based on specific criteria.

Here are some examples of Graph endpoints for SharePoint.

    - Retrieve a list of all SharePoint sites:

        GET https://graph.microsoft.com/v1.0/sites

- Get information about a specific SharePoint site:

  ```
  GET https://graph.microsoft.com/v1.0/sites/{site-id}
  ```

- Upload a file to a document library:

  ```
  POST https://graph.microsoft.com/v1.0/sites/{site-id}/drive/
  items/{library-id}/children
  ```

- Retrieve items from a SharePoint list with specific fields:

  ```
  GET /sites/{site-id}/lists/{list-id}/items?expand=fields(select
  =Column1,Column2)
  ```

- Create a new item in a SharePoint list:

  ```
  POST https://graph.microsoft.com/v1.0/sites/{site-id}/lists/
  {list-id}/items
  Content-Type: application/json

  {
  fields: {
  Title: CSR543,
  RequestTitle: dw relcoation,
  RelatedTo: {
      ChoiceValues: [Equipment]
  }
  }
  ```

2. Microsoft Graph and Teams:

   - *Retrieve Teams and channels*: Microsoft Graph allows us to fetch information about Teams, such as the teams a user belongs to, the channels within a team, and the members of a channel. This enables programmatic interactions with the Teams structure.

   - *Create and manage Teams messages*: We can leverage Microsoft Graph to send messages to Teams channels or chat conversations, retrieve message history, and perform actions such as deleting or updating messages. This facilitates integration with external systems and automates messaging workflows.

- *Access Teams events and meetings*: Microsoft Graph provides functionality to work with Teams events and meetings. This includes creating and updating events, retrieving attendees and schedules, and managing meeting details. Developers can build calendars and scheduling features into their applications using this capability.

- *Manage Teams users and permissions*: With Microsoft Graph, we can programmatically manage Teams users and their permissions. This involves tasks such as adding or removing users from Teams, assigning roles and permissions, and controlling access to Teams resources.

Here are some examples of Graph endpoints for Teams.

- Get a list of all Teams that the user is a member of:

  GET https://graph.microsoft.com/v1.0/me/joinedTeams

- Get information about a specific SharePoint site:

  GET https://graph.microsoft.com/v1.0/teams/{team-id}

- Send a message to a Teams channel:

  POST https://graph.microsoft.com/v1.0/teams/{team-id}/channels/{channel-id}/messages

- Add a user to a Team:

  POST https://graph.microsoft.com/v1.0/groups/{group-id}/members

These examples showcase the versatility of Microsoft Graph when used in conjunction with SharePoint and Teams. By leveraging these capabilities, we can create powerful applications that integrate and interact with these services, enabling automation, customization, and enhanced collaboration experiences.

> **Note** You can explore more about Microsoft Graph end points in Graph Explorer: `https://developer.microsoft.com/en-us/graph/graph-explorer`. Here, you'll get the whole set of end points Graph provides and an interface to test queries.

Project Progress Review

Let's assess our progress in developing a modern workplace for Cloudhadi, at the end of this final chapter.

Throughout this chapter, we accomplished significant milestones in enhancing the Cloudhadi portal. We successfully integrated the service portal web part into Microsoft Teams, enabling business users to conveniently create and view requests directly within the Teams platform. This integration streamlines the user experience and promotes seamless collaboration.

Furthermore, we developed a chatbot that allows users to interact with a live bot and create requests through chat-based conversations. This feature adds an additional layer of convenience and accessibility for users.

By implementing these features, we have addressed the use cases UC-SD2 and UC-SD4 listed in the section "Service Portal Use Cases" in Chapter 2.

We covered most of the requirements outlined in Chapter 2. This book has provided you with an example at least for each of the technical areas, in the outlined requirements. However, there are still a few remaining requirements that can be implemented to further enhance the digital workplace for Cloudhadi. I encourage you to explore those requirements and consider implementing them for practice.

As you move forward, I encourage you to continue exploring and expanding upon the foundation we have established. There is always room for further customization and improvement to meet the unique needs of organizations.

Summary

In this final chapter, we explored important components of the suite of Microsoft products and services, including Teams, Power Virtual Agents, and Microsoft Graph. We began by providing an overview of Teams and how we can leverage SPFx web parts within the platform. This integration allowed us to extend the capabilities of SharePoint Online and enhance collaboration within Teams.

Our focus then shifted to Power Virtual Agents (PVAs) and the creation of a chatbot. We learned how to develop a chatbot using PVAs, enabling interactive and automated communication with users. This added another layer of functionality to our SharePoint-based solutions.

Lastly, we briefly touched upon Microsoft Graph, the unified API endpoint that provides access to data and resources across Microsoft 365. While we didn't delve deeply into Graph, we highlighted its significance in the broader context of the Microsoft ecosystem.

Throughout this book, we've covered various aspects of SharePoint Online design and development. We explored customization and configuration options, including forms, workflows, and search. We also discussed the integration of modern technologies like React, the Power Platform, and Teams into SharePoint development. Our approach has focused on fundamental concepts and design planning to help you build effective solutions for the Clouhadi modern workplace requirements.

Remember, this book served as an introduction, and there is much more to discover and explore in the world of SharePoint and the broader Microsoft ecosystem. I hope you enjoyed this journey and found the insights valuable. Thank you for reading, and best of luck in your future SharePoint endeavors!

Index

© Hari Narayn 2023
H. Narayn, *Building the Modern Workplace with SharePoint Online*,
https://doi.org/10.1007/978-1-4842-9726-1

T

U, V, W, X, Y, Z

Printed in the USA
CPSIA information can be obtained
at www.ICGtesting.com
LVHW060546170924
791293LV00006B/606